Keats Community Library

B06670

D1578420

WARM UP THE SNAKE

This book is dedicated to my dear wife, Patricia,
who prefers to be addressed as "Pat."
So, dear Pat, this is to thank you formally
for your patience, your good humor, and your
marvelous ability to keep me relatively sane
as I write (and rewrite) this book.

With love and admiration,
John

The first time I met my executive editor, LeAnn Fields, she suggested I offer a commentary on my reasons for writing this memoir. Primarily, the idea came from Pat, who was tired of hearing my rants about the paucity of meaningful work in television today. "Put it down on paper," she would say. "Don't tell it to me." There was also a more compelling subtext. She wanted me to rent an office somewhere so she could enjoy solitude at home without having to endure my stream of muttered complaints. Another impetus came from my good friend Dr. Mike Leavitt, who thought the idea of writing a book would be good therapy—especially for Pat.

On reflection, the idea took shape following a freelance job interview. After almost fifty years as a (mostly) successful director, and having attained a measure of stature in the industry, it was unusual for me to be asked to "audition" for work. During my most productive years, commitments generally stemmed from past successes, and employment often resulted from a simple phone call. However, since it was a new day, I felt that young "show runners" were entitled to a face-to-face discussion, so I advised my agent that I would have no ego in the matter and to accept the invitation to meet without a firm offer.

Arriving at the production office, I was greeted warmly by the executive producer and her coproducers and staff of writers. The young executives regaled me with stories of how they had all grown up on my television work and urged me to share inside tales on many of the series that delighted them in their early years. Such camaraderie filled the conference room that the meeting lasted over an hour, with so much laughter that it felt like a cocktail party among old friends. The interplay was so pleasant that we all seemed reluctant to get back to work discussing the project. But that part of the process also went well, and with a sense of accomplishment the meeting came to a close. The executive producer stood up, took my hand, and said with genuine affection, "I feel like I'm shaking hands with a legend." I said goodbye to a room full of smiling and appreciative faces.

The feeling of well-being vanished as I drove away from the studio. As I reviewed the interview my thoughts turned to baseball, and to the proverbial aging shortstop who can't go to his left anymore. When that happens, no matter how great the career may have been, the cliché says the body is telling you it's time to hang up your spikes and walk away from the game. That which applies to baseball players also has meaning for directors. That nice young woman who called me a legend meant it as a compliment. But legends are dangerous. They threaten the rookies because they know too much. Legends get elected to the Hall of Fame. Legends get put on a shelf along with their trophies. But legends don't get hired.

It was no surprise to me when I didn't get the job, and I concluded that Pat and Dr. Mike were right. It was time to write a book.

Regarding the title, I had intended to name the book *Release the Pigeon and Warm Up the Snake*, for reasons that will become evident in chapter 13. When I mentioned this to my friend, the author Al Slote, he swiftly said that any work with that title would end up in the pet section in most bookstores. He advised me to shorten the phrase and add "A Hollywood Memoir." I'm indebted to Al for his valuable suggestion, as well as his friendship over many years since our Ann Arbor days.

By the way, my valued editor, Jerry Roberts, thought that "Pigeon" seemed too tranquil for a Hollywood memoir, preferring the menace implied by the other half of the menagerie. I'm happy to accept his suggestion.

In addition to Jerry, many thanks are due to Mike Grudowski who did a masterful job of "polishing" the final manuscript.

One day in the middle of 1970, I received two telephone calls, one right after the other, in an occurrence of what one could be tempted to describe as lightning striking twice. Looking back on five decades of work in television, I can tell you: You don't get many days like this one. One of the calls came from Mary Tyler Moore, telling me she was about to shoot a pilot for a new television series. She asked if I could meet with Jim Brooks and Allan Burns, who wrote the script and would act as executive producers. The other call came from Norman Lear, who wanted to send me a draft for a pilot he was about to produce. Unfortunately, the demands of a weekly series meant I would have to choose between the two.

After I read both submissions, I was immediately taken by the Mary Tyler Moore work. The script was intelligent, well thought out, and, above all, *funny*. Reading Norman Lear's work, I kept rubbing my eyes as I encountered language I had never heard on television before. Surely, Lear did not expect words like "spics" and "spades" to be uttered on CBS.

As I read on, though, the relationships in the script Norman was offering captivated me. I found myself laughing my head off at characters who were real, recognizable, and hilarious. I reread both scripts and thought about them intensely. I met with Norman, who showed me the two pilot episodes he had produced for ABC with his partner, Bud Yorkin. Both versions (with different casts) had been rejected. This third effort would be for CBS. When I asked Norman about the unusually explicit language, he said management had assured him they would go along. He had been promised this in part because Lear's script had been watered down considerably from its British ancestor, *Till Death Do Us Part.*

I had my doubts about the network's ability to live up to this commitment, but the attempt intrigued me. When Norman asked my opinion of the old pilots, I told them I thought the lead characters, played by Carroll O'Connor and Jean Stapleton, were wonderful. But the supporting actors, played by different people in each pilot, were not in the same class. These included the Mike and Gloria characters as well as the next door neighbor, Lionel. None of this group of six actors, I said, should be retained for the CBS pilot. I left Norman, saying I would like a day to think over his offer. But the truth was, I had practically made up my mind already.

As a courtesy, I met with Brooks and Burns and passed on *The Mary Tyler Moore Show* with great reluctance, because I was certain it was going to be a huge hit. I telephoned Mary and told her how much I enjoyed reading her pilot episode, but I was going to opt for the Norman Lear vehicle because it was so outrageous. I reminded her about how well she and I had worked on *The Dick Van Dyke Show* and that I would probably join her later if she would still have me. This would be after Norman's series disappeared without a trace despite the valiant try we would give it. I had no doubt that it would never see the network light of day, because of its uncompromising use of language. But I couldn't resist directing something that appeared unique.

I telephoned Lear to discuss compensation, as I was currently acting as my own agent in television. At that time, I believe the Directors Guild of America (DGA) called for minimums of $750 per half-hour, with in-demand directors averaging about $1,250. I was in the $2,500-to-$3,000 range. So when Lear said he could only pay $1,000, I was dumbfounded. Having burned my bridges with Mary, I asked Norman how he could justify such a cut for an established director. His reply stunned me: His entire budget was about $80,000! This included the actors' compensation, writing, directing, producing, the below-the-line crew, stage facilities, and so on. I choked out, "What kind of film budget is that?" The answer was that it was not a film budget at all. Apparently, CBS wanted the series but not enough to have it filmed. It would be shot on *videotape*—much cheaper than film—at the CBS Studios on Fairfax Avenue, in Los Angeles. I told Norman that as much as I loved his script I couldn't cut my established price that much. After lengthy conversations, we worked out a compromise: I would work for $1,500 an episode, but we would break new ground by applying the DGA residual percentages to an imagined compensation of $3,000.

Of course, this would only apply if there were reruns, which hardly seemed likely at the time. But the compromise would help me in future bargaining with others, and it allowed me to save face and direct the script, which I desperately wanted to do. Money was not really the issue; probably I would have accepted the deal at any price. But please don't tell Norman.

All in the Family has been praised for presenting groundbreaking television, but at the time it was no sure thing. Soon after I began directing the first episode of the series, I became aware of a stranger standing behind me. I have always had a firm rule banning visitors from the control room, so I asked if there was something I could do for him. He said he hoped I could, because, as he phrased it, "my ass is on the line with this show." He then introduced himself as Bob Wood, president of CBS. I told him I would do my best, and since it was a camera rehearsal in progress, I didn't object to his presence. Mr. Wood had indeed taken a big chance. Late in 1970, CBS had decided to shed its rural image by eliminating shows like *The Beverly Hillbillies, Green Acres,* and their ilk, replacing them with relatively sophisticated urban comedies. But it was rare—if not unheard of—to broadcast the kind of uninhibited language for which we would become known.

It's easy to understand Mr. Wood's nervousness, but it didn't make us pull any punches in the pilot episode. We all thought the first show went marvelously well, but the story presented in the second episode let me down. Compared to the first week, it was limp and lacked the bite of the pilot, which introduced all the main characters and used language the second script lacked. For example, the second episode dealt with Archie writing a letter to the president. Using actor Rich Little to do a voiceover impersonation of Richard Nixon, the camera saw, through a fantasy effect, the whole family watching TV. We see Archie proudly imagining the reception his marvelously composed letter will receive at the White House. There was nothing wrong with this satirical idea, except that, in staging the scene, I was forced to compose a static picture as the audience listened to three pages of material. It was funny to hear "Nixon" praising Archie as "one great American." But while that kind of writing works for radio, it falls on its face in a visual medium. More significantly, as the introduction to a new series, it failed to show the conflict inherent in Archie's interaction with the rest of the family.

After we had shot six installments of the series and were facing our imminent debut on the air, the network, true to form, began to get cold feet. First, they scheduled us at 9:30 on Tuesday nights, opposite powerhouse movie slots on both ABC and NBC. In addition, someone in management had decided it would be better to open the season with the weaker episode (the second one shot) rather than the explosive pilot. Norman Lear asked my opinion of the network's order. I told him, "I'm in no position to make such a heady decision. You and Bud Yorkin have a whole lot more at stake than I do. But I sense you want to fight them, and if it were up to me, I would argue strenuously to put the pilot on first." Lear responded, "They're threatening legal action if we persist." My answer was, "If the network is allowed to dictate content, you've lost the show anyway. I think it's urgent to stand fast, but again, the financial risk is all yours. Nevertheless, I'll back you up to the best of my ability." I also told Norman that if the second show ran first, I had no intention of finishing the current episode, and that I would walk away from the series rather than submit to the kind of network tyranny that promised to doom the program before it ever got a chance.

This colloquy went on the entire week of rehearsal for the sixth episode. As we approached opening night, things really got hot. On any given Tuesday, we would tape a dress rehearsal in front of a California studio audience from 5 to 6:30 PM, and then do the final show at 8 PM. Our first broadcast was scheduled to air at 9:30 Eastern Time. We were informed that Lear and the network were in furious last-minute talks, and that CBS had said they would mount Episode No. 1 and Episode No. 2 on separate tape machines. The push of a button would decide the argument.

Having finished the dress-rehearsal taping, we all gathered in my control room to watch the 9:30 New York feed. I had bet that they would put on a substitute program and allow the matter to drag on, but I was wrong. As our clock showed 6:30 in California, the images of Carroll O'Connor and Jean Stapleton appeared, singing the opening song. We knew we were on the air, but we still had no idea which tape would run. We held our collective breath—and then the first line of dialogue proved CBS had decided to go our way.

At the time, this appeared to be our triumph, but it was the network that really won the day. They had given in, but in so doing had set the stage for making enormous profits. Still, high ratings did not materialize instantly. For a time, we languished in the Tuesday slot and, indeed, we were told after the first thirteen episodes that there would be no second season. Canceled! We were all depressed, for it had been a wonderful, if all too limited, experience. But of course, that was not really the end of the story.

Having been denied a pickup for a second season, I took my family to the Hawaiian island of Kauai, where at lunch one Sunday we were served by a Japanese waitress. Apologetically, she asked if she could collect on the bill early, since she had to leave. In the spirit of a languid weekend, I asked, jokingly, what could provoke such haste on a lovely, sunny day. There was a TV show that came on at three, she replied, and she didn't want to miss it. What show? I asked. She replied, "It's called *All in the Family*." Without revealing my connection, I asked what it was about the program that appealed to her. "It's Archie Bunker," she answered. "That's my husband!"

If a Japanese woman in the middle of the Pacific Ocean was making this connection, I thought, something unusual might be happening. Sure enough, when we returned, CBS had received feedback of this nature from thousands of other people. Word of mouth saved the day. That summer, reruns of the initial thirteen episodes showed ratings promise, and CBS reconsidered and switched us to Saturday night. Eventually, *All in the Family* would lead off a blockbuster Saturday lineup at 8 PM, followed by *M*A*S*H*, *The Mary Tyler Moore Show*, *The Bob Newhart Show*, and *The Carol Burnett Show*. During my four-year tenure as director, our program would achieve a 62 share of audience: out of every 100 television sets in use, 62 of them were tuned to the Bunkers.

CHAPTER
2

People often ask me how I got started in show business. The answer, I suppose, is poverty. I had returned to the University of Michigan after serving in the Air Force during the Second World War. Although the G.I. Bill was a godsend, paying tuition and a small stipend for books and incidentals, it wasn't enough. So I took on several odd jobs. I served breakfast at the Michigan Union, washed dishes at the Kappa Sigma house for my lunch, and drove a taxicab on weekends.

An opportunity for a different kind of employment unexpectedly fell into my lap. I had taken several courses in radio production from a marvelous teacher, Professor Garnet R. Garrison. Having worked as a director at NBC Radio in the late 1930s and early 1940s, he became a wonderful mentor, and in my senior year he urged me to consider getting involved in radio production and, subsequently, in that advancing new form of entertainment, television. So when I heard about a new radio station beginning to operate just outside Ann Arbor on Packard Road, I was eager to learn more. As a waiter, I earned thirty-five cents an hour, and tipping was expressly forbidden at the Union, so you can imagine my interest when I found out the station was offering a dollar an hour for people who could read the news as it came off the Associated Press wire, and who could double as disc jockeys.

Along with two other students, I applied for the job, and suddenly I was in show business—sort of. The station, WHRV (for Huron River Valley), was limited to 1,000 watts and assigned a frequency of 1,600 kilocycles, which presented a small problem. Before 1946, the radio spectrum in the United States ended at 1,560 kilocycles, but that year the band was extended to 1,600, making the new station silent for all except the few who owned new radios. To increase our audience, the station owner advertised in local newspapers that without charge, an engineer would come to people's home and adjust old radios to receive the station's signal! In this manner we probably doubled our listeners to a couple of hundred.

One Saturday evening, our employer convened a meeting of his weekend staff and said he wanted to fill some air time with broadcasts of the University of Michigan basketball team, about to begin its season. He asked which of us knew enough about Big Ten basketball to become our play-by-play man. I had written a sports column for my high school newspaper, though I had never attended a college game. So I promptly volunteered, claiming superior knowledge of the sport. The owner pronounced me qualified and assigned me to broadcast the game against Minnesota the following week.

Having had my bluff called, I hustled off to Wahr's Bookstore to buy a volume explaining the rules of college basketball. Next, I found the courage to approach the athletic director, Fritz Crisler, a man who had coached the Michigan football team to many a championship. I soon learned that basketball at Ann Arbor was hardly a huge draw. After a string of losing seasons, the "crowd" that showed up for a game numbered in the hundreds in a fieldhouse that could hold five thousand. When I asked him where I could set up to broadcast the games, Mr. Crisler shrugged. He said there had never been a demand for such a facility and he had no place to put me. I asked if I could have my station build a wooden "box" suspended from the rafters at midcourt, and he said, "Okay," with little enthusiasm or interest.

The station owner agreed to build such a contraption, which I had to reach by climbing to the top of the fieldhouse and then descending through the girders to my aerie in the sky. It proved satisfactory, if a little unnerving, and I recruited a friend to act as my "spotter," to point out who had the ball from time to time. I managed to get through the first night somehow and, to everyone's surprise, Michigan won. I felt more confident the next week and Michigan won again. And again! After the team had won six in a row, the fieldhouse began to fill to capacity for every game. As fans found they couldn't get into the sold-out arena, the station became overwhelmed with requests for engineers to adjust their radios to 1,600 kilocycles. I became a minor celebrity as my broadcasts began to reach a growing audience. When it came time to play the powerhouse Indiana and Iowa teams, their broadcasters advanced on Fritz Crisler, asking for space to report on the resurgent Michigan team. Crisler would say, "We have no room for you." Then he would point to my box in the sky and say, "Talk to the guy from WHRV." When they did, I made a deal for them to pick up my broadcasts for about $25 per repeater station. I now had a limited Big Ten network listening in.

When Michigan, unbelievably, finished the 1948 regular season undefeated, I approached the station owner and said he would have to send me to New York's Madison Square Garden to cover the team's appearance as Big Ten champions against other regional winners. He looked at me as if I had lost my mind and protested: "I don't have that kind of money for a basketball game!" I reminded him of the monster he had created. "If we don't carry the games," I said, "the villagers will be at your door with torches, and they will burn down your station for having deprived them of the sports narcotic you have provided." As the color drained from his face, I suggested a way out: "I think I can get a commercial sponsor for the broadcast, and for a modest fee I'm certain the athletic department will allow me to travel with the team by train to New York."

After getting his permission, I hit pay dirt on the first try—the local Ford dealership agreed to sponsor me with a shoestring budget. But the station owner laid down some draconian conditions. He said that no one would accompany me, that I would have to make all the press arrangements for a broadcast booth with the Madison Square Garden authorities, that I would have to hire my own radio engineer from a local New York station, and that I was only permitted to engage the telephone company's cheapest "Class D" line. This meant Ann Arbor could hear me speak at a prearranged time, but I could converse with them only by making a telephone call to synchronize our clocks before the broadcast.

I was left almost lightheaded by the notion that I would be dealing as a member of the press with the management of fabled Madison Square Garden. Nervously, I managed to secure credentials and a broadcast location, and made contact with an engineer from a small Bronx radio station, WBNX. I set up the line with AT&T and was suddenly in business. Surprisingly, everything went smoothly, except that Michigan came in fourth in a field of four. In consecutive games, two

legendary players, Ralph Beard of Kentucky and Bob Cousy of Holy Cross, made mincemeat of our defense.

On the train ride back to Ann Arbor, I reviewed the New York experience and decided I had found the backstage preparations more interesting than the actual broadcast. I determined that sports broadcasting would not become my life's work, and my thoughts turned to directing and producing.

The University of Michigan was on an accelerated trimester schedule in those days, so I raced through my B.A. degree and earned a master's in record time. When I consulted Professor Garrison for advice on my next move, I was appalled to hear him suggest, "Go to Grand Rapids—it could be a chance to break into television." I said, "If I do that, in five years I might be ready for Detroit. In another five I might make it to Chicago. If I'm still alive, I might finally reach New York. I think I'll go straight to New York. My parents are living in Queens and they'll put me up until I can land a job in Manhattan." Garrison said, "New York will break your heart."

He had a point; I couldn't find work there for nearly seven months. The best I could do was to get a job at a small radio station in Freeport, Long Island. It was a 250-watt outlet with a transmitter close to the Atlantic Ocean, which tended to increase its power somewhat. The station owner was a tyrant and so tight-fisted he allowed us only one small light bulb, which barely illuminated the small hallway to the restroom. I quickly learned that I was one of a long line of mistreated announcers who seldom remained in his employ. I lasted a week and went back home.

My father was a carpenter, and he offered to hire me as a laborer to begin "real work" instead of chasing my show business fantasy. After six days of back-breaking lifting, I quit and resumed venturing into New York in search of less painful employment. I was living rent-free in my parents' small apartment in Rockaway Beach, a long subway ride from Manhattan. In terms of my later career, though, the experience proved invaluable, as I was able to store away my father's frequent comments until they were repeated years later by Archie Bunker, addressed to his son-in-law, "Meathead." To survive without asking for money, I lived on the government stipend granted to veterans: $20 a week for 52 weeks.

I would make the daily trip into Manhattan to hang out at the Kaufman-Bedrick coffee shop, located on the lobby floor of the RCA Building, home of NBC Radio and Television. While nursing a cup of coffee, I would read discarded editions of *Variety*, the show-biz newspaper, in hopes of gleaning information that might lead to work. Also, I could sit near real professionals who would pause in the shop on the way to their offices upstairs.

Before I left Ann Arbor, Professor Garrison had mentioned the name of one of his former students, Walter McGraw, who had become a director for NBC Radio. I nervously steeled myself to make an introductory telephone call to McGraw, and was surprised and delighted when he suggested meeting at the RCA coffee shop the next week. McGraw couldn't have been nicer, although he, too, was out of work. In subsequent meetings, I met Walter's wife, Peggy, a writer who was also between jobs. One day over coffee, Walter was musing about what radio shows were popular at the time. The two hits that came to his mind were *We, the People* and Jack Webb's *Dragnet*.

In analyzing why these two productions worked so well, McGraw suggested that *We, the People* drew a large audience because it involved real people telling stories about incidents that had truly involved them in some way. One problem for the show was that ordinary folks were nervous reading a script live on the air, but fans generally overlooked this, entranced by the tales of abduction and murder. Listeners were hooked by the reality factor. In Walter's opinion, *Dragnet* presented a kind of reality in dramatic form. Jack Webb's "just the facts, ma'am" method of underplayed acting appealed hugely to audiences, who were invited into the "real" world of police detectives.

McGraw wanted to marry the two formats with an idea for a show he called *Wanted*. The idea centered around a weekly hunt for a major felon who would become the object of a nationwide search. Borrowing from the two previously discussed hits in a classic show-development formula of A meets B, Walter proposed interviewing in their homes—where they could feel at ease—the real people who had witnessed a crime, the ones acquainted with the escapee, or those who had served time with him. They would tell their stories in a relaxed session that could be tape-recorded and edited into a smooth narrative.

I had no idea if the technology available at the time could accommodate this, or if it would meet network standards of engineering quality. But McGraw told me that since Bing Crosby had made a huge investment in the Ampex Corporation, pioneers in the creation of high-quality audiotape recordings, most networks were leaning toward taping. At that time, programs originating on the West Coast had to be transmitted at 5 PM in Hollywood for reception at 8 PM on the East Coast. This required popular entertainers such as Bob Hope and Jack Benny to do another complete show at 8 PM for the West Coast. This irked star comedians and singers who wanted to do only one performance a night. Although the 5 PM shows were recorded on acetate discs, the audible hiss on some of those platters caused the networks to refuse to permit replays until Crosby convinced NBC to allow rebroadcast with the new, improved tape system. Walter said they now had a "portable" recording unit—it weighed only 60 pounds—that a radio technician could carry into people's homes. The interviewer would use standard microphones, ensuring quality control. I was invited to join the McGraw enterprise at a salary of no dollars a week, although I would be welcome to join them for lunches and dinners. It was an offer I couldn't refuse.

Peggy and Walter set about the research to start the program by telephoning or writing crime reporters throughout the country, asking them to search their newspaper morgues for prominent stories in which the felon remained at large. For this service the reporters would receive $25 per lead. If their subject ended up on the air, they would earn $25 more. Between meals, I helped staff the phones. Eventually, we compiled enough juicy stories for Peggy to write a radio script telling the tale, connected by the voices of real people who had made contact with the wanted man. No actors would be used except for the narrator, Walter, who would introduce and close each weekly episode. It required some twenty to twenty-five voices to tell the story, always concluded with McGraw imploring the public, "Catching this man is now up to you," or words to that effect. In another innovative stroke, the McGraws contacted the Hearst newspaper chain, whose papers nationwide would publish a mug shot of that night's star miscreant. This would sync with a radio cutaway in which listeners were told to look at the Hearst paper in their locality, with the Texas announcer saying, for example, "See page three of today's San Antonio Light," while New York's broadcaster was announcing, "Turn to page two of the Daily Mirror." It would be wonderful cross-promotion.

Before any of this could hit the airwaves, though, NBC had to put up $5,000 to make the radio pilot, a sample of where the series intended to go. In pursuit of this goal, the McGraws invited me to join them for my first network pitch meeting. With great excitement, I finally rode an RCA elevator up to the executive offices. I had no idea how much this initial network meeting would resemble the many that I would attend over the next fifty-plus years. Network executives may not have been cloned yet, but I am convinced they are all the product of the same damaged gene pool. Only a network executive, for instance, could have had this exchange with one of my writers twenty or thirty years later:

WRITER: What did you think of the script?
EXECUTIVE: I don't know. I'm the only one who's read it so far.

Naturally, at this first meeting I said nothing, and the McGraws conducted the pitch. When they had finished, the executives huddled for a moment, then advised us that they saw merit in the project but would only support us if the show were about criminals who were in prison, not free. But what about the title? Wouldn't that negate the basic premise of the show? No, they liked that—*Wanted* was "catchy." Walter argued briefly that the "heat," or tension, of the series would come from the felon running loose in society, but he soon gave up and agreed to produce a sample episode about a man locked up.

I soon found myself with Walter on a railroad crossing somewhere near a penitentiary in Western Pennsylvania. A young man was incarcerated in the institution, which we could see from the tracks, and his mother told her tragic story while we stood outside in a steady drizzle. Walter did all the work, while I watched. His technique seemed to work quite well, particularly later, in the homes of other interview subjects, whom he instantly put at ease with his patience and courtesy. Also, I noted that because of the prior input of the local crime reporter, Walter sometimes knew the history of his respondent better than the person himself recalled. In a second or third recitation by the witness, Walter would gently suggest incorporating a fact or quote that the speaker had stated for publication in the past, but had forgotten in the intervening years, which helped move our story forward. Later, when I became the field producer conducting the interviews, I leaned heavily on Walter's methods. It was incredibly useful training for becoming a director.

Returning to NBC's executive suite with the finished tape, we played our work for the small group of bosses, who met briefly, then returned with a novel idea. They found the idea of a program about wanted criminals intriguing, but they thought a story about a man already incarcerated lacked "heat." The leader of the pack suggested, "Why not do a series about people who escaped, who are loose in our society?"

McGraw taught me a great lesson that day. Without missing a beat, he said, "That's a terrific idea!"

Once NBC had approved *Wanted*, Walter, expressing more confidence in me than I felt in myself, assigned me to travel to Philadelphia to interview the warden of Eastern States Penitentiary. The subject who would kick off our series was the legendary bank robber Willie "The Actor" Sutton, who had escaped from prison some months before. As a twenty-four-year-old novice with no experience visiting prisons, I approached the menacing stone edifice with trepidation. The penitentiary had been built in 1825 and looked like something out of Dickens, but I took courage from the business card I had been given, identifying me as an employee of the NBC Radio Network. I presented my credentials to a prison guard and told him my engineer and I had an appointment to see the warden. Shortly, we were ushered deeper and deeper into the dank interior of one of the most frightening structures I had ever set foot in. Many steel bars and corridors later, we reached the warden's office, with my imagination running riot. What would this terrifying man look like? Probably huge, beefy, tough as nails, with the personality of a monster, I thought.

As we entered the dragon's lair, I was stunned to see, seated behind a sprawling desk, a man no larger than a jockey. He looked like Jimmy Gleason, a thin character actor in movies of the 1930s and 1940s, and wore a porkpie hat and yellow socks encased in brown loafers, which rested arrogantly on his desk with a penny stuck in each shoe. The warden was clearly Irish, with an East Coast accent. Trying to disguise my amazement, I introduced our radio engineer, who was now gratefully resting his sixty-pound tape recorder on the carpet.

I asked the warden if we could conduct our interview while sitting in the cell that Willie Sutton had occupied. He agreed, and we set off through another labyrinth of endless halls and iron-barred gates until we reached the last cell in a long row. As we arrived, a terrified inmate sitting in the cell looked up fearfully. The warden gestured, saying "Get outta there," and the man scampered into the care of one of the guards who had accompanied us.

As we entered the cell, I noticed one wall had been partially plastered. I was told that Sutton, with the help of several confederates, had started digging a tunnel from this very spot. It had taken many months and, when finished, measured more than ninety feet long. From newspaper reports I had learned that eight other men had escaped with Sutton. All had been rounded up practically the first day except for Fred Tenuto and Sutton himself, both of whom remained at large. One of the accounts I had read concerned one of the escapees—a man named Van Sant, who had been grilled mercilessly, after his capture, about how the prisoners had disposed of the enormous pile of dirt their tunneling had unearthed. Van Sant had held out for some time but finally said, "All right, I'll tell you." A stenographer was summoned to take down his testimony, and with an attentive audience listening carefully, the prisoner said, "We dug a long time and had no place to put the dirt until we figured out the perfect answer." "Well," said the guards, "what was it?" "We dug another hole," Van Sant answered, "and put the dirt in there." The account didn't describe what the general reaction was, but presumably the authorities were not laughing. It was later learned that the prisoners had systematically flushed the sand down the prison's ancient toilets. Modern prisons know all about this today, and now routinely monitor water flow in search of excess soil deposits in the sewage systems.

Now the warden sat on a cot in Sutton's cell, with the engineer and me on a facing bed, while I held the microphone. I began by offering a mild instruction, something like, "Please begin by stating your name and position and finish with words to the effect that the subject's whereabouts were not known at that time." This enabled us to segue into the next tape seamlessly. My off-mike comments were never to be heard on air; only the speaker's voice would appear in the program. McGraw had taught me to signal the engineer to start the tape apparatus with a surreptitious nod of the head, and to minimize the presence of the mike by maintaining close eye contact. This made the microphone and the entire process less intimidating, allowing the subject to talk more freely. Our warden that day, though, needed no instruction and no help.

Quietly, he began. "This is Warden Cornelius J. Burke"—he pronounced it "Boyk"—"of the Eastern States Penitentiary. I once spent a day visitin' the federal penitentiary at Alcatraz." (I wondered where he was going, but nodded encouragement to go on.) "At that time, they had there a population of 4,368"—this number and the next one may not be accurate, but the ratio is close—"4,368 of the most vicious, most dangerous prisoners we've got in this country. Here at Eastern States, we have a population of 6,474, and every one of those men is just as dangerous and just as vicious as anybody they got in Alcatraz!" Having made the case for his boys, the warden modulated his tone, saying, almost wistfully, "And among those men at one time was Willie Sutton"—he paused—"who has since left us." At this, the urge to laugh was overwhelming, but I managed to maintain eye contact, and bit my tongue until it bled. Warden Burke went on: "Now all the time Willie was here, he never gave us no trouble. But we knew he was thinkin'. We knew he wanted to leave this place udder than the right way, and by the right way, I mean goin' out that gate!" He spoke this last line with all the intensity of a road company actor delivering the closing speech of a florid melodrama as the curtain falls.

The warden's testimony was so compelling, it was the only time I ended up using a tape without extensive editing. We broadcast his entire interview. He even managed to teach me something about sound. Thinking about the background noises in the prison, I had imagined we would hear nothing but clanging gates and echoing footsteps. Instead, the warden's comments were underscored by some catchy Dixieland music. Without prompting, he explained that we were hearing the inmate band rehearsing for a concert. The man clearly had show business in his veins.

Another incident from my time at *Wanted* illustrates how, while telling a story, some people select words that a screenwriter wouldn't dare submit. In Cleveland one day, I interviewed a man whose neighbor had been murdered during a robbery. His recitation went something like this: "I thought I heard shots coming from Charley's house, but I wasn't sure. Some time later, I noticed the light on in his kitchen, and the back door open a crack. I tried to push the door, but somethin' was blockin' the thing. I finally got it open and found it was Charley who was stoppin' the door from openin'. There he was, layin' in a pool a' blood. I reached down to feel for a pulse and there wasn't much pulse, because just then Charley was takin' his last gurgle." The word *gurgle* was terribly graphic, and devastatingly cold. If I were writing a script, it never would have occurred to me.

The Cleveland police identified Charley's murderer as one Edward Sadowski, who had fled the city and escaped, probably to Mexico. The chief of detectives insisted that he had long since left town. On the night we broadcast the Sadowski case, I was in Seattle, trying desperately to get a recording from a former FBI agent, now an attorney in private practice, regarding another case. The ex-FBI agent insisted that he couldn't comment on any situation with which he had been involved because of a rule of silence imposed by FBI Director J. Edgar Hoover. This prohibition applied, apparently, to all agents current and retired, and he insisted I would never get him on tape. I asked the man if he was acquainted with our show. When he said no, I invited him to dinner and to listen to that night's episode.

At the hotel, when I turned on the radio to listen to the local NBC affiliate broadcast *Wanted,* I was startled to hear our narrator, Walter McGraw, saying that instead of our normal opening, we were about to hear from a special guest, the Cleveland police department's chief of homicide, Captain David Kerr. I knew Captain Kerr, having taped his comments some two weeks earlier, so I listened intently. "Last week," he announced, "we cooperated with *Wanted* in putting the spotlight on an at-large murderer who we believed had run from our jurisdiction. I told the interviewer that Edward Sadowski was long gone from the city and probably holed up somewhere in Mexico. After the broadcast, however, our switchboards lit up with calls, as they do every week after this show is broadcast, and of course we track down every lead. One of these tips led us to an apartment where we found a man crouching under a bed. Sure enough, it turned out to be Mr. Sadowski. When we ordered him to raise his hands, he came up firing a pistol, and our officers put a bullet in his head, two in his chest, and three more in his abdomen. Needless to say, the subject offered no resistance."

The former FBI agent was entranced. "What a great show!" he exclaimed. "I'll give you the recording you want." Not only that, but he also filled a void we needed to complete an episode we were working on in Virginia. It turned out to be a real coup.

Speaking of J. Edgar Hoover, when McGraw had first contacted the FBI, he was brushed off with a typical "not interested." McGraw said, "Okay, we'll deal with state and city authorities," which we did. Once we were on the air, we began to do quite well without federal assistance. In fact, when we started catching criminals on a regular basis—four out of the first seven we broadcast—Hoover became interested in joining us. McGraw blew him off.

One day, while working in the Southwest, my engineer and I missed a plane out of Albuquerque on our way to Denver, where we had reservations at the Brown Palace Hotel. Because of our late arrival, the hotel had given away our rooms, but the management was kind enough to register us at one of their other properties. Arriving in my room, I called New York to let Peggy and Walter know I was all right. "You're at the such-and-such hotel in Denver," Walter said.

"How did you know?" I asked.

"Hoover's office called to say, 'Your boy Johnny isn't at the Brown Palace. He's checking in to the such-and-such,'" from where I was calling. Apparently, the FBI had a tail on me. That may have been comforting on one level. But it suggested that I was in a high stakes game for which I had not knowingly volunteered.

An experience in Philadelphia further convinced me that I should think about moving on. In researching the story of Fred Tenuto, who had escaped from the penitentiary with Willie Sutton, I met a pair of homicide detectives named, improbably, Patrick McGurk and Dennis McColgan. Thanks to my NBC expense account, every evening with them was spent eating and drinking in famous establishments well beyond their means as city employees. Something the officers kept doing caught my attention, and I asked naively, "How come you guys always select a table where you can sit with your backs to the wall?"

"Easy," one of them responded. "Police always want to sit where they can see all the action in a restaurant. And did you notice we always keep our right hands free to grab a weapon if necessary?" I hadn't noticed, but it suddenly hit me: "In the event of shooting, wouldn't I be in the line of fire? What should I do in that case?" Both cops answered together: "Duck!"

As part of the Tenuto investigation, I wanted to tape a bartender working in a saloon at the corner of Tenth and Watkins Streets in South Philadelphia. Nobody at the police station was eager to take my engineer and me to the location, even though I offered some expense money to anyone who'd come along. At last, one tough sergeant said he would accept the fee I offered and would accompany us if we would stay calm and do exactly what he told us.

It was a hot, sunny day, and the officer told us to wait outside while he entered the bar through the front entrance. As he entered, the rear door practically exploded open, with a bunch of men running as if for their lives. When we were invited to join the sergeant inside, he was repeating softly to the dimly lit and ominously quiet room, "This isn't a pinch. Be easy." As things settled down, I approached the bartender and began to ask a few questions. He appeared terrified, and finally stammered, "Look, you better get out of town. They say Tenuto is living somewhere near here, and he won't be happy to see you."

I stayed just long enough to tape the man. And I began thinking about looking for a slightly different line of work.

There's an incident that's said to have happened in the early days of television, during a live dramatic broadcast. One of the actors, playing a man sitting in an airplane, completely forgot his lines. So he said to his seatmate, "This is where I get off," which is exactly what he did. I have no idea how the crew wriggled their way out of that one.

At the dawn of television, live production was the only game in town, and what you saw was what you got. The phrase "working live" is meaningless today, with the advent of sophisticated editing. In the digital age, the ability exists to reconstruct scenes and create venues that could not exist in reality. But when I started out, there were no retakes, no ability to fix any errors. So there are countless examples of the gaffes and horrors associated with that primitive era of production, some of which became legends of a sort.

One example of this is amusing now in hindsight, although it couldn't have been to those who endured the moment: In a notable TV production of *Hamlet,* Maurice Evans walked downstage in the set of Elsinore Castle, and began the famous soliloquy, "Now I am alone . . ." Unfortunately, he was not. He had unexpectedly been joined by a rather rotund stagehand, crossing upstage behind him. Things got worse when the workman stopped, looked off into the wings, where presumably others were waving at him to get off, then looked toward Evans. When he realized where he was, he did a giant take and dropped to the ground, where he slowly inched his way along, making a painfully slow exit while trying to look inconspicuous. Because the camera had on a wide-angle lens, for an extremely long shot, every excruciating moment of his crawl was manifest to the world, as Evans bravely pressed on with his Shakespeare. I didn't witness that particular episode firsthand, but I did get a chance to live through some similarly humorous (though at times terrifying) events that characterized working live before millions of people.

In 1950, when NBC decided they wanted to present a TV version of *Wanted* and asked me to continue with the series, I said, "No way." I was becoming too identifiable as it was. A radio tape unit was conspicuous enough, and I could only imagine the attention the lights of a TV film crew would have attracted. However, I did use some of the NBC contacts I had made in radio to ask for an assignment within the expanding television network. When I was asked what job I had in mind, I said I would like to become a director. This request was greeted by laughter. People became directors, I was told, only after serving time as stage managers. I said that was okay if a position were open, but I was told I probably would not be interested, since the position paid only $80 a week (for my work on *Wanted,* I had been earning $250 a week, plus expenses). To their surprise, I accepted the job with alacrity, and began my career in the new enterprise near the bottom of the food chain.

Some of my fellow stage managers of the period, I should note, went on to achieve distinction. Among them were Arthur Penn, later a distinguished Broadway director who also directed the films *The Miracle Worker* and *Bonnie and Clyde;* Jack Shea, who became a three-term president of the Directors Guild of America; Paul Bogart, who followed me when I left *All in the Family,* and Dominick Dunne, later a famous novelist and journalist. But back then, we were twenty-five or so young upstarts, assigned to a windowless office—formerly a large supply closet—on the 28th floor of the RKO Building in Radio City. The place was furnished with three desks and an equal number of chairs. We were not expected to use the facilities other than to write our daily reports, but things became so crowded from time to time that we appealed to our supervisor, Roy Passman, for some relief from the stagnant air. Our pleas fell on deaf ears, though not for lack of trying.

One day I asked the property department to lend me a stuffed canary in a cage, and hung the bird upside-down from its perch. Knowing the time of Mr. Passman's arrival, we brought together as many of our group as possible, and filled the office with "victims" demonstrating various forms of simulated oxygen deprivation. When our boss passed our door, I pointed to the lifeless bird and said, "Our canary just died. Can't you help us get some air?" This got us nowhere. Nor did the scrawled message, "For the love of God, Montresor," affixed to our closed door. Foolishly, we imagined Passman had read Edgar Allan Poe's *The Cask of Amontillado* and would remember the dying man's cry as the last brick is mortared into place, ensuring his death by suffocation. No such luck.

Finally, I got our scenic department to paint a 28th floor perspective of Manhattan, and we installed this simulated window on our blank wall. For this occasion, we gathered everybody who wasn't on assignment at the moment, and we packed the space like the Marx Brothers' stateroom scene, staring out at the "view" as Passman approached. This stunt did have an effect, apparently, because the next day workmen appeared and broke through part of one of the walls, creating an opening about two feet from the ceiling. Management had relented, giving us a trickle of air filtering in from the adjoining space. It was not the great solution we had sought, but it did grant us a little victory at the expense of our petty chief.

Jack Shea and I were constant thorns in Passman's side, because we preached union doctrine any chance we could. There had been a relatively toothless union known as the Radio Directors Guild, now renaming itself the Radio and Television Directors Guild. Shea and I joined immediately, even though the outfit was not recognized officially and, therefore, was not a closed shop requiring membership within the industry. Most of our group signed up when Jack and I began to talk solidarity, and before long we were on our way to becoming a serious bargaining unit. While we proselytized, we began to live by certain rules of behavior we invented. We proclaimed brashly, "The union requires us to approach our jobs in a prescribed professional manner." If we made our claims sound forceful and official enough, agency or other nonnetwork production units accepted our "rules." In time, even the networks signed on to these standards, and they became codified. Eventually they formed the basis of today's collective bargaining agreements as they relate to stage managers and associate directors.

One day I was called in to Passman's office and asked if I would be willing to travel to Los Angeles for a special job. I was instantly suspicious. Was I being sent away because I had been a ringleader in tormenting the man? I never voiced the thought, but Passman went on to say I had been chosen because, along with Arthur Penn, I was considered an excellent stage manager. In 1951, live television originated only on the East Coast and could be seen as far west as the Pacific Ocean. West-to-East transmission was not yet possible, but the network was about to inaugurate a coaxial cable to enable it. Therefore, novice stage managers needed to be trained in the techniques required to service programs such as *The Colgate Comedy Hour.* Passman said it would be our task to recruit likely candidates and teach them how to provide network coverage.

I grumbled something about being banished to a wasteland and demanded to know how long the job would take. Passman said we'd be needed for just two weeks, and I agreed to go for that long. Also assigned with Penn and me was a fellow named Bud Yorkin; I believe he was an associate director at the time. I had never met the man, but he would one day own the *All in the Family* franchise along with Norman Lear.

I arrived in California on a magnificent October day and checked into the Knickerbocker Hotel, where I had stayed once during my *Wanted* days. The sunshine was marvelous, and I soon lost my New York scowl, especially after reporting to the El Capitan Theater and finding the chief carpenter and his crew polite and welcoming. This was a far cry from theatrical workers on the East Coast, where every day provided a new confrontation. Our first recruit was a young actor named Jack Smight, later a polished film director who crafted *Harper* and *Midway.* Jack was a quick study and became one of the regular stage managers on *Colgate,* where Bud Yorkin served as associate director. Arthur Penn and I continued to find other candidates, and the two weeks passed rapidly. We were still recruiting and teaching when we were asked to extend our assignments six weeks longer. I informed the company that I would remain in town that long, but that would be it.

As the six weeks ended, though, I had become so thoroughly addicted to Los Angeles that when management asked if I would consider staying on permanently, I immediately replied, "Gather up my belongings in New York and have them shipped." I have never regretted this decision, although at the time I was sorry to see Arthur Penn refuse the long-term offer and return to New York. I would miss his friendship and his wise counsel on many occasions. Of course, Arthur made the right decision for himself, becoming one of the featured directors on *Philco Playhouse* and, later, the Broadway stage. I think he decided to return to New York after walking with me down Hollywood Boulevard one day in late November. A series of "Christmas trees" made of green tin had been installed over each lamppost on the street, trimmed with white paint to simulate snow and bathed in brilliant sunlight. It was a bizarre sight to our New York eyes. They didn't call the place Tinseltown for nothing. "If I ever see this and call it normal," Arthur said, "I'll know I've stayed here too long."

During my days as an NBC stage manager, before and after my move to the West Coast, I witnessed plenty of foul-ups that no one could have invented. One day I was assigned to monitor the time and placement of a live commercial insert within a program, produced by an outside advertising agency. The program featured "Dunninger, the Mental Wizard," a see-all, know-all "mentalist" act. As the NBC representative, I had little to do but sit in the control room behind the production team and observe the action with my notepad at the ready. The first two sales pitches went as planned, but as the program neared its end, the director became concerned that time would run out before the final commercial. He instructed the stage manager to "give Dunninger a speed-up and signal we have one minute to go."

The stage manager obeyed, but the mentalist's pace continued as before. The director called, "Give him thirty seconds!" No response. "Speed him up, we're not going to make it!" Pandemonium reigned as the performer talked right into the NBC system cue, cutting off transmission. The last commercial was lost: disaster. I made my notes, and joined the angry mob as they boiled out of the control room and confronted a bewildered Dunninger. "We lost the last commercial!" the agency men screamed. "Why didn't you take our cues?"

"What cues?" Dunninger asked.

"The three or four speed-ups, the one-minute, and the thirty-second cues we gave to the stage manager."

Dunninger was irate. "Why don't you put the son of a bitch where I can see him? What do you think I am, a *mind reader?*"

One of my other early assignments at NBC was working as one of the stage managers on *The Kraft Television Theater,* produced and directed by employees of the J. Walter Thompson advertising agency. The show was a one-hour drama presented weekly, featuring excellent writing, above-average casting (frequently using performers who customarily worked on Broadway), and a pair of interesting directors. We stage managers were never privy to what occurred before the production moved into Studio 8-H each week, since we were only employed for one day of camera rehearsal and another ten to twelve hours the following day when the live broadcast took place. It was plain, however, that a well-oiled machine was at work. The director Stanley Quinn would "dry"-rehearse in a venue outside NBC for a full week, using a bare hall with the "sets" marked on the floor with tape to indicate doors, windows, and the like; rudimentary props stood in for the real thing. Proper sets, props, and costumes were never used until the company arrived at NBC, when the assigned stage managers were expected to learn the entire production—with its myriad cues—while staying out of the way of the four or five cameras. While this company worked on its second week of rehearsal and its two days in studio, the other director, Maury Holland, would be mounting his play in the rehearsal hall vacated by Quinn. This weekly alternation appeared to work quite well for the agency, and I was granted the invaluable chance to observe two completely different approaches to drama.

Stanley Quinn was a perfectionist who, in my opinion, occasionally overprepared. He demanded and achieved a perfectly workable solution each week, sometimes at the cost of inhibiting performances. On the other hand, I felt Maury Holland was a bit too loose. He was more interested in camera effects than in the humanity inherent in a particular piece. Holland was addicted to shooting through fireplaces, opening hinged pictures to allow a camera to poke through, moving an entire wall to provide an unusual angle. All this is acceptable, but it shouldn't be overdone, as Mr. Holland discovered one night to his regret.

During the live broadcast that evening, Maury lost his way. Following my carefully marked script, I told Tommy Noonan, our chief carpenter (stagehand), to flip open a wall that had been rehearsed to move when a particular line was spoken. The line was read, I gave the cue, but unhappily, in the control room Holland called the wrong camera, which revealed a group of rattled actors performing in front of a set piece that had miraculously opened behind them. There, in full view of the world, Tommy Noonan stood with his hands on a tip-jack, looking offstage obediently in my direction, waiting for his next cue.

I was hidden by a flat, out of view, with a monitor next to me, bemused by the scene I was witnessing on national TV. There were the actors emoting, and Tommy Noonan looking offstage expectantly, and a boom operator in the deep background, sitting on a set not yet in use, munching on an apple.

"Tommy," I said quietly, addressing his image on my TV set, "close the wall." I could see my puzzled crew foreman on TV mouth the words, "Close the wall?" When I said yes, still concentrating on my monitor, Tommy give an elaborate shrug as he restored the set to its proper order. The expected blast in my earphones did not materialize. Instead, a kind of deranged, strangled laughter came out of Holland's mouth.

"You work for ten days" he began with an almost quiet giggle. Then he said, bitterly, "You rehearse long hours"; that gave way to demented laughter. "You spend all kinds of money"; Then the technical director's voice broke in: "Maury, should I take camera three?" The director's choked response was, "Take anything you want, it doesn't matter anymore . . . The whole wall . . ." He punctuated this last utterance with restrained yet hysterical mumbling. I derived from the situation an invaluable lesson in the craft of directing: Don't try to overproduce effects or get too technically cute.

Another episode at NBC involved a director we derisively nicknamed Captain Video because of his many gaffes. Our hero one day was directing a "remote" at a Navy yard dock, where the battleship *New Jersey* was moored. Looking through the camera as he set up a shot, he found the framing to be off. Waving his hands to accompany his order, he shouted, "Move the boat four feet to the left!" The "boat" was 45,000 tons of warship secured by giant hawsers, and it wasn't going anywhere. Someone suggested gently that it might be easier to move the camera, and this was done as the perplexed "captain" watched.

Quite the opposite kind of director was Fred Coe, a soft-spoken Southerner who produced and occasionally directed *Philco Playhouse,* a superior dramatic series. Even the best, however, can run into difficulty, as happened when Fred directed a live broadcast of *Cyrano de Bergerac*. To create a mood at the beginning of the final act when the protagonist, mortally wounded, enters the garden of the nunnery, Fred called softly, "Fade up . . ." The picture resolved into a moonlit exterior, as he whispered, "Cue the leaves . . ." From above, autumn foliage gently floated to earth. Almost inaudibly, Coe spoke into his control room microphone, "Cue the nun," as leaves continued to fall softly in the moonlight; the nun did not appear. Slightly louder, Fred said, "Cue the nun." More leaves, no nun. Louder still: "Cue the nun!" With no nun in sight and the stage lull beginning to constitute a crisis: "CUE THE GODDAMNED NUN!"

By then, every member of the crew had removed his headset to avoid hearing loss, and so the roar from the control room was piped through twenty-five pairs of earphones and directly into the boom microphones, broadcasting it nationwide. To make matters worse, the nun finally appeared onstage as if she'd been shot from a cannon.

Commercials weren't immune to these kinds of miscues. In Hollywood, early in 1951, I was ordered to stage-manage a live commercial cut-in from an NBC studio on Vine Street—a ludicrous assignment, to me. Up the street at the El Capitan Theater, the main event, *The Colgate Comedy Hour* starring Dean Martin and Jerry Lewis, was being put together. This ambitious production required a full orchestra, singers, dancers, sketches to be rehearsed, and so on, and every minute was needed to mount the one-hour live show. By contrast, we had the exclusive use of a giant stage to spend a full day rehearsing a one-minute pitch for a brand of frozen orange juice called Snow Crop. The advertising agency had gone to great lengths to hire a famous film actor, Fred MacMurray, to sell the item, and I suppose the nervous ad men who buzzed about the set wanted to get their money's worth. So we ran through the short script endlessly. The product was fussed over, lit and relit, the commentary discussed as if we were presenting Ibsen and rehearsed until we wanted to throw up. MacMurray became so annoyed by the constant repetition that he began to refer to the product as "Snow Crap." The crew laughed. The agency men frowned.

As the day wore on, though I agreed wholeheartedly that we had over-rehearsed the spot, I said to MacMurray that I thought the constant repetition of "Snow Crap" might become so embedded in his unconscious that there could be a slight danger of him saying it "on the night." He laughed at the thought, and kept on mispronouncing. Of course, you have already guessed what happened.

When our spot was broadcast live and MacMurray said the evil words, I thought the agency reps would commit mass suicide. It reminded me of the famous *New Yorker* cartoon showing Procter & Gamble executives gathered around a pool in various poses of disbelief and horror; it was captioned, "The day the Ivory Soap sank at P. & G."

My stage manager days at NBC gave me the pleasure of working with many legendary comedians, including the wonderful Jimmy Durante. This extraordinarily talented and gentle man was terrific in rehearsal, magnificent on the air, and always pleasant to the entire working crew. His show was part of *The All-Star Revue,* an umbrella title for a weekly variety show featuring great comedians, with Jimmy one week, Ed Wynn the next, Olsen and Johnson another time, then Victor Borge, and so on. The series was staged in New York on what was formerly America's only "Ice Theater," featuring a giant stage and seats for more than five thousand spectators. It was a brilliant venue for production, and as stage manager I had control of seven floors of fly galleries, myriad curtains, drapes, tormentors, teasers—the whole works. The Center Theater gave one a feeling of power seldom experienced on such a scale. The span of the stage was breathtaking and featured three working rectangular elevators, which allowed the use of different levels for a variety of theatrical tricks. Superimposed on the three lifts was a massive turntable, an engineering marvel.

When Durante closed his show each week, he would walk into his "dressing room" set, which featured an upright piano. Depending on the time remaining on these live broadcasts, Jimmy would sing a few bars of his closing song: "Goodnight, goodnight, it's time to say goodnight . . ." On a command from the control room, I would cue Durante to get up from the piano, move upstage, and put on his hat, at which time the grips would be signaled to pull apart the back wall of the set. The camera would now see Jimmy walking away into a distant blackness, moving through a series of illuminated white circles, diminishing in size as he moved far upstage, and finally speaking his closing line: "Goodnight, Mrs. Calabash, wherever you are." I never found out what the reference to Mrs. Calabash meant, but the sequence was emotionally moving for some reason, and it almost brought tears to my eyes every time. I wish I could remember the name of the creative director who came up with a novel twist one week, but fifty-five years have intervened and I can't recall. The stunt, however, remains with me to this day.

The home audience eagerly awaited the closing bit each time Durante performed. One night, however, our director decided he wanted to create a surprise by using the massive turntable. The dressing-room set was erected on the turntable itself, and Jimmy was seen among the five thousand spectators in the theater. On cue, he began walking out of the audience, ascended the stage steps, and entered the dressing room while the camera followed his action. As he stepped into the set, the camera pushed in with him so that the scene showed Durante in his familiar closing position within the "walls" of the enclosure. As he began playing the piano, I cued the engineers to rotate the turntable 180 degrees. This movement, undetected at home, happened swiftly, so that when the back walls of the set were pulled apart, Durante exited, not into the customary circles of light, but back into the audience he had just left! It was a phenomenally successful shot, and people talked about it for weeks afterward, trying to figure out how the magical effect was pulled off on a live broadcast.

Before I left New York, in addition to my work on *The Kraft Television Theater,* I had been assigned to *The Jack Carter Show,* a one-hour, Saturday-night sketch-variety program occupying the slot just ahead of Sid Caesar and *Your Show of Shows,* which ran for ninety minutes. Jack and I later became good friends in California, but while I worked his show, he appeared to be neurotically driven and compulsive, full of manic energy that somehow fueled his onstage persona. He was a very funny man when he worked before an audience, but he was tortured in rehearsals, frequently working himself up into a fury. Jack would never deliver his opening monologue in full voice when he rehearsed. He would sort of mumble the words for timing purposes; he wanted to keep his material fresh for the night. We never got to hear the jokes until we were on the air. It was surprising, then, to hear him say one day, "This is the first time I've had flop-sweats in a rehearsal." Someone explained to me that "flop-sweats" described the malady that visited a comic if he was bombing in front of an audience. I was puzzled, and naively asked a veteran crew person, "How does Jack expect us to laugh if we can't hear the material?" The answer left me more confused than ever. "Mr. Carter wants it both ways. He doesn't want his stuff to get stale, so he just moves his lips when he rehearses. But he expects you to get the jokes, because he hears them in his head perfectly and the monologue is real funny, so why aren't you laughing with him?"

In Manhattan, the *Carter* show was produced by Ernie Glucksman, a genial man who had worked the Borscht Belt in the Catskill Mountains of New York. The producer was somewhat of a restraining hand on Jack, and I watched Ernie carefully as he put the troupe through its paces in rehearsal. We occupied the Seven Arts Room of the Edison Hotel, just off Broadway, and I was assigned as second stage manager on Fridays and Saturdays only. My job was to "hold book" during run-throughs, cue the talent as directed, run a stopwatch on everything, and generally maintain order the following day. That's when we would load into the Hudson Theater, a venerable house so old that it still had gas-fired footlights, artifacts of theatrical history, although they were no longer in use.

It was always an early call on Saturday mornings, and the theater was cold and barren as I reported for work. The stage crew was busily hanging scenery when Jack would arrive, his overcoat draped around his shoulders, invariably in a peevish mood. He would begin to complain about the scenery even though someone would explain to him patiently each week that there were no lights set as yet, some of the painting needed to be finished, and so forth. None of this registered. Jack would utter imprecations to the effect that NBC was short-changing him, that all the money was going to Sid Caesar. But when the audience arrived for the live telecast, he always came through.

As soon as we wrapped our show each Saturday night, most of us repaired to the Blue Ribbon, a restaurant and bar next door, where we drank German beer and watched the program we all regarded as "the real thing." That was *Your Show of Shows*, daring and magnificent week after week. Sid Caesar, Carl Reiner, Howie Morris, and Imogene Coca performed the work of Sid's enormously gifted writing staff, which included Neil Simon, Mel Brooks, Larry Gelbart, Woody Allen, Selma Diamond, Danny Simon, Tony Webster, Lucille Kallen, Joe Stein, and

Mike Stewart—an incredible array of talent led by head writer Mel Tolkin. Mel was a transplanted Russian who once read the sign "No U Turn" as "No, *you* turn." This last came to me from Carl Reiner, who frequently quoted the remark with delight.

Watching Sid and Carl was a university course in comedy, and I'm certain that viewing that remarkable series informed my future work. Sid and his wife, Florence, are now our neighbors in Beverly Hills, and we have dinner or one of Sid's special breakfasts frequently; he's a wonderful cook. My wife, Pat, has asked him on occasion to describe an incident she may have heard about, and it's one of the great pleasures to watch him drift into character and regale us with a brilliant pantomime or a run of his double-talk in French, Italian, German, Japanese, or whatever the accent may be. He's a national treasure.

Before I left New York, I got to eavesdrop on one other priceless scene involving a legendary NBC personality. *Kraft Television Theater* was not the only tenant of the RCA Building's Studio 8-H; the studio also housed the famous NBC Symphony, conducted at that time by Arturo Toscanini. The ninth floor of the studio featured a balcony from which it was possible to watch a rehearsal of the great orchestra, provided one stayed out of the famous maestro's sight. While listening to one of these run-throughs during a break from my stage-managing duties, I watched as the volatile conductor had a bit of a run-in with one of his hapless musicians. Apparently, this man kept hitting false notes, even after Toscanini had corrected him numerous times. The leader was patient for a while, but after yet another misstep, Toscanini shouted, "Pick up your instrument and leave. You are fired!" The musician did as he was told, but as he reached the exit, he turned and yelled back, "You're a no good son of a bitch." Without hesitation, Toscanini hurled back his response: "It's too late to apologize."

In 1952, having served NBC as a West Coast stage manager, I was upgraded to associate director (AD), and then assigned to work with director Bill Bennington on two memorable occasions. The twenty-fifth Academy Awards ceremony was scheduled to be broadcast live for the first time, and Bennington and I were chosen to oversee the event. The master of ceremonies at the Pantages Theater that night was Bob Hope, and each presenter was an actor or actress who had won an Oscar in the past. It was an awesome assemblage of stars, many of them, particularly the women, deeply concerned about how they would look on television. To soothe these anxieties, NBC had hired Hal Mohr, an Oscar-winning cameraman, to consult with our lighting engineers.

Hal was a giant of a man who calmed down the ladies simply by his presence. But he couldn't do much about electronic shooting other than offer friendly advice to the crew. As AD, I carefully monitored the time allotted each presenter, and created a lengthy rundown chart indicating where we were supposed to be at any given minute during the broadcast. All went according to plan, until Milton Berle refused to acknowledge the frantic speed-up signals being thrown at him. He was hysterically funny, but our efforts to speed him up proved fruitless. Uncle Miltie finally wound down, but we had to cut deeply into the time given other acts. Ultimately, we made it off the air "on the button." I believe it was one of the only occasions when the ceremony finished on time.

My next assignment with Bennington was to cover Florence Chadwick's attempt to swim the Catalina Channel, in Southern California. This was purely a stunt to show the versatility of television coverage, but planning the event placed a heavy burden on our engineering depart-ment. We used two cameras operating out of a remote truck that had been driven onto a World War II-era LCT (landing craft tank). This was a small vessel just big enough to contain the truck and a couple of studio lights that could illuminate the swimmer throughout the night. A third cameraman boarded a platform high above the stern of the little craft. His job was not to photograph anything, but solely to point his equipment toward Catalina Island. The electronic output of our remote unit was fed through his dish into the void. On the island, engineers would pick up the signal from the boat and relay it to Lookout Mountain in the Hollywood Hills, then on to NBC's broadcast transmitters on Mount Wilson. At some point, approximately midway across the channel, our cameraman was to turn his unit to face the mainland. It all sounded suspicious to those of us who were ignorant of technical matters, but we were assured the system would work.

Of all the people associated with this venture, I felt most sorry for that third cameraman, Armand Poitras, who had the difficult task of pointing his device into the dark, using only his headphones to hear whether he was "on the beam" or had to pan right or left to keep the signal focused. All this took place on an extremely cold night, with all of us exposed to the elements for eleven or twelve hours.

At Catalina's Isthmus, it was bizarre but exciting to see Florence Chadwick, who had conquered the English Channel and other major crossings, enter the water at about 10 PM, wearing goggles, her body covered with grease. She would be accompanied across the channel by a rowboat containing her trainer, who was not allowed to touch her but could occasionally offer some kind of sustenance by means of a bottle tied to a stick. A flotilla of small boats carrying reporters and photographers accompanied us, as well as several crafts holding men armed with rifles. When I asked about this, I was told they were there to ward off any sharks that our lights might attract. I laughed to myself at this notion, believing the gunmen were really just there to hype the program. I wasn't laughing some time later when I learned the Catalina Channel is known as a hunting ground of the great white shark, an immense predator that can exceed twenty feet in length.

Having been warned about the cold, I had dressed warmly. Inside our truck's control room, though, the temperature soared as the electronic equipment gave off waves of heat. Also, something none of us had counted on began to happen. Because of the swimmer's slow speed, the skipper of our boat had to throttle back to about one knot per hour. With two engines running, it became too difficult to maintain proper camera distance, so we had to shut down one engine. To maintain some kind of headway and stability, the helmsman would alternate running first one engine, then the next. Also, as I learned that night, the channel was well known for producing the nightly "Catalina chop," an exceedingly restless sea. With the chop, the alternating engines, and a boat that floated like a cork without a tank to weigh it down, a certain malaise began to circulate.

In the control room it was worse. The combination of heat, the rocky image of Miss Chadwick rising and falling with the swells—all of this motion repeated on the bank of video screens—and the bumpy pitch and roll of the boat itself, began to take its toll. One by one, the crew would turn a shade of green, then absent themselves for a quick trip to the open air. I laughed because I had a cast-iron stomach, and even ate a sandwich as others were bailing out. At one juncture Bennington, too, felt ill, and he turned the director's seat over to me as he raced for the railings. After some time, he returned to see me insouciantly munching away at my lunch, but then my turn arrived. Perspiring freely, I raced to the deck and headed for the nearest rail—only to be interrupted by our announcer, who was rapidly running out of things to say about Florence Chadwick. Despite my frantic attempts to wave him away, he approached, grabbed me gratefully, and said to the unseen television audience, "Here's one of our directors up for a breath of air. John, what can you tell us about covering this wonderful event?"

It may have been the cold air, or the shock of suddenly appearing on live television, but I somehow managed to control my shaky insides enough to be interviewed. I felt rather foolish. Here I was, wearing a fleece-lined jacket left over from my Air Force days, fighting nausea, and feeling as cold as I can ever remember feeling, and there in the water was a plucky woman swimming hour after hour in a choppy sea fit for polar bears. I mumbled a few platitudes and escaped to the warmth of the control room. Although the night wore on endlessly, I was told later that much of Southern California apparently stayed with us. Station KNBH (as it was known before becoming KNBC) gathered a huge audience for the broadcast.

Sadly, as dawn broke, the tide had turned against Miss Chadwick, and she was beginning to weaken. We could see Dana Point, our destination, looming gray on the misty horizon, and we began to cheer our heroine on. To encourage her further, volunteers dove into the water to swim by her side. Former Olympic medal winners Buster Crabbe and Johnny Weismuller, each of whom had portrayed Tarzan in films, were among those who matched her stroke for stroke, but the attempts were futile. With the coast only a stone's throw away, she signaled to her backup team that she was finished, and they hauled her onto their boat and covered her with blankets. It was a sad ending to a gallant try.

When we signed off, we had our own rescue to effect, helping Armand down from his camera operator's perch. Practically frozen, he had stayed manfully at his post above the stern the entire time we were on the air. Later, we learned from our crew on Catalina that before we reached the halfway point across the channel that our technicians had almost lost the ability to maintain a viable signal. Engineers on the island were collecting our output with their receiving dish before retransmitting to Lookout Mountain. It was imperative for them to keep the boat's electronic output centered, but as our little craft chugged slowly toward the mainland, the invisible beam we were sending began to drift toward a stand of trees. Since line of sight had to be maintained at all times, the signal would be lost if foliage or solid wood interfered. Fueled by panic, the engineers began to chop down the offending trees as the beam drifted toward the grove. Fortunately, our boat soon arrived at the midpoint and we were able to aim the signal directly to the mainland, sparing Catalina any further deforestation.

Florence Chadwick tried the Catalina swim again some years later. This time she made it across. But there was no television crew assigned to record it.

I had gotten my start in broadcasting back in college because of poverty; my first assignment as a director happened because of illness. In 1953, I was associate director for Sid Smith on a live broadcast starring the famous opera singer Ezio Pinza. As I recall, the show was supposed to go on at 5 PM, but at 4:15 Sid was stricken with food poisoning. Our producer was trying desperately to find an emergency replacement. It was a fairly complicated musical hour, with a live orchestra, and it would have been impossible for any unfamiliar director to step in on such short notice. I told the producer I could do it.

"Who are you?" he said.

"I'm the associate director, and I've been through all the rehearsals. I can manage it." I was exhibiting a confidence I didn't truly feel, rolling the dice. But it was a thrill to see my name as director painted on a big card hastily constructed by the art department. (I saved the artifact for years, until it perished under an overflowing coffee pot.) Zsa Zsa Gabor was our guest on the show, and she did her usual glamorous turn despite having been scared witless by a crazed stage manager, who told her, "You realize we're on live, but don't worry about being seen by millions of people with no chance of fixing a mistake, like if you forget your lines." The idiot laughed uproariously at his wit, and I spent the next ten minutes undoing the damage. Fortunately, the show went very smoothly and my producer was exceptionally pleased.

The Pinza show was sponsored by RCA, attempting to sell new television sets. Every other week, the same sponsor would star the singer Dennis Day, and I was soon asked to take over that program.

My fondest memory was directing an episode featuring a visit by Jack Benny, the incredibly gifted comedian I had idolized since radio days. I had been privileged to work with stars on many other shows, including Danny Thomas, Lucille Ball, Ed Wynn, Eddie Cantor, Donald O'Connor, Olsen and Johnson, Jimmy Durante, Dinah Shore, Ben Blue, and even the fabulous Buster Keaton, who appeared on *The Jack Carter Show* when I was a stage manager. But Jack Benny was the most gentle and cooperative performer I had ever encountered up to that time.

My first day as a film director almost didn't get started. Having made my debut as a live director on the Pinza broadcast, and then serving as an NBC staff director, I was soon offered a chance to direct a three-camera film, *I Married Joan,* starring Joan Davis and Jim Backus. When Phil Weltman, my agent at William Morris, had called to say he had set up an interview with Joan Davis, I pointed out to Phil that I had never directed a film show; in fact, I had never seen one being shot. Weltman brushed aside the comment and told me to meet Miss Davis and her producer, Pinky Wolfson, at Joan's home in Bel Air.

I didn't even know what to wear for such a meeting and, after much thought, I purchased an expensive (for me) sport shirt at Sy Devore's shop on Vine Street. Never having driven through the intimidating portals of the Bel Air gate, I wound about nervously past some of the world's most expensive real estate, finally stopping in front of Joan Davis's mansion. The house was imposing, and Joan appeared stiff and judgmental. Mr. Wolfson looked somewhat sympathetic and tried to set me at ease, but all I could think was, "What am I doing here under such false pretenses?" It was a hot, sunny day and I was grateful for the iced tea that was offered. That was the best part of the interview, which I felt had been a disaster.

I was astonished, therefore, to learn I had been offered two episodes to direct at a fee of $750 per installment. This posed a dilemma. NBC was paying me $300 a week, supposedly for a year's work. But I had no contract, and the network routinely laid people off whenever production slowed down. The $750 was tempting, but there was no guarantee beyond two weeks. Also, because it was a filmed series, I would have to join the Screen Directors Guild, whose initiation fee at the time was $1,500. My agent pointed out that since the Davis show was a William Morris "package," the agency would not take the customary 10 percent commission from my two weeks' pay. This happy accommodation would still leave me with no money to live on after my entry into film land. But what the hell, I had rolled the dice before. I quit NBC and plunged headlong into an uncertain abyss.

As I faced my first shot for the series, which involved Jim Backus making a call from a telephone booth, there were hot lights burning, and almost a hundred people on the set were hushed into silence by my assistant director, Joe DePew, who then called, "Quiet, roll 'em." Cameras rolled film. The sound man called, "Speed." The clap-stick was activated, and a respectful silence ensued. I watched all this with great interest, for what seemed like an eternity. Then Joe touched me and whispered, "You've got to say 'Action.'" After that embarrassment, my debut episode went surprisingly well so I approached the second installment of the series with considerably more confidence, little knowing I was in for a test that could have abruptly ended my career.

At risk of overgeneralizing, it has occurred to me that the second episode of a series often appears to be weaker than the first. (This also seems true of second-night performances in the theater.) Maybe it's only a perception caused by a letdown in excitement after the opening, but this phenomenon would occur with both *The Dick Van Dyke Show* and *All in the Family,* and it hit with force in the second Joan Davis episode. The script that week felt much less interesting than the first episode and presented a host of difficulties. But after five days of grueling rehearsals, I felt we were ready for camera day on Saturday (this was before industry custom shortened the work week to five days). We were granted one day of rest, but since we often shot until midnight on Saturdays, those Sundays always seemed like only half-days off.

With heavy "scoop lights" hanging low and burning hot, I took my position behind the three cameras and two microphone booms that covered the fourth wall of our set. I needed to stand there to observe the movements of all the cameras and, indeed, the entire scene, including the actors some fifty or sixty feet beyond. Knowing where I planned to use a close-up, I had to watch the rolling cameras to be sure they came to a stop in time for the required edit. Also, I got into the habit of watching the assistant camera operators to see if they changed focus when necessary. Most importantly, I wanted to listen to and evaluate the acting as the scene progressed. It was like a three-ring circus, with the director having to have eyes in the back of his head to take it all in.

With the huge crew shushed into silence in anticipation of the order to roll cameras, Joan unexpectedly called me from the considerable distance that separated us.

"John," she called. "John . . ."

"Yes, Joan?"

"John, I don't think this bit is funny."

I was dumbfounded. After five days of rehearsals, I thought we had solved all the flaws in the script. In the crushing silence that descended, all I could think to say was, "It's been funny all week."

"No," she countered, "I don't think it's working. Come on up here and show me how to make it funny."

This was an outrageous request and it sent a shiver of fear down my spine. Time seemed to stand still as I reviewed the situation in my mind. Later I was told that I had responded instantly, but to me it seemed like an eternity. I said, with some force, "Show you? For Chrissake, if I could *show* you, I'd be standing where you are, making $30,000 a week. *You* show me, and I'll tell you if it's funny."

Everybody on stage began to applaud. Apparently, this was an old cruel trick Joan played on unsuspecting directors. I later learned that several of my predecessors had indeed attempted to "show" her how to be funny. Joan Davis was a great physical comedienne, and no mere male could act out a humorous shtick better than she could. Directors who were thus humiliated never got invited back. Somehow my forceful response helped earn me employment for the next thirty episodes.

I learned a lot about comedy from that talented but tortured woman who cursed like a longshoreman. She was given to extreme moods and sometimes bitter outbursts. I heard her ask the writers one day, "Why can't our scripts have some of that fucking whimsy?" I'm not sure it was whimsical, but one episode required Joan to bathe a young chimpanzee in the kitchen sink. During the action, soap got into the monkey's eyes and he bit Joan on the hand. She exploded in pain and innovative invective. Filming was over for the day, and our star went to the hospital for precautionary shots.

She recovered completely but the chimp died.

CHAPTER
4

In the early days of television, obstacles sometimes appeared in the guise of special requests from sponsors, some of them so absurd that today they seem incomprehensible. While stage-managing a variety show sponsored by Ford, for instance, I was thunderstruck when the advertising-agency representatives looked askance at a painted backdrop showing a view of Manhattan. We were told this image of the city would not be allowed, because it included the famous Chrysler Building. Since Chrysler was Ford's competitor, we were forced to paint over the offending structure, appeasing the sponsor by altering the New York skyline!

On another occasion, I had directed a scene in a Western saloon featuring cowboys drinking beer. Our sponsor was the Schlitz brewing company, and the resident company overseer approached me and asked why the saloon's patrons were not drinking bottles of Schlitz. The brand in question, I pointed out, did not yet exist in 1870. Nevertheless, I was urged to have the bartender serve bottles of Schlitz. I opted instead to have the cowboys drink whiskey.

Another memorably bizarre request came from, of all people, a future U.S. president. In 1955, I was selected by ABC-TV to direct the Main Street Parade for the opening day of Disneyland. In preparation, I was dispatched to Anaheim to the 160 acres of orange groves being transformed into a giant amusement park. Walt Disney had decreed that the facility would open on July 17, but when I arrived Main Street was still an unpaved stretch of California dirt. With a sense of desperation, crews labored around the clock to complete artificial lakes and rivers, rides, and storefronts. The City Hall building had been completed, along with the fire station next to it, and I reserved a portion of the structure for my control room. The rest of Main Street was a Potemkin village of false fronts disguising empty space.

Having turned over my center of operations to the technical crew for wiring, I then spent much of my time selecting camera positions on rooftops and plotting the parade route. ABC had arranged for us to share the same food service as the park laborers throughout our preproduction phase, so one day as the whistle blew for lunch and I headed for the mess tent, someone fell into step with me.

"You going to lunch?" said the voice. "I'll walk with you."

"Sure," I said, and then realized that my companion was none other than the great man himself, Walt Disney. Still in my twenties, I was awestruck to find myself walking with this semimythical figure, and I struggled to think of some way to strike up a conversation. After a moment, I ventured, "You know, Mr. Disney . . ."

"Call me Walt," barked the voice.

I couldn't do it. I started again, assuming that the message proclaimed on a familiar poster of the period—"For the children of the world, we present Disneyland!"—was a safe subject. "Mr. Disney," I said, "this is a wonderful thing you're doing for the children of the world."

"What did you say?"

I repeated, "This park—what you're doing here—is so great for children." He stopped walking and looked at me, an expression of incredulity suffusing his face. "Don't you know anything?" he said. "Kids don't have any money."

If I had harbored any doubts about the American system of capitalism, that remark forever dispelled them.

When opening day arrived, two well-known announcers had been chosen to narrate the festivities, Art Linkletter and Ronald Reagan (who, although I disagreed with most of his agenda once he entered politics, was one of the most affable people I ever worked with). The governor of California, Goodwin Knight, would formally dedicate the park at the Main Street flagpole. Miraculously, the street had been paved at three that morning, just in time for the parade. Alas, with the world's press in attendance, many reporters' wives found their high heels sinking into the not-quite-hardened asphalt.

I had other problems, although Art Linkletter was not one of them. He had asked me if he could station himself on a balcony overlooking

Main Street. I asked, "Is it the balcony that features that big Kodak Film sign?"

"Why yes, how did you know?"

"Someone told me you own that concession."

He laughed, and I said, "It's okay with me, if you're comfortable standing there." Linkletter was a superb ad-lib commentator. He could have stood on his head and delivered a wonderful broadcast.

Ronald Reagan, on the other hand, arrived a bit late, and then asked to see the script. Surprised by the question, I said, "There's no script. It's a parade."

"I know," Reagan said, "but what do I say?"

I could only respond, "Well, if I were describing it, I might offer something like, 'Here comes Mickey Mouse, there goes Minnie, this looks like Pluto . . .'"

But Reagan was not to be denied, and we finally provided him with written "talking points" about the Disney characters he would see.

To a large degree, Hollywood is a product of the culture that surrounds it, and some oddities that appeared in programs were simply reflections of the era—unfortunate ones at times. In 1959, when I was directing an episode of the popular series *Riverboat*, starring Darren McGavin, I arrived on the set one morning to observe the assistant director setting background action. Universal had a beautiful full-scale sternwheeler on its back lot, and the colorful surroundings looked entirely appropriate for a scene purporting to take place in 1840 Memphis. Something caught my eye, though, and I asked the assistant director how he was creating the illusion of antebellum activity on the waterfront. "I'm having stevedores loading bales of cotton," he said. "I can see how you're staging the activity," I replied, "except all the extras you've selected are white. In the mid-nineteenth-century South, only black slaves would be loading cotton." It was disheartening to have the AD look at me strangely and say, "Did you expect me to hire black extras? We don't do that."

I stopped the all-white activity and ordered different background action more appropriate to the time. But the encounter caused me considerable anguish, unpleasant feelings that it rankles me even now to recall.

By that time, I had bargained my way into working on dramatic series. In 1957, when I had just completed a wonderful year directing *Our Miss Brooks* with Eve Arden, CBS asked me to take on a new Eve Arden show at the finish of the season. For some time I had looked with envy to directors like Arthur Penn and John Frankenheimer, who were working on the prestigious drama anthologies *Philco Playhouse,* *Climax,* and *Playhouse 90.* I agreed to do the new comedy only if CBS would promise me a straight dramatic program after four weeks of work with Eve. I would return to comedy at their discretion after an episode or two of something serious.

As the fourth week of my contract approached, I reminded the CBS powers that they owed me something. I had hoped for an assignment on *Playhouse 90* but was told that *90* as well as *Climax* were completely booked. When I waved our agreement before them, they responded weakly, "The only thing we own is *Gunsmoke.*" I said, "It's a drama, isn't it?" They gulped and said, "Yes, but you've never directed a Western, have you?" I said, "I've never even seen a Western being shot!" Since I had them over a contractual barrel, though, I was assigned, with their great reluctance, to direct the next episode of the hit series.

In selecting actors for my dramatic debut, I met with Lynn Stalmaster, the well-known chief of casting for the series, and asked him to bring in some applicants for the role of the principal bad guy. In came a host of recognizable performers, all of them with heavy Southern or Western accents. "I've seen all these guys before," I said. "Is there anybody new you can bring in? How about some angry young man from New York?" Stalmaster practically fell off his seat. "A New Yorker in a Western?" he said. "Are you crazy?" I said with a smile, "Where do you think the bad guys came from in the late nineteenth century?" Billy the Kid was born in Brooklyn, after all, and Bat Masterson had died there in 1923. Probably many of the well-known gunfighters had come from the same troubled Eastern streets. I also pointed out that the frontier-era railroads era provided easy exchange of citizens from New York to all points of the expanding West.

Reluctantly, Stalmaster brought in a freshly minted New York actor, just off the proverbial train. I was in luck. The man read his scenes brilliantly, and I offered him the job at once. He had one concern, however: He didn't know how to ride a horse. I admired his candor but assured him the part didn't require any hard riding. There was only one scene in which his character holds up a stagecoach and is discovered sitting on horseback in the middle of the road.

During the three days of location shooting, the young actor performed with an intensity that was riveting. He even offered to do his own stunt when the marshal dispatched him in a gunfight, and he did the job perfectly. Only one thing remained, his close-up sitting on the horse. Now, picture horses are well trained and accustomed to all kinds of riders. But our visitor from the East must have unwittingly transmitted some message to the animal. You could practically read the horse's mind: "I think there's a guy from New York sitting on me today." The animal became skittish and refused to stand still, until we placed a wrangler below camera to stroke his legs. Our actor became increasingly nervous as the number of takes mounted, but I assured him we would get the shot if he remained patient. When take twelve was announced, someone shouted, "Put him on a ladder!" But I squelched the notion and continued photographing the "cowboy close-up" I felt was right for the moment. By this point, four wranglers were assigned, one to a leg. After five or six more takes, one of them remarked, in a stage whisper audible to the world, "And this kid calls himself an actor." After we finally printed the shot, I took the relieved New Yorker aside, thanked him for his performance, and offered some friendly advice: "Everybody is making Westerns now. If you want to work regularly, I suggest you take riding lessons as soon as possible." Clearly, he paid attention. The next time we met, I was directing an episode of *Bonanza* and the actor, Pernell Roberts, now playing Adam, galloped along expertly with the rest of the Cartwright clan.

Casting against type wasn't our only experiment for that episode. In setting up the "long shot" to reveal the bandit brandishing his weapons, I had asked our cameraman, Fleet Southcott, if we could mount the camera on top of the stagecoach in order to shoot over the teamster and the four horses, come around a bend, and discover the holdup man in that fashion. One of the crew said, "The camera will shake." That was the effect I was looking for, I answered. The sound man wanted to know how he was expected to provide his electrical connection to the camera. I said, "Wouldn't it be possible to drive your truck behind the coach and link up by using a long cable?"

Clearly, my notion was not popular with the crew, but to his great credit, Southcott said, "Hold on. We've been on railroad tracks for so long in the way we're making these pictures, maybe it's time to try something new." The camera was mounted on a "high hat" secured to the top of the stagecoach, and the shot, shakes and all, went off without a hitch. Some years later, watching the director Tony Richardson's motion picture *Tom Jones,* I saw a jiggling camera used to great advantage throughout the production. Today, a "nervous camera" is used effectively wherever TV series or feature pictures are made.

That wasn't the end of the *Gunsmoke* episode, though. Some time after wrapping the production, I attended a screening of the first rough cut, along with the producer, Norman MacDonnell, among others. The lights dimmed, the screen lit up, and as the film unreeled I sank lower and lower in my seat. A thirty-minute episode dragged on for what seemed like hours. When the sluggish marathon finally ended, the lights came up on a room filled with shocked silence. When nobody spoke, I asked who the cutter had been. A cautious hand went up, and I asked our producer if I could have some time in the cutting room to give "a few notes." The grim response was, "Go ahead—anything you can do to save this thing."

For the next three days I worked with the editor, shortening here, lengthening there, replacing a long shot with a close-up. Finally, we showed the new edit to MacDonnell and his staff. To my immense relief, the film came alive and ran with excitement. Our producer was so pleased, he hired me on the spot to finish the rest of the season, alternating with one of the regular directors, Ted Post. A final irony occurred that year when the Academy of Television Arts and Sciences awarded the Emmy for Best Editor to my colleague in the cutting room. I have a photograph of him holding the statue. He graciously signed the picture, "This really belongs to you."

Gunsmoke was the first Western I worked on, but not the last. A year or so later, while we were shooting an episode of *Bat Masterson.* a series that starred Gene Barry, the script that week called for location work that would simulate the exterior of a posh San Francisco gambling hall, with a rear exit that led to rocky terrain overlooking a precipitous drop into the Pacific. We broke the scene down into parts. We chose a cliff near Marineland, an aquatic attraction in Southern California, to photograph a hazardous stunt involving the "murder" of a character as the villain of the piece casts him into the sea. The crew built the interior of the casino on stage. But the outdoor shot showing the front of the establishment proved difficult, until our location department came up with a solution.

The Hollywood Hotel boasted a beautiful turn-of-the-century façade, but it was located on busy Hollywood Boulevard. When I was told of this extraordinary selection, I was skeptical until I visited the site and realized that if we trained the camera head-on to the hotel, thus avoiding traffic on the boulevard, we could "dress" the area with extras wearing period costumes. By covering the sidewalk with dirt we were able to use horse-drawn carriages to deliver patrons to the "casino." As long as we showed nothing behind us, and eliminated the sounds of traffic, the illusion would work. After I had rehearsed the scene and turned over the set for lighting, the hotel manager approached me and asked if I would like to meet one of his longtime residents. The legendary Mack Sennett, of Keystone Kops fame, lived there in retirement, and I was delighted to meet this almost mythic character. He was a bit frail, but alert and articulate. During our talk, the conversation turned to comedy, and Mr. Sennett expressed a thought that has stayed with me through the years. It was a simple statement, but extraordinarily perceptive. He said, "The audience will not laugh if it is mystified."

Back to *Bat Masterson:* We set up camp on a high plateau near Marineland, on the Palos Verdes Peninsula near Los Angeles, to prepare the complicated stunt involving the death of one of the characters. In discussions with the stunt supervisor, I pointed out that the bit had to look dangerous, but as always I stressed safety. Ideally, I said, I would like to place the camera on a high setup overlooking the cliff, with the stunt man in the foreground holding on to a precarious perch. The "heavy" would stamp on the victim's hands, causing him to lose his grip and fall away, traversing a steep slope in the middle distance, with ocean waves crashing ashore in the far background. The problem facing the crew, and making the job exceptionally dangerous, was the extreme pitch of the terrain. The steepness would make the falling man accelerate too rapidly. Unless he could slow down somehow, he could quickly lose control.

The solution, the supervisor explained to me, was to have the falling man disappear briefly behind some brush that the greens department would place on the hill. Behind the first clump of shrubs, another member of the stunt crew would be anchored into the mountain. This man, hidden from view, would apply a body block to the faller, slowing his speed but allowing him to reappear from the camouflage so the camera could see his continued descent. Once more he would disappear behind a lower group of greens, where another anchored stunt man would deliver the next slowing block. Finally, the victim would appear once more, briefly, until he vanished behind a third installation of shrubbery. At this point, a final colleague would catch the falling man and stop his descent.

I was assured that every contingency was covered and the stunt was completely safe. With some misgiving, I had the camera set up, crossed my fingers, and called, "Action." At first everything went as planned. Our man went behind the first set of greens, came out, disappeared behind the second set, emerged again, and headed for the final stop. Then, to my horror, something kept falling after the third position.

I gulped and told the camera operator to continue rolling. I was convinced that our stunt man was doomed as he gathered momentum, along with a cloud of soil and rocks, eventually falling into the sea far below. I croaked "Cut!" fearing the worst.

To my immense relief, our man stepped out safely from behind his final shrub. On being stopped, he had apparently dislodged a large boulder, which had continued all the way into the ocean. It was a fantastically successful shot, starting with a close-up and ending with an uninterrupted fall into the sea. But the situation left me somewhat traumatized. I was never again comfortable directing dangerous stunts.

I had first met Gene Barry, the star of *Bat Masterson*, when he was cast as the new gym teacher on Eve Arden's series *Our Miss Brooks*. The new member of our fictional school was athletic-looking and handsome, and his addition to the company was meant to arouse feelings of jealousy in Mr. Boynton, the shy teacher who was the object of Miss Brooks's affections. The notion of sexual competition employed an age-old formula that was common in what Robert Guillame (who decades later starred in *Benson*) used to call "adventures in sitcom land." In this case, the old recipe flopped.

In our first rehearsal, something odd began to happen. Each actor seemed to be jostling the other for position on stage. Neither could seem to find a comfortable place to stand, and they continued to circle each other as the scene progressed. This bizarre waltz went on for some time, until I finally called a break and took Gene Barry aside. "What's going on?" I asked. He said, "Didn't my agent tell you I've got to look camera-right to camera-left? You've got me facing the other way." I answered truthfully, "Your agent has said nothing to me, but just out of curiosity, why?"

"Because I want the camera to see only the left side of my face. That's my best side."

I laughed. "Boy, that's tough. Eve Arden has the same idea. She can only be photographed featuring her left side, and she was here first."

The new gym teacher was hastily dispatched. The next time I ran into Gene, I was directing Westerns and he was playing Bat Masterson, the foppish lawman who dressed elegantly, with a derby hat and a fancy cane that frequently doubled as a weapon. Gene was well suited for the role, and since he was now the star of the series, he could indulge his desire to look right to left anytime the mood struck him. Which, of course, was always.

At times, the hazards of location shooting arose in ways one could never foresee. On a scouting trip preparing to shoot another Western around that same time, I had found a beautiful pristine meadow of mustard flowers. I thought it would make a great shot to see our wagon train rolling through a virgin landscape. So I asked the location manager to rope off the area carefully so that no trucks or equipment could spoil the ground before we made our long shot showing pioneers crossing through unspoiled America. I had selected a nearby hill from which to photograph what promised to be a colorful shot, and I was relieved to see my meadow still undisturbed as I arrived on the morning of filming.

Directors generally have to be alert to everything going on around them, so as I headed for morning coffee, my ears picked up a whispered conversation between the first and second assistant directors. The second was saying something no director wants to hear on a distant location. Although he tried to keep his voice low, he clearly said, "I thought he was on your bus."

This ominous remark could only mean an actor left behind at the studio, and I could only hope it was not a key player. Naturally, when the agitated assistant reported to me, I learned that it was someone I had planned to use in the first shot. A group of close scenes had been planned for the early morning hours, before the sun was high enough to shoot the meadow shot, and so I juggled the schedule around the missing actor, and we managed to improvise enough work to keep us going. Meanwhile, the second assistant was dispatched to phone home base, with orders to transport the missing performer to our location as soon as possible.

I vamped with close work for about an hour, glancing from time to time at the sky. Finally, the sun broke through, and I figured another thirty minutes would give us perfect light. It was time for the company to move to the hill and set up the camera for my highly anticipated meadow shot. The wagon train was stationed just out of sight, preparing to enter left-to-right and make a camera-right exit. The camera came up to speed, and just as I was about to wave a cue to the waiting wagon teamsters, a yellow speck appeared in the distance: a bright yellow cab, heading directly for the camera! This horrible apparition was making deep tracks through the field of mustard, ruining forever the location I had lusted after. The taxi's passenger turned out to be our missing actor, who had taken it upon himself to make up for being late. Later, the wagons were photographed rolling through a portion of the field using a medium shot, but the vast expanse I had visualized evaporated forever.

I later learned that, as the day ended, the tardy actor cornered the first assistant director and asked to be reimbursed for the hefty cab fare. That was one conversation I was happy to miss.

Another unwanted-vehicle-on-the-set moment from the late 1950s sticks in my memory. I was directing yet another Western on the Universal back lot when I observed, to my amazement, a tram carrying tourists, rolling through my location. I yelled at my assistant to get the offending vehicle out of the shot, only to be told that the tram had priority over the needs of a shooting company. It seems Universal had embarked on a new business, one that was destined to grow in size. Now the studio tour occupies its own vast acreage as part of an enormous entertainment complex.

The tram no longer impedes production, but that day the vehicle sailed right by the camera and all of us becalmed workers. When I remarked to the crew that since we were not getting paid extra for appearing as part of an exhibit, it would be appropriate to turn our backs on the camera-toting tourists until they disappeared. When the front office confirmed to me that the tour would continue to disrupt production time, I refused to work at Universal for more than thirty years, never returning until the 1990s. Even then, I accepted only indoor work on stages.

During the time I was making Westerns, I had several opportunities to return to New York to direct other series. One was a sitcom pilot starring Walter Slezak. Having agreed to replace the original director, I arrived in New York and was met by the playwright Howard Teichman (who had written the hit Broadway play *The Solid Gold Cadillac*), CBS program executive Marlo Lewis, and Robert Weitman, a senior vice president of the network. This was a formidable group to have taken the trouble to meet with a mere director. It seemed to indicate the value the network placed on this pilot. During the limousine ride back to Manhattan, Mr. Teichman waxed enthusiastically about the set being constructed for the pilot. "CBS has spared no expense," he beamed. "They're allowing us to duplicate the Oak Room of the Plaza Hotel!"

Not certain I had heard correctly, I asked, "Did you say duplicate? Isn't that a two-story space within the hotel?"

"Absolutely, and we're having it copied! Would you like to see the construction? They're assembling it right now at the 57th Street mill." Such enthusiasm was not to be dampened, and I readily agreed.

Upon entering the scene shop, I was astounded by the din and the extraordinary number of busy carpenters, some of them perched on scaffolding high above the mill floor, constructing stately pillars. Some were even engaged in finishing the tops and the backs of some of the columns. I thought, If this were a high-budget feature-film production, there might be some excuse for such wasteful construction, but with multiple cameras and an audience in attendance, there would never be a need to photograph a master-shot reverse angle. No one would ever see the fine craftsmanship being lavished needlessly on the dark side of the set.

Something else struck me, and I asked where we intended to shoot the pilot. I was told we'd be working at the Hy Brown Studios, on 24th Street in the Chelsea District. I wondered if I could speak with the chief carpenter, and after we were introduced, I asked the man if he was familiar with Hy Brown's facilities. When he said yes, I asked, "Could this set you're building fit into the space available on 24th Street?" He laughed and said, "No way. Why do you ask?"

Whether it was inexperience on the part of our triumvirate or the previous director's fault, someone had dropped the ball. Even if one wants giant scenery on stage, it is important not to build units in one piece. Tall flats must be constructed in segments no taller than five feet, nine inches, so that they can be broken down and fit into railroad freight cars for touring. These dimensions were long ago dictated by the size of a boxcar door. Also, pieces of that size can easily be loaded into trucks for a drive across the city. In addition, the scenery had to be light enough for stagehands to load it into the theater. One can have as many five-foot, nine-inch pieces as desired; they are simply hinged together after transport.

Our unhappy group had ordered construction of the proverbial boat in the basement, with no way to get it out. When the shock began to wear off, one of my hosts stammered, "What do we do now?" I suggested that we send everybody home for the day, and schedule a meeting with our art director. Fortunately, we had enough time to redesign a more modest Oak Room using much of the material already gathered. The crew accomplished this without too much damage to the budget, the scenic effect was more than convincing, and we mounted a successful production.

But the look of the blood draining from the faces of my three hosts, when they realized the blunder, is a look I will never forget.

CHAPTER
5

One day in 1961, during my "Western period," while I was attending a Directors Guild of America (DGA) board meeting, the director and producer Sheldon Leonard asked me if I'd like to leave the mud and dust for a while and direct a new show he was preparing, to be played indoors before a studio audience. Carl Reiner would be the producer, and the star would be Dick Van Dyke.

Naturally, I agreed to the interview, which did not start off on a particularly graceful note. When I arrived at the Reiner home to meet these gentlemen for the first time, I shook hands with Dick and told him how much I had enjoyed his performance in the off–Vine Street production of *Vintage 60,* a modest musical from the previous year. In his usual self-effacing style he mumbled, "That was Dick Patterson." Fortunately, both Carl and Dick overlooked my faux pas, and the meeting went uphill from there. In fact, it launched a mutual admiration society that has lasted for almost fifty years.

When offered employment, it was my custom at the time to sign on for only two episodes. I reasoned that if the company and I get along well, we could agree to more episodes. If we didn't hit it off, nobody need be embarrassed by the director's swift departure. Why ask for two commitments? Because in the first week, one could get unlucky and draw a less-than-brilliant script, or encounter some unforeseen disaster. The second installment would give the director a chance to recover. If both scripts are poor, it's best to duck out quickly anyway. For the *Van Dyke* show, Carl Reiner delivered two excellent scripts, although the first one played slightly better when it was put on its feet.

From the start, I couldn't believe the outstanding talent of the company of players. The only cast member I had known beforehand was Rose Marie, who had worked with me on an episode of *Gunsmoke*. Performing wildly against type, she had played a salty country woman of indeterminate age. When she had come in to read for her part in the Western, Rosie hit every possible nuance, and I offered her the job instantly, on one condition. "The woman you're playing is seen chopping firewood," I told her. "Would you be willing to remove the polish and cut your nails?" Through the years, we've enjoyed many a chuckle over this first meeting. During the *Gunsmoke* episode, I had actually had to prevent Rosie from inadvertently stealing a scene by being *too* funny. During a dinner scene, her action was to dish out food for the five or six ranch hands seated around a table. The men carried all the dialogue; the woman had no lines. However, as the scene progressed, Rosie paid close attention to everything being uttered, reacting facially to every comment made. I took her aside after the first rehearsal and said, "The way you're playing this, nobody will hear a word these guys are saying. She looked surprised and asked, "Wasn't I doing it right?" "Too right," I said. "What I see is a very actively engaged actress delivering a wonderful sketch performance. But this isn't a comedy piece. The woman is not, and should not, be part of the dialogue." "What should I do?" she asked. "Serve food," I said, "Your turn to speak will come later."

On my first day at *Van Dyke*, I was thrilled to see how marvelously the cast responded to anything asked of them. They rehearsed as though they had worked together forever. The rehearsal went so well that as the day ended, I realized we had staged the entire thirty-minute piece. The players were ecstatic and couldn't wait to come back the next day. Then it hit me—this was Wednesday. The live performance wouldn't happen until the next Tuesday! When working with a single camera, the strategy calls for rehearsing until the scene is ready to commit to film, then shooting before the material can grow stale. But this applies only to short takes, which sometimes consume mere seconds, rarely more than four or five minutes. With a three-camera production like that on *Van Dyke*, though, the play is presented from Act One to the finish, and my foolishly rapid staging had set us up for a tired, boring production on the night. I was the football coach who had prepared his team for the big game with a week to go.

The next day, the world's most enthusiastic actors showed up to continue at the previous rehearsal's fast pace. I stalled, drinking multiple cups of coffee. When I finally faced the group, they were straining at their leashes. I complimented them on their work the previous day, then told them I wasn't sure about the furniture placement. Puzzled, they all thought the room had been set up just right, but I asked their indulgence as I had the prop men rearrange the sofas and chairs. When they finished, I began a rehearsal that by design did not flow easily. Despite several uncomprehending looks from the cast, I kept putting obstacles in their paths. The day ended with the players muttering unhappily. The following morning, Friday, I told the company that they had been correct; the furniture had been placed better the first day. I apologized for wasting Thursday, and after the set dressers had restored the room to its original configuration, we returned to Wednesday's blocking. The performance that Tuesday night was terrific, and I never explained my apparent craziness to any of the cast until several years later. The experience taught me a great lesson. From then on, I always took care to advance staging incrementally, never shooting for perfection on the first day of rehearsal.

The process that Sheldon Leonard and Carl Reiner created to prepare for each episode of the *Van Dyke* show is one that I have used, when I had control, on every series I have directed since. Simply put, every Wednesday morning we would gather around the table and read a script that was intended to be produced the following week. The cast would read through the entire script once, while our great script supervisor, Marge Mullen, clocked it for a rough timing. Sheldon always attended these readings, and he would comment briefly on the "arc" or "spine" of the show. He had an uncanny ability to put his finger on potential flaws, and while he wasn't always right, his batting average was incredibly high. At this first reading, which I always referred to as "the reading of the will," the actors were invited to comment about lines that affected them or constructions that seemed awkward. Their opinions were received with respect, but not yet discussed in depth. That process waited until the following week, after the writers had delivered a second draft.

When someone had finished talking, one of us might turn to ask Sheldon a question, only to find that he had slipped out of the room. He perfected this technique so well that we began to refer to him as Lamont Cranston, the Shadow of radio fame. Sheldon also employed this method of escape during DGA board meetings, so often that it became customary to create a one-dollar betting pool containing our guesses as to what time he would slip out that day.

During our table readings for *Van Dyke,* after we had made rough comments on the second draft of a script, the writer—usually Carl, and later the team of Bill Persky and Sam Denoff—had a week to work on changes and additions. We would then turn our attention to the current week's program, which had gone through the same process a week earlier. This reading was also done nonstop, with no comments, and timed again. Then we would read again—this time line by line, and everyone was now invited to ask questions and discuss the text fully. It was terrifically valuable to get the actors' inputs while the writers were there listening, to address in advance problems that might otherwise cause endless delays on the set. It's sadly different in television today, to see writers so protective of their work that they refuse to entertain comments from the very people who have to direct or speak their words. By ignoring the actor's process, they eliminate much of the richness that characterized television during its golden age.

After this table reading, lunch would be called, and then the cast assembled on stage to begin rehearsals "on our feet." Here the genius of Sheldon and Carl (and years later, in a similar fashion, Norman Lear) became manifest: I would be left alone. As director, my job was to stage the action, and if something didn't work I was expected to fix it. Left to our own devices, we could invent physical comedy, try different approaches, allow departures from the original text. In rehearsal, I would never tell an actor how or when to move on a given line. I encouraged them to find their own way and helped them only if they got entangled, or if they found a spot that couldn't be photographed in the multiple camera method of shooting. During these rehearsals, I always put the script aside and listened to the lines as if I were a member of the audience. Sometimes I'd query an actor, asking why they spoke a particular line, and he or she would typically answer, "That's what's in the script." I'd point out if the line didn't make sense there. Was there a better answer than the one that had been written? Occasionally, we'd venture off on a tangent that led us into new territory, allowing us to explore a more interesting comedic road. Sometimes the departure wouldn't work, but frequently it led to gold. The real test came on Friday nights, when we did a run-through for

Carl. Often he applauded our efforts; at times he questioned the deviation. But he always appreciated the attempt, because experimentation and deeper investigation invariably led to better performances. During rehearsals, I never allowed visitors on the set, believing an actor should be free to try anything that could help him develop a character, without worrying about looking foolish in front of an audience.

On camera days—Mondays and Tuesdays—anybody was free to attend "blocking." By that time the performance was relatively set, though by no means complete. Our process allowed us to make improvements right up to the last minute, although needless tinkering was discouraged. Shooting a three-camera film, as we did for *Van Dyke,* we played before a single audience, giving one performance in sequential fashion, just like a theatrical play. That performance began at 8 PM and usually ended by 9:30 PM. Because the show was filmed, postproduction enhancements were possible. But since the cast was so well rehearsed, the episodes never needed extensive editing.

Friends have often asked me what it's like to have a series canceled, particularly when you know the work has been good. It's always a bit painful, but never more than when it is announced too late to find other work. In the case of *The Dick Van Dyke Show,* we were confident that we'd be renewed for another season after completing our first year, in 1961. So we were disappointed, to say the least, when we heard the series was to be terminated. Mary Tyler Moore seemed to take the news harder than most. I remember her mourning what we thought would be the final episode: "This is the last time we'll be reading a new script together." "This is the last time we'll have a rehearsal." "This is the last time we'll do a show together."

During the making of the first six episodes, the cast and I customarily went out for dinner or a drink after completing an installment. One night, Morey Amsterdam had suggested we go to the Crescendo, a Sunset Strip nightclub where Morey had performed many times. I can't remember the show we saw, but I recall our group standing outside waiting for the parking attendants to bring our cars. This was kind of a sad day, I commented, because it would be the last time we would be able to gather together so publicly. When I was pressed to explain myself, I said I had been in similar situations in the past—that our first show would air that week, and from then on their celebrity would force us to meet in more private venues. As the youngest member of the troupe, I said, Mary would probably be the most vulnerable, because the others had all been there before. Needless to say, she and the rest of the cast adjusted just fine.

Some time after receiving the cancelation notice, it was fantastic news all around when we learned that Sheldon Leonard had convinced our sponsor, Procter & Gamble, to give us another season, although the company agreed to fund only half of each episode. Sheldon convinced Kent cigarettes to sponsor the second half of the series, and serendipitous scheduling that placed us behind the successful *Beverly Hillbillies* gave us just enough rating points to survive.

By 1963, we even had opportunities to break new ground with the series, culturally speaking. In hindsight, the episode that stirred up some controversy for us seems quite tame and innocuous today but it caused a furor back then. The episode, which Persky and Denoff had written, was called "That's My Boy??" This was the writing team's first effort for Carl Reiner, I believe, and it was terrific. The plot spun off of the fear that gnaws at some parents concerning their new baby: Is it really theirs, or has the hospital made some terrible mistake?

In the script, a series of coincidences at the hospital alarms Rob Petrie (played by Van Dyke) into believing that they have brought home the wrong infant. Although Laura (Mary Tyler Moore) will have none of this nonsense, Rob tries to convince her otherwise:

LAURA After all the excitement today, it's kind of nice to be alone.

ROB Yeah—just the two of us.

LAURA The three of us.

ROB Oh, yeah [*nodding to bedroom*]. The little stranger . . . uh . . . baby!

LAURA You know, Rob, I didn't realize we had so many friends. Everything . . . the gifts and the flowers were just beautiful. Say, Rob, who sent those?

ROB Which?

LAURA The ones we got when we were leaving the hospital. In all the excitement I never even looked at the card.

ROB Neither did I. *[Crosses to flowers, finds card, reads]* Congratulations and much love . . . Dick and Betty Carter.

BOTH Aahh!

ROB *[Frowns]* Do we know a Dick and Betty Carter?

LAURA *[Thinking]* No. Maybe it's someone from your office.

ROB No. The only Dick and Betty Carter I know are Phil and Edna Greenbaum.

LAURA *[She picks up card envelope from table and looks at it]* Oh . . . this explains it. These are for Mrs. Peters in room 203. It's been going on all week. They kept getting us mixed up. You know . . . Peters, 203 . . . Petrie 208 . . . the names and numbers look alike.

ROB *[Frantic]* They got everything mixed up.

LAURA One night . . . *[smiles]* I even got her rice pudding!

ROB What did you say?

LAURA That I got her rice pudding.

ROB *[Meaningfully]* You got her rice pudding!

LAURA Yes—which means she probably got my blueberry tart.

ROB Among other things.

LAURA As a matter of fact, that envelope they gave us today—that was hers.

ROB It figures. That's it. That's how it happened. I knew it!

LAURA Rob, why are you getting so excited—it's only flowers. We'll return them.

ROB *[Mumbles]* Yeah . . . we're not bringing up the wrong flowers.

The plot develops, with Rob finding more and more "evidence" that they have brought home a child belonging to the Peters family, who in turn have the Petrie's baby. Next-door neighbor Jerry convinces Rob to telephone the hospital to discuss the situation. With Laura asleep, Rob agrees, but as he crosses to phone, it rings.

ROB Hello! Yes, this is Mr. Petrie . . . Who? *[Covers phone with hand. To Jerry]* It's Mr. Peters!

JERRY What does he want?

ROB What do you think? *[Into phone]* Uh, yes, Mr. Peters, I know we have something of yours . . . and you have something of ours. A basket of dried figs? *[To Jerry]* They got Laura's aunt's figs, too. *[Finding it hard to break the news]* You don't know, then? Uh . . . this is going to be pretty hard to tell you, Mr. Peters, but . . . well, how can I put it? Um . . . *[Fresh attack]* Mr. Peters, you do know that there is a tremendous similarity between a three and an eight . . . if you close up the open side of a three, you've got a perfect eight . . . What? Yes, this is Robert Petrie. Now, you know there's a great similarity in our—Yes, I am one of the writers of the Alan Brady television show . . . Well, I'm glad you think our show is funny, but I really would like to get this thing settled . . . Uh . . . you know there is also a great similarity in our names—Petrie and Peters—and both our wives did give birth at the same time in the same hospital, and the hospital was very busy . . . What am I getting at? Mr. Peters, may I ask you a personal question? Who does your baby look like? . . . Well, our baby doesn't look like either of us neither. *[Beat]* I think I'm making myself very clear. We have each other's babies. *[Very seriously]* How do you want to handle this? . . . Yes, I am Robert Petrie the comedy writer, but I can't see any humor in this situation . . . Mr. Peters, may I have your address, please? . . . I see . . . No, that's fine with me as long as we settle it tonight . . . Fine . . . you got my address from the hospital . . . Fine. *[Hangs up]*

JERRY He's coming here?

ROB Yeah. He said his wife felt like getting some air. They were going to drop off the dried fruit anyway. Boy, he's taking this pretty lightly. Some people just don't care whose baby they bring up.

Laura enters from the bedroom and Jerry beats a hasty retreat. Rob attempts to convince Laura that they must exchange babies with Mr. and Mrs. Peters, who are on their way.

LAURA Rob, nothing in the whole world will convince me that the baby in that crib is not ours.

ROB I don't blame you, honey . . . You just can't face the facts . . . Poor kid!

[The doorbell rings]

ROB There are the Peters now. Laura, prepare yourself!

LAURA Rob, nobody is taking this baby, do you hear—nobody!

ROB Laura, I think you'd better go to your room. I'll handle this.

LAURA I'm staying right here!

[Rob opens the front door]

VOICE *[offstage]* Hi, we're Mr. And Mrs. Peters.

ROB *[Startled]* Come in.

[A young, attractive black couple enter—Rob, mouth agape, as they enter carrying a basket of figs and smiling broadly]

MR. PETERS Would you like to swap some figs for some flowers?

In 2006, the exchange seems unremarkable. But in the climate of 1963, both the network, CBS, and the sponsor, Procter & Gamble, objected strenuously to the script, not wishing to play a "racial joke" on their program. Both entities insisted they would not pay for this episode, fearing it was too charged for the times. Objections notwithstanding, Sheldon and Carl stepped up boldly and said the company would play the pages as written. If our live audience indicated any objection to the material, the producers would junk what we had shot and pay for it themselves. On the other hand, if the audience reacted positively, they would release the episode as per usual.

Under this draconian condition, a lengthy conference ensued about how the joke should be delivered. Could it be straightforward, with the black couple entering with little preamble, or should there be some exposition or "pipe" introduced to change the situational dynamic? Dick Van Dyke was shooting *Mary Poppins* at Disney, when we arranged a lunchtime meeting with our star to talk about the episode. Carl opened the discussion by declaring that there would be no animus if the black family had control of the joke—hence the lengthy monologue written for Rob on the telephone. If Mr. Peters could stop the situation at any time while on the phone, there would be no need for the couple to make an actual appearance. Consequently, the repeated references in Rob's side of the phone conversation indicate that Mr. Peters was laughing at the craziness presented by the writer of a famous television comedy.

When the black couple arrives, the script laid out this exchange:

ROB Why didn't you tell me on the phone?"

MR. PETERS And miss the expression on your face?

ROB Yeah. Did I give you a good one?

MR. PETERS A beaut!

In casting, I looked for the handsomest, least threatening black actors I could find, finally settling on Greg Morris and Mimi Dillard, both of whom filled the bill admirably. I drilled them to display huge smiles and not to speak too soon. They were perfect, and the audience responded in three stages. First, they issued a surprised gasp, then a rolling laugh, followed by sustained applause. The episode went on to become one of our most memorable broadcasts, prompting hundreds of letters of approval, and not a single letter of complaint. We had delivered what I believe was television's first racial joke—the first in good taste, at least—and at the same time, a not-too-subtle commentary about the abilities of a black child in our society.

Having won over the audience, we used our "tag"—a little afterpiece that followed the final commercial—to go a step further. Fastforwarding out of the flashback to the hospital incident, we shot the following exchange:

MEL Rob, that's a fantastic story. So everything worked out fine.

ROB Well, things didn't work out as well as we'd expected.

MEL What do you mean?

LAURA What are you talking about?

ROB You know the Peters's little boy, Jimmy? He's in Ritchie's grade at school?

LAURA Yes?

ROB Top of the class, straight As. Our Ritchie—bottom of the heap. I still think we got the wrong kid!

That same year (1963), when I began preproduction on a feature film called *The New Interns,* I suggested to the producer, Bobby Cohn, that we make one of the lead interns a black man. The studio opposed this idea initially, arguing that it would cost us severely in Southern communities. I argued that what we lost in the South we would gain in Detroit. Despite management's misgivings, I convinced the powers in charge that I could cast Greg Morris as a lead and hit the racial issue right on the nose. I was proven right in Detroit as well as in the South, where audiences accepted, and at times even applauded, Greg's careful portrayal.

One day at lunch, Dick Van Dyke dropped a casual reference to his brother, someone never before mentioned. Carl Reiner pounced on Dick, asking if the brother was in show business. When Dick said yes, Jerry worked in Southern clubs, Carl immediately began thinking of a script for the show. When he pressed Dick for some characteristic behavior that he could incorporate into Jerry's guest appearance, Dick revealed that his brother sometimes sleepwalked. That's all Carl's fertile mind needed to build an episode around a character who was shy in his waking moments, but totally uninhibited while asleep. Eventually, he wrote what became a famous two-part episode called "The Sleeping Brother," and Jerry Van Dyke flew out to join the company.

Jerry appeared shy and somewhat laid-back at the first table reading, and spoke haltingly as he read his part, which struck me as a difficult job for any actor since it required him essentially to act two different parts. I think Jerry was intimidated by the professionalism of the regular cast, all of whom were comfortable in their parts and approached the table reading with a confidence that must have overwhelmed the newcomer. When we got on our feet in the first staging rehearsal, Jerry staggered uncertainly, carrying his script and trying to integrate his movements while the others glided through. I had a sinking feeling. Not sure what to do, I acted on instinct and slowed the operation considerably.

First, I called a five-minute break and idly asked our prop master to throw me a football while I thought things over. When the break ended, I continued tossing the ball to anyone who wanted to play receiver, and soon invited Jerry to participate. He joined in willingly, and after a few minutes of this, I asked him if he had any tape or film of the act he performed in clubs. He said he had a two-inch tape, which could be played only at a major facility such as the CBS Studio. I phoned Carl's office and suggested we all go over to Fairfax Avenue to view Jerry's tape, and he thought it was a fine idea.

The entire cast of regulars joined us in this little expedition, and we were soon watching Jerry on tape play his banjo and deliver short jokes, à la Henny Youngman and his violin, or Morey Amsterdam and his cello. Unfortunately, Jerry's roadhouse jokes featured hoary old-timers, such as, "How do you tell a happy motorcyclist? By the bugs on his teeth." In our series, Mary Tyler Moore frequently spoke the line "What are you going to do, Rob?" whenever Dick's character was faced with a problem. So when I ran into difficulty on the set, Rose Marie was fond of teasing me by directing the line at me. Sure enough, in the parking lot as we were leaving, she sidled up to me and said, "What are ya gonna do, John?" I delivered my answer in the same rhythm Morey used: "Shuddup."

God bless Carl Reiner, who saw in Jerry's banjo playing a device to allow him to perform outrageously as the brother who told uninhibited jokes while he sleepwalked. Carl got to work immediately, adding this behavior to the script while I dragged my heels in rehearsal by throwing around the football. By wasting Wednesday's rehearsal and part of Thursday's, I think I was unconsciously slowing down the rest of the company so Jerry could find a comfortable pace. On Friday, his work noticeably improved, and I suspect Dick spent some time with his brother over the weekend—by Monday, his acting had improved exponentially. On Tuesday night he delivered a smashing performance.

When the cast gathered for Wednesday's reading of Part Two, Jerry was as elated as the rest of us. But once we arrived on stage for our first rehearsal, I found him throwing the football. "What are you doing?" I asked.

"Throwing the football, like we did last week."

I looked at him as if he were crazy. "Are you kidding? We don't have time for such nonsense. We're here to work. Places, everybody."

A different guest appearance on the show didn't work out quite so well. When Jamie Farr was a young unknown, he was cast as a delivery boy bringing sandwiches and coffee to the *Alan Brady* writers. In the episode, when Morey Amsterdam says his coffee is the one with eight lumps of sugar, Jamie's line was, "Eat candy. Why ruin good coffee?" Since this was his only line, Farr was cast for a single day of rehearsal. But he had trouble from the beginning. He tried, "*Why* ruin good coffee?" and then, "Why *ruin* good coffee?" and then, "Why ruin *good* coffee?" I even tried something I almost never did. I gave him a line reading and asked him to repeat it. No luck.

Along came Rose Marie: "What are ya gonna do, John?"

"I think he may be tone deaf," I remember telling her. "But don't worry, it's only a line. He'll come through with the audience." Wrong.

During the performance, Jamie mangled the line again, and we finally got it right by doing a pick-up after the audience had left. This time I read the line, and Jamie repeated my emphasis correctly.

Some thirty-five years later, I was changing planes at O'Hare Airport in Chicago when I noticed Jamie approaching. By then he had long been famous for his role as the cross-dressing Corporal Klinger in *M*A*S*H*, and we had a moment of mutual recognition. Without either of us breaking stride, I pointed at him and he said, "*Why* ruin good coffee?" We continued walking past each other as I shook my head, saying, "Still not quite right, but don't worry. We'll get it in a pick-up."

While we were filming the live performances of *The Dick Van Dyke Show*, I used to do the "warm-ups," talking to members of the audience between takes. During one episode, Mary Tyler Moore was seen preparing breakfast while the studio audience looked on. During one lull in shooting, a woman in the audience asked what substitute we used for the eggs Mary was supposedly cooking. The woman had heard that if a scene called for ice cream, for example, studios always used scoops of mashed potatoes as a stand-in, since the hot lights would quickly melt the real thing. I suppose that may have been true if potatoes had been rounded into balls and placed in sundae dishes to act as set decoration for a banquet scene, but I don't think it would work with an ice cream cone. Truth be told, anytime I had occasion to shoot a scene with ice cream, I used ice cream, particularly if a child actor were involved.

Imagine trying to get a youngster to express joy while licking mashed potatoes!

Since I had time to kill during a scene change, I thought it would be fun to ask the audience what they thought we used for eggs. They came up with many ideas for substitutes, some of them bizarre but none of them useful. When they ran out of suggestions, I advised them that we had given the matter serious thought, and after much study, we decided the best material to use was—eggs.

Some folks remained skeptical. Sitting only fifty feet away, they had watched Mary first crack, then drop two eggs into a pan, followed by the familiar breakfast sound of frying. Even after the scene had been shot, and Dick Van Dyke had eaten Mary's cooking, some diehards still asked, "So what did you use for eggs?"

Before *Van Dyke* had become a hit show, it was not easy to attract an audience to fill our 300 seats. So the stands were sometimes occupied by agents, relatives, friends of the family, whomever. These were among the worst audiences possible. Agents who had read the script on behalf of their clients often laughed before the punchline, throwing off everybody's timing. Wives, husbands, and "significant others" were also a pain. Occasionally one could spot them mouthing lines along with their loved one on stage. Having prompted the actor at home, the relative was only interested in seeing his or her favorite deliver speeches properly, and usually gave little thought to laughing. A few network executives committed even more egregious offenses, ostentatiously reading the week's script as if it were an opera libretto. Their noisily flipping through the pages distracted entire rows of people from reacting properly to the play.

This mattered because our entire purpose in playing before a "live" studio audience was to record their laughter in conjunction with the material. We wanted to earn their laughter without relying on a laugh track. We wanted them to respond when something was funny, not only to keep us honest in the writing, but also to let the players on stage hear that the spectators appreciated their work. The best audiences always consisted of people who knew the characters well but had no clue what line was coming next.

The audience during the filming of one episode really set us back on our heels. We kept hearing a particular section explode with laughter three or four sentences after the delivery of a funny line. This not only puzzled us but also completely destroyed our timing. Later, we learned that a large number of seats had been reserved for a Japanese group that spoke no English. The interpreter was getting the jokes, but by the time he translated them, the boat had sailed. In any case, I wondered, how on earth did the translator ever manage all of our idioms delivered like rapid-fire? Rose Marie suggested that the interpreter was a stand-up comic in Japan, and he was just doing his act, and not translating our show at all. She may have been right.

In 1963, around the same time I was directing *The Dick Van Dyke Show*, my agent, Bill Meiklejohn, informed me that he might be able to make a deal for my services with Hal Wallis, the legendary producer, to direct feature films for theatrical release. Intrigued by the prospect, I signed on, with visions of directing classic cinema along the lines of *Casablanca*, which Wallis had produced along with successful English costume pieces. When my first assignment with Wallis turned out to be *Wives and Lovers*, I accepted, content to begin my cinema career with something lightweight, expecting that something more substantial awaited me down the line.

First, though, I appealed to Mr. Wallis about the movie's title. I didn't like it, because it seemed to me people might confuse it with the novel *Sons and Lovers*. I was instantly overruled; Wallis liked the title. I also struck out when I heard a catchy tune with the same name as the film. I played a recording of it for Wallis and suggested it might fit in to the movie somehow, helping generate publicity. He turned it down flatly, although the song "Wives and Lovers" later became a giant hit.

When I signed on to direct the film, I was excited to learn that it would be a vehicle for Shirley MacLaine, who was under contract to Wallis at the time. However, a legal dispute caused the deal with Shirley to fall through, and the wonderful Janet Leigh was cast in the lead role opposite Van Johnson. Both of these popular stars were gems to work with. I enjoyed both their professional approach to the work and their friendship, particularly Janet's, which endured until the day she passed away. The cast also included Ray Walston, a delightful star of the Broadway stage; Martha Hyer, a cool femme fatale type; and Shelley

Winters, the Academy Award-winning actress whose performances I had often enjoyed. They were consummate professionals—with one notable exception.

For the first four or five days of shooting, the production rolled along with amazing speed and efficiency. Working exclusively with Janet and Van, we were almost a day ahead of schedule, and Wallis beamed with pleasure and compliments when he viewed the dailies. Then Hurricane Shelley arrived. Wasting no time, she proceeded to make her first day of shooting a nightmare. After rehearsing a scene to the actors' apparent satisfaction, I had turned over the set for lighting, a rather long and tedious process. Eventually, our first assistant director, Danny McCauley, told me that Lucien Ballard, the director of photography, and his camera department were ready to shoot. Shelley answered the call to the set for filming, where she promptly indicated she wasn't happy about the position she had chosen during rehearsal. She would prefer to be on the other side of the stage.

It has always been my practice to allow actors to select their own movements initially, subject to my final approval. I've found that respecting the actor's instincts in a scene benefits the production in the long run. An actor finding his or her own way in a scene is far happier, I have learned, than one who has been told to stand here or move there on a particular line. Naturally, though, one can't allow chaos to prevail, and at times a director must step in with corrections. Shelley had selected her own position on stage, and I felt it was consistent with the scene's intent. To completely alter this blocking would have necessitated a total relight, which would cost us several production hours. I suggested we shoot the scene as rehearsed, and after some grumbling, our diva appeared to go along. But I soon learned what had apparently prompted her to ask for such an enormous delay: She hadn't learned her lines! Not only did she exceed ten or eleven takes for one scene, but she actually boasted that in her first film, the brilliant director George Cukor had done ninety-four takes with her on one scene. Obviously, Mr. Cukor had a lot more patience than I.

Winters committed every possible sin, changing interpretations for take after take, never settling down to one performance. Her work was so enervating that Janet Leigh and Van Johnson each came to me separately, asking me not to print a scene in which they appeared exhausted, just because she had managed to get one take correctly. I promised them I would do my utmost to protect them from her shenanigans.

At one point near the end of the day, I'm afraid I lost my cool. After Shelley had delivered yet another subpar performance that she appeared to like, I said we would do another. Shelley then said loudly, "Okay, why don't you print mine and then I'll do yours." This was too much. It was almost six o'clock and the production had lost all sense of momentum. "I print what I approve," I said, "and I disapprove of everything you've done today! Wrap it up, Danny!" McCauley pulled the plug, the stage went dark, and we finished a day behind schedule.

I called Hal Wallis, told him what had happened, and implored him to replace Winters. But Wallis told me, "Look, she's a seminame and she's working cheap. I'm not going to replace her. Her money is so low we can afford an extra day or two. Everybody has trouble with her. Use it as a learning experience."

Next, I phoned my friend George Stevens, who had directed Winters successfully in the classic *A Place in the Sun*, as well as in the more recent *Diary of Anne Frank*. I asked if he had trouble with her, and he laughed and said, "She likes to be punished. I would often give her a 6 AM call and make her sit in her dressing room for a whole day without using her until she became more tractable. She enjoys attention, even if it's negative attention."

"It's easy for you to take that kind of time," I said. "I'm on a forty-five-day schedule."

"Hit her with a two-by-four once in a while," Stevens replied. "She'll love you for it."

I never went quite that far. But one day when I was viewing my dailies, Shelley slipped into the projection room, uninvited, and said when the lights came up, "Hey John, I'm good in this thing. I've got a hunch you and I are going to do a lot of films together." My reply was unequivocal: "Bullshit, Shelley. This is it!" She loved it.

In time, I found that many directors shared my feelings about this difficult actress. One day at dinner, I asked Guy Green about his experience with Winters in his film *A Patch of Blue*. Guy dropped his silverware clumsily and said, "Please don't mention that name during dinner." Carl Reiner, who has never said an unkind word about anyone, once phoned me to ask about Shelley. He was casting her as

Alan Arkin's mother in his film *Enter Laughing*. I advised him to pass. Too late, he said; he had already cast her. But life with her couldn't be too bad, could it?

Some time later, Carl called to tell me what a disaster she had been. Apparently he wanted some reaction shots of Shelley sitting in a theater audience. Carl said he would play all the parts offstage, and if anyone could perform this task superbly, it's Carl, who is a brilliant comic as well as a first-rate director. Winters would have none of it. She insisted he assemble the entire cast to play their roles off-camera. Carl patiently told her they had all been dismissed and were off the clock. But Shelley was so adamant, Carl eventually lost his temper and vowed he would do without her reactions—what he already had in the camera would suffice.

The final irony: Shelley Winters received the best reviews of my debut film. Her method of operation was clear: cause enough film to be exposed, and some suffering director (as I became in the cutting room) would wade through the pile of dross she delivered, select the best takes, and manufacture a performance out of them. Academy Award, anyone?

I never tried to cast this difficult and manipulative person in any of my subsequent films, although she visited when I was directing other pictures and attempted to make contact. Using George Stevens's model, I generally spoke rudely to her, which worked for a while. But then she decided to libel me with a completely fabricated story in a book she had written. I contacted my attorneys, proved that her concoction was libelous, and had the offending passages removed from subsequent editions of her nasty literary effort. In fifty years of working with some of the most professional actresses in our business, most of whom were simply marvelous to work with, she is the only actress I have actively disliked.

After completing *Wives* and waiting for my next assignment from Wallis, I received an offer from producer Bobby Cohn, of Columbia, to direct the sequel of his successful melodrama *The Interns*. My agent cleared this proposal with Wallis, and I was soon ensconced at Columbia, preparing *The New Interns*. I was able to sign Lucien Ballard to serve as my director of photography again, which gave me a great sense of security. But the script disappointed me, and I asked the writer to do some revising.

After accepting many of my notes, he delivered a draft that still didn't satisfy me, so I asked Mr. Cohn if I could take a crack at the script. He approved, and several weeks later I came up with a photoplay I could live with. Bobby and the studio were equally pleased, and I began preparation with a light heart, even though the actor selected to play the lead role, Peter Falk, declined Columbia's offer. Falk was kind enough to meet with me one day at the studio, and he pleasantly explained that the large cast and multiple storylines contributed to his bowing out. "With all these people involved in the piece," he said, "I don't think I can score in this film."

I was sorry to see Falk go, but happily, we replaced him with George Segal to play the central character. Before we met, I had neither seen nor even heard of George, but his serious demeanor when discussing his role impressed me. During the many weeks of production, he was wonderful—thoroughly professional, finding deep nuances, imbuing the character with a burning intensity that commanded the stage. To borrow Peter Falk's words, he "scored" magnificently.

Because we had a modest budget, I cast *The New Interns* with many fine performers I had worked with and respected in television. These actors were not known for their feature work, and therefore did not yet command high salaries. But many of them went on to head-line features (Dean Jones at Disney, George Segal in several major films) or star in landmark TV series: Telly Savalas in *Kojak*, Barbara Eden in *I Dream of Jeannie*, Greg Morris in *Mission: Impossible,* Stefanie Powers in *Hart to Hart,* and Dawn Wells in *Gilligan's Island.* George Furth worked with me later on other series, including *All in the Family,* and went on to become a successful Broadway playwright. Inger Stevens, a lovely, talented performer, unfortunately passed away at too early an age.

Among many amusing incidents that occurred during the shoot, one stands out in my mind. In that era, many actors with ethnic names had changed their billing to something the studios felt sounded more "American." Thus, Archibald Leach became Cary Grant; Bernie Schwartz became Tony Curtis. George Segal maintained the name given him at birth. Possibly that was what caught the attention of a reporter working for the *Jerusalem Post*, who arrived on our set one day with a photographer and interviewed George and me. Before he left, the correspondent requested a photograph to be made of him standing between actor and director. Of course, we agreed, and we lined up.

From the camera's viewpoint, George was standing on the right side, with me on the left. Just before the flash, George called out, "John, would you trade places with me?" I agreed, and after the picture was taken, I asked, "What was that all about?" George laughed and said, "I outfoxed you. My publicist said I should always maneuver to be on the side I picked for the photo. That way I get top billing."

"Ordinarily true," I said, "but this shot is going to be published in Jerusalem, where top billing is read right to left."

The look on George's face was priceless.

Another amusing incident took place during the picture's final shot. I had placed the camera on top of our highest piece of equipment, to photograph some action featuring our cast and a large contingent of extras. The crane started in close to the action, then pulled back slowly to photograph the monumental steps and imposing façade of Los Angeles County Hospital on a busy morning, as the end-of-film music took over. The shot was a bit tricky and required a number of retakes to get it right in one continuous movement. Each take required the repositioning of a host of people, not to mention the crane and its attendant crew. In the midst of one of these agonizing and time-consuming pauses, a spectator, who had been watching for several hours, approached me cautiously and said, "May I ask you a question?" I nodded absent-mindedly, and she asked, "Why do you take the same picture over and over again?" I said, "Do you realize how many theaters there are in this country?" She nodded, apparently satisfied.

Speaking of sideline spectators, George Stevens once shared a story that occurred when he was filming *I Remember Mama*, in 1947. A large section of a San Francisco location had been "dressed" to look like 1906; the crew had disguised telephone poles to simulate trees, judiciously covered all signs, and carefully camouflaged every other visual that looked current. After setting up a long shot of the neighborhood, Stevens overheard a conversation between two ladies standing among the spectators. "Is this picture in color?" said one of them. "Don't be silly," said the other. "They didn't have color in 1906."

A friend of mine, Bob Sweeney, told me something when we worked together on *Our Miss Brooks*, back in the 1950s, that has stayed with me for a lifetime. Bob came to work one day after spending the weekend visiting relatives. An uncle had remarked, "Bob, I saw your show the other night and it was awful. Why do you act in such terrible productions?" Bob had answered, "Uncle Joe, you're a carpenter, and sometimes you're given Cuban mahogany to work with. Other days, you're asked to build something out of third-rate knotty pine. You'd rather work with the rare wood, but since you're a professional carpenter, you go to work every day and try to do the best you can. Sometimes we get great scripts, sometimes they're not so hot. But since I'm a professional actor, I show up every day for work the same way you do." Bob's wisdom applies to directing as well, and his words have frequently sustained me when I struggled with a knotty-pine-level script.

After I finished *The New Interns* at Columbia, I returned to Paramount and my contract under Hal Wallis, where I was dismayed to learn that my next assignment was to work with Elvis Presley on a film called *Roustabout*. At the time, I was not a fan of Presley's music, although I have found merit in it since then. As for his acting ability, I thought he was stiff and unconvincing. But a job is a job. And we had the good fortune to also cast Barbara Stanwyck, a brilliant actress, to portray Presley's boss at a carnival, and the equally terrific performer Pat Buttram as the "wise old hand" of the outfit.

Elvis was always polite and affable, never addressing me as John, but always as "Mista Rich." His willingness to take direction surprised me, and his work ethic in keeping up with Miss Stanwyck and Leif Erickson, who played one of the antagonists, impressed me. It turned out to be a pleasurable experience, and I kept myself interested by trying a few camera tricks that appealed to Presley, and later to Hal Wallis.

Early in the picture, one of our musical numbers required Elvis to ride a motorcycle while singing an upbeat song. The production schedule called for three days of process shooting on a special stage, with Presley sitting on a motorbike in front of a rear-screen projection device. This is painstaking and boring labor, and I had always viewed the results of such work as stiff and unreal, with its often flickering images. So I wondered aloud one day if it was possible to film the song live on an actual location. I had heard Presley knew how to ride a motorcycle, so I broached the idea with the departments involved. The technical people instantly said it wouldn't work, because an acetate record was always used when committing a musical number to film. The artist would customarily record the song first, then, when the camera is turning, sing in sync with his own played-back phrasing. Instantly, both the music and sound departments objected to my notion. "If you tried to shoot live," they argued, "how would you keep the disk from skipping a groove or two on a bumpy road?" Naively, I asked if it were possible to use audiotape on the camera truck and beam the sound back to Elvis. It had never been done that way, I was told; the tape recording couldn't be synchronized with the film. But when I asked for a test to be conducted, the tape held sync perfectly.

Then I approached our star and asked if he'd be willing to sing to playback while riding the motorcycle. We would shoot with two cameras, I explained, one for the long shot and one for the close-up. Presley was delighted to do it that way, the scene looked terrific, and we saved almost three days of shooting. Hal Wallis loved it.

During another scene, at a roadhouse, Presley came upon some nasty college types and their girlfriends. The script called for three beautiful coeds, and Wallis and I convened a "cattle call"—a detestable practice, in my opinion, in which twenty or thirty young lovelies show up to compete for three parts, only one of them a speaking role. These girls were all knockouts, so I arbitrarily selected a blonde, a brunette, and a redhead. Wallis agreed, and I picked one of the girls to speak the line. On location, though, the lady I had chosen couldn't deliver the line properly, and after four or five attempts, I asked one of the other extras to take it. This young woman, a breathtaking beauty, delivered the line flawlessly, in one take. While setting up for the next scene, I thanked the young woman, who told me this was one of her first jobs in film, and that she was going to be a big star one day. Without really believing it, I told her I was sure she had a great future. Her name was Raquel Welch.

The scene in the roadhouse continued with an exchange of insults that lead to a pitched battle outside in the parking lot. The college boys gang up on Elvis, and he defends himself valiantly in a fight scene carefully plotted out by our stunt coordinator and his team. During the rehearsal, Elvis approached me and asked if he could do his own stunt. I couldn't believe this request. If anything happened to him, I pointed out, we would have to shut down the picture. But he continued to plead his case, saying he had a black belt in karate and knew how to conduct himself without anyone getting hurt.

It was not his skill that concerned me, I said. "What if the stunt man you're fighting throws a bad punch? The reason we employ stunt people is to avoid having our stars suffer injury. The insurance company would never allow this and neither would Mr. Wallis."

Elvis then played his trump card. "I'll take full responsibility if anything happens," he said. "I really want to do this." I had him repeat this promise in front of many witnesses, and against my better judgment, I reluctantly agreed. You may have guessed what happened. Our hero looked terrific doing his karate moves, but then the stunt man's boot struck Elvis's forehead just above the eye, bringing the fight, and the day's shooting, to an abrupt end. Presley was rushed to a local hospital as I was driven to a pay phone to tell Wallis. Thankfully, our associate producer, Paul Nathan, was one of the people who had heard Elvis plead his case. Nathan had contacted Wallis before I could, allowing Vesuvius to vent a bit before I called. The producer summoned us all to a meeting the next day, and a slightly chastened Elvis showed up sporting a hospital bandage on his head. Fortunately, the wound was not serious, but the mishap threatened to slow us down considerably, until I had a brainstorm.

I reminded Wallis that in our story, after Presley has finished his song on the motorcycle, he is forced into a field by the Leif Erickson character, who was driving a Jeep. Using a stunt rider for Elvis, we had already shot the sequence with the machine crashing through a fence. I suggested we could attribute Presley's laceration to the motorcycle crash. With skillful makeup around the wound and a carefully applied bandage, we kept filming without significantly altering our schedule, and the bandage eventually disappeared as the real Elvis recovered.

Another camera trick arose later in the picture, when our leading man sang to the romantic interest (Joan Freeman) while the two rode a Ferris wheel, before the carnival opened for the day. Once again, the production schedule called for extensive process shooting, using a background plate to show movement while Elvis and Joan sat in the foreground. To photograph the film destined for the process camera, I decided to ride the wheel myself, looking backward from one of the swinging seats. To my disappointment, my eye told me that the plate would have great interest only when something colorful came into view: the merry-go-round or other rides, balloons, or pennants. As soon as the seat rose into the air, the background became dull: lots of blank sky and flat ranchland.

When I returned to earth after my test ride, I sought out Lucien Ballard and asked him how high our equipment could reach. I hoped to shoot the full number on location without using process, provided that the camera could hold a two-shot throughout the song. The crane could do what I asked, Lucien said, but we needed to keep the camera from bumping at its high point or shaking when the chair hit bottom. A rope was attached to the underside of the camera so the grips could "lead" the movement as the chair of the Ferris wheel came over the top at relatively high speed. The shot required six men to cushion the camera as it reached the low point, and the camera operator, Dick Bachelor, and his assistant, Davey Walsh, had to focus and follow the moving target throughout the number. Because the grips would have to absorb the shock of slowing and stopping the apparatus on their knees, we couldn't expect them to rehearse the routine more than once for the rehearsal and once for the take.

I took Elvis aside, explained what I was doing, and asked him to rehearse carefully to maintain perfect lip-sync without the need for retakes. It had to be done in one shot, with no chance to cut away. Once again, I was delighted to see him respond positively to the challenge. On the take, Presley was perfect, and the song and the camera movement were beautifully integrated. I had even discovered that we could adjust the timing of the Ferris wheel to match the beat of the music. It became a memorable shot, and saved us another three days of production time. Wallis was entranced by the number and heaped praise on me, wondering how we had managed to bring it off.

After working with the editor and delivering my rough cut, I was still basking in the euphoria of having invented at least two interesting production numbers without the need for editorial intervention. So I was flabbergasted, when I watched Wallis's version of the film, to find that he had interrupted the Ferris wheel sequence by inserting a cut of the ride's operator. We had seen Elvis ask the man to start the machine as a "test run," so why the cutaway? I cornered Wallis one day and asked why he had tampered with something he had praised so lavishly.

He replied, "It's necessary to see who's controlling the ride." I couldn't believe my ears. "All you've done," I sputtered, "is prove to the world that we didn't do the number in one take! The cut to the operator ruins the whole effect!" Wallis was adamant, and since he owned the movie, that's the way it was released.

Several weeks after the film debuted in theaters, I asked to see the great man in his office. I had visited my attorneys and dictated a codicil to my last will and testament, which I had brought with me. I told Wallis I had mentioned him in the document, and he appeared very interested; his expressioned softened and became unnaturally sweet. "Really?" he said. "You've mentioned me in your will?"

I replied, "Would you like to hear what I have written?"

He nodded yes, so I unfolded the paper and read: "If I should die before Hal Wallis, which is probable, because I'm working for the son of a bitch, I direct that my body be cremated and my ashes blown into his eyes."

The wording startled Wallis into resuming his customary frown. Then he just stared at me, finally saying, "You're making this up."

"No," I said, "it's true, it's all legal, and it's there to remind me forever of your arbitrary editorial decision on the Ferris wheel shot." The codicil remained in my will until Wallis left this earth for that great cutting room in the sky. When he died, I had the paragraph removed. Still, of all the arbitrary decisions I've seen producers make through the years, the cutaway from Elvis and the girl still rankles me the most.

Something George Stevens once said to me helped me on the set of *Roustabout*. Early in my career as a director, I was humbled when viewing Stevens's great Western *Shane*. I thought I would never achieve anything on that level, and of course I haven't, preferring—or being compelled—to work in more confined spaces. George became a good friend when we both served on the Screen Directors Guild's Board of Directors. I asked him one day if he had ever experienced insecurity while directing. He laughed and said, "Many a morning, when you walk into that cold, dark universe of a film stage and realize you don't have a clue in your head about what to do, a sense of near panic hits you."

This put me at ease, I found it so humanizing, and I asked, "So what do you do?" George's reply served me well during many a production. He said, "Nothing will happen until you say something, so I always tell the cinematographer 'Put the camera here.' That gets everybody moving. After that, I can change my mind, but the important thing is to get started. Otherwise people get the idea they can sit around." In line with his advice, I have always followed the precept of getting the first shot early in the day. For every five minutes wasted in the morning, the schedule suffers disproportionately at day's end. It's one of the reasons I hate morning lateness by actors. It's disrespectful of the crew, who have arrived on time, and it's extremely rude to fellow actors.

One morning on the set of *Roustabout,* Barbara Stanwyck, a model of professionalism, was standing in her marks at 9 AM, the precise moment the call sheet had indicated, her lines firmly in mind, makeup and hair completed. That day, Elvis Presley, who usually arrived on time, didn't show up until 9:30. I was fuming, and took him aside and said, "I know you're the most important person in this picture, but that actress standing on the set waiting for you was a huge star while you were still a kid. It's thoroughly unprofessional to keep anyone waiting, particularly that lady."

Elvis sheepishly apologized, saying, "I'm sorry, Mista Rich, it won't happen again." And it didn't.

I suppose there are exceptions to this principle. I have been told, by Jack Lemmon and Billy Wilder, that Marilyn Monroe habitually arrived late while shooting *Some Like It Hot.* Lemmon thought this showed her insecurity. "She couldn't present herself until she felt ready to face the camera that day," he said. Wilder was asked if her lateness drove him crazy. Billy replied, famously, "Look, if I wanted somebody to be on time and to know the lines just perfectly, I've got an old aunt in Vienna. She's going to be there at five in the morning and never miss a word. But who wants to look at her?"

Despite Wallis and the Ferris wheel run-in, I again directed Elvis Presley for his company in *Easy Come, Easy Go.* This time the singer was cast as a Navy frogman who finishes his tour of duty and gets involved in a search for buried treasure. At one point in the script, Elvis joins a beautiful society girl, who lends her yacht for the treasure hunt. An underwater fight scene was filmed in the clear waters off Florida, with a stunt man doubling for Elvis. When the fight was over, "Elvis" swam up out of camera to exit from the depths.

We were now prepared to continue the sequence off the coast of Catalina with Elvis himself breaking the surface of the water and swimming over to the boat. Clad in frogman gear that matched the stunt man's costume, our star looked perfect as I described the shot to him. He should go into the water, I explained, submerge briefly for a count of ten or so to allow the water to calm, then pop up and swim over to the yacht. At this, Elvis looked at me apologetically and said, "I can't do that, Mista Rich. I can't swim."

I thought about this for a moment, then said, "Okay, we'll costume one of our stunt men and he'll swim to the boat. You won't have to swim at all—just go over the side, and I'll have the camera pick you up as you leave the water and climb the little ladder." This too was unacceptable, as Elvis said he couldn't go into the water at all—it made him too nervous. "Okay, I'll have the stunt man reach the deck and I'll pick you up taking off the mask and flippers." This met with his approval and that's the way we shot the scene.

Once again, I was in for a surprise when I viewed Hal Wallis's final cut. This time it was an odd piece of film spliced into the underwater action scenes. Apparently, Wallis had decided to insert a close-up of Elvis to cut into the stunt double's work, but he hadn't consulted me or asked me to supervise the shooting.

Because of Elvis's insecurity, it was clear they wouldn't have shot anything near real water, so whoever directed the moment had set up a very tight head shot of the star, so as not to reveal that he was standing on a Paramount stage. The anonymous director chose to heighten the illusion by splashing Elvis with buckets of water and photographing his face as he looked through the glass of a small fish tank. The little aquarium featured a few tropical specimens darting in front of Elvis, who wore a scuba mask and looked intensely in different directions to fit into the previously filmed fight scene. It was a disastrously amateurish piece of work—probably the most embarrassing attempt at "movie magic" I have ever witnessed.

After delivering *Wives and Lovers* and *Roustabout* to Wallis's evident satisfaction, he informed me that for my next assignment he wanted me to direct *Boeing-Boeing*. The play had been a huge hit all through Europe, playing to packed houses in London, Paris, and Rome for several years. Having secured the film rights, Wallis told me to fly to London to view the stage production. I heard him make vague references to being in England himself, and that he was preparing to sail over on the luxury liner *France*. Somewhat facetiously, I remarked that since I had never been to Europe before, nor sailed across the ocean, would it be all right with him if I crossed by sea, rather than flying? To my immense surprise, he said it would be okay, but told me to book on the next crossing. To my relief, his largesse did not extend as far as having me by his side on the same voyage. With mounting excitement, I flew to New York and met with Wallis's silent partner, Joseph Hazen, who entertained me royally in his huge Park Avenue apartment, filled with an extraordinary collection of nineteenth- and twentieth-century art. It was a heady experience to be surrounded by such opulence, and it put me in the mood for embarking on the great steamship.

When we left the harbor at twilight and sailed majestically into open water, I was astonished to view my birthplace, the peninsula of Rockaway Beach, to my left. As we approached Ambrose Lightship, I was transported to my childhood, when I had spent many lonely nights on the boardwalk, viewing the blinking light and imagining the continents lying just beyond the beacon. What a surprise to learn that it wasn't Europe off the starboard side of the vessel—it was Sandy Hook, New Jersey! The phrase "Travel is broadening" hit me with a significance I had never before experienced.

Unmarried at the time, I was fortunate to meet an attractive lady on board, and we dined together in the lavishly appointed restaurant. As we docked in Southampton, she agreed to accompany me on the boat train to London. Determined to learn the unfamiliar coinage of pounds, shillings, and pence, I practiced by ordering refreshments in the bar car. But nothing prepared me for the commotion that greeted the crowd of travelers as we descended from the train. A large contingent of photographers and reporters was on hand, obviously there to meet someone of importance. As flash bulbs went off, it gradually became clear that the mob was photographing us!

Out of the center of the jostling group emerged a smiling Hal Wallis, introducing the chief of Paramount's London publicity department, who oversaw the gaggle of reporters, as well as several attendants to see to our luggage. When I introduced my surprised companion, Wallis greeted her with uncharacteristic warmth as we were ushered to a chauffeur-driven limousine. In the car, before dropping the woman off at a relative's apartment, I tried to explain to her that I wasn't really all that famous, but I don't think she believed me.

After I'd been deposited at the Dorchester Hotel, arrangements were made for me to attend the West End production of the play, and I realized at once that it was a giant European hit because its driving issue was satirically poking fun at American sexual proclivities in the jet age. I felt that a film based on this theme would do extremely well in foreign markets but probably wouldn't be received happily by U.S. audiences. Wallis disagreed with my comments—but pleasantly—as he continued to ply me with cocktails and dinners and to arrange daily sightseeing trips with his driver and Jaguar sedan. I began to think of my employer as the enormously wealthy drunk in Charlie Chaplin's *City Lights,* a man who befriends the little Tramp, lavishing gifts, luxurious lodging, and fabulous food when he is drinking, only to turn vicious and hostile when he sobers up.

During my European idyll, however, Wallis's reputation as a hard-driving, tightfisted producer was nowhere to be seen. So I took another chance, suggesting that perhaps I should go to Paris as well, to see the play in its French incarnation. To my pleasant shock, the producer instantly agreed, and booked me into one of the finest hotels in Paris. After seeing the play again, and listening to the appreciative roar of the French audience, I phoned Wallis and repeated my earlier assessment about its prospects with American moviegoers. At the conclusion of our talk, during which Wallis continued to ignore my worried statements, I had another wild brainstorm—what the hell?—and asked, "Wouldn't it be productive if I flew to Rome to experience the play in its Italian version?" In addition, I continued, since Eddie Anhalt, the writer of the screen adaptation, was living in Italy at the time, wouldn't it be wise to meet with him and discuss the work in great depth? Once more, Wallis played the generous host, agreeing to first-class travel, per diem expenses, and a suite on the Via Veneto. Clearly I was being treated as the fair-haired boy, and clearly the era of good feeling would eventually end.

It did, when I was summarily ordered to fly home (no luxury liner this time) to have serious talks with the chief in his inner-sanctum office at Paramount. There the boss greeted me with considerably less charm than he had displayed on the continent—*City Lights,* indeed—and asked what I thought of casting Jerry Lewis and Tony Curtis in the lead roles. A more interesting pairing, I told him, would be Dick Van Dyke and Jack Lemmon; or Jack Lemmon and Tony Curtis. When Wallis asked who Van Dyke was, I explained that Dick was coming off four or five brilliant years on TV and could handle comedy on a much more sophisticated level than Jerry Lewis's slapstick. As for Tony Curtis, I had seen his terrific work in *Some Like It Hot* and thought he would do the role great justice. But I feared that working with Jerry would infect Tony's comedic impulses, with Lewis falling back on familiar shtick rather than aiming for honesty. I didn't see the over-the-top comic as a believable romantic lead, but Wallis was convinced he had a winning combination, and my protests went unheeded. After casting three beautiful stewardesses—Dany Saval for Air France, Christiane Schmittmer for Lufthansa, and Susanna Leigh representing England—along with the magnificent Thelma Ritter as the put-upon housemaid, we were ready to begin shooting in Europe.

In France at that time, Jerry Lewis was the most revered American performer, a living legend. When my assistant director, Danny McCauley, and I drove to Orly Airport to meet the morning Lufthansa flight bringing Jerry to Paris, the number of suitcases he had brought was astonishing. Apparently, one trunk contained nothing but socks; I had heard he never had socks laundered, but simply discarded them after one wearing. Rumor also had it he would wear a tuxedo only once. I was now ready to believe another improbable story I had heard, that Jerry's annual bill at Sy Devore's Vine Street haberdashery was in the vicinity of $300,000—and these were 1965 dollars! Danny had to arrange for extra transportation for Lewis's luggage. The star himself was whisked off in a Cadillac limousine. Later, we learned that he found his suite at the Ritz to be unsatisfactory, and he promptly moved out to a location unknown to most of us.

On the set, my fears about Lewis's behavior began to manifest themselves almost from day one. Tony Curtis was fastidious about his clothes, always impeccably groomed and dressed, and Jerry loved to step on his co-star's shoes just before a scene began to be shot. Tony tried to act like a good sport and carry on, but clearly he was not happy about it. Every time Tony returned to his dressing room for freshly polished shoes, Jerry convulsed with laughter.

I was never certain why Lewis indulged in this inane behavior. It may have been the way he kept a light tone on the set when he was shooting his early comedy films with Dean Martin. Whatever the reason, I tried to avoid becoming too dictatorial, but all that changed one day when he dragged out another relic behavior from his television years. Years earlier, when I worked as a stage manager on *The Colgate Comedy Hour*, I had often seen Jerry, during rehearsal, stealthily approach Ernie Glucksman with a pair of scissors. At the propitious moment, Jerry would cut off the hapless producer's tie, causing gales of laughter from the crew and orchestra. One day on the *Boeing-Boeing* set, Lewis resurrected this allegedly hilarious bit just before filming a scene, using Tony as his victim. Naturally, the gag disrupted production, and while waiting for Curtis to return to the set with a new tie, I took Jerry aside and reminded him we were filming a major motion picture, not some cut-up TV sketch show with everyone acting like kids.

Lewis looked at me as if I had said something stupid, began to laugh, and stepped toward me, wielding his scissors with obvious intent. I whispered to him, "Jerry, if you try to cut my tie off, I will kick you in the balls in front of the entire company. Don't do it. Don't even think of doing it."

He looked stunned, and said soberly, "Boy, you're serious. You really mean it, don't you?"

I answered without hesitation, "You can find out real quick. Cut my tie, but first check to see if you're wearing an aluminum cup."

He thought this over for a moment, and then put away his prop. I never saw him use it again, and while I regretted having to threaten him, I believe I needed to draw a line in the sand. For the rest of the film, our relationship could be described as polite, and dedicated only to the business at hand. Monkeyshines disappeared, Tony's shoes remained polished, and everybody's ties emerged unamputated. Several critics, incidentally, noted that Jerry's performance in the film seemed adult and controlled, a welcome departure from his usual screen persona.

Tony Curtis was a more focused actor than his co-star, but he did have his idiosyncrasies. For instance, the Cadillac limousine that had been secured for him disappointed him. He demanded a large black Citroen, which was the automobile of choice for diplomats visiting the city. Unfortunately, a major international conference was in session, and it appeared that every Citroen limousine in town had been reserved for ambassadors. This explanation did not satisfy Tony, and to my amazement he refused to enter the Cadillac. Danny McCauley subsequently reported to me that a Citroen had been located in Madrid. I could not believe the company would go to such lengths, but apparently shipping a limo from Spain to France is no problem if the star is big enough, or vain enough, or both. At any rate, the limo made Mr. Curtis happy, and I confess he did his job well.

Another strange mishap marked our Paris shoot as well. Davey Walsh, the assistant cameraman on Lucien Ballard's *Boeing-Boeing* staff, was wrapping up his equipment one Saturday evening after we had shot part of a taxi chase on the Champs Elysee. I left the scene at about 11:30 that night. On Monday morning, I learned to my dismay that a drunk driver had struck Davey and a French camera loader shortly after the company finished work that Saturday. I visited the two victims at the American hospital and learned that the French assistant had sustained minor bruises, but Davey had suffered broken bones in one of his legs, leaving him with a permanent limp. Today, David Walsh is a first-rate director of photography, and I'm pleased at his progress through the years. But I have always felt a little guilty for having selected the camera position that led to the injuries.

Many years after the incident, Paramount attorneys phoned and told me that I had been named in a French lawsuit, alleging that as the director in charge I bore responsibility for the 1965 accident. Alarmed, I asked what the defense would be and was told, "There's no real defense required. We simply plead you guilty and the whole thing goes away. We've done this many times before."

"Hold it," I said. "I have no intention of pleading guilty to any wrongdoing, since I did nothing wrong. On the night in question, I wrapped up my work, leaving paramedics and police on the scene under the supervision of the French production manager. If there's any fault to be assigned, check with him. I intend to visit France many times in the future, so I refuse to be identified as a confessed criminal for the convenience of Paramount's attorneys." With much grumbling, the lawyers followed through on my demands, and the French magistrate who heard the case eventually declared me innocent. I visited Paris recently, and I'm delighted to report that I didn't see my photograph on display in any French post offices.

There was another curious epilogue to that film project. During the making of *Boeing-Boeing*, I had become friends with actress Dany Saval and her husband, the noted composer and conductor Maurice Jarre. Maurice had already earned worldwide recognition for his monumental score for *Lawrence of Arabia*, and David Lean had once again commissioned him to write the music for *Doctor Zhivago*. The studio had decreed a December opening for *Zhivago*, and my friend complained about the tight schedule. It was no surprise to see him retreat into concentrated thought from time to time in that summer of 1965.

One night back in California, while having dinner in the Jarres' Hollywood Hills home, I noticed Maurice begin to absent himself from the conversation and lapse into one of his silences. After a moment, he apologized for having to leave the table, and took his place at the piano. He played out a series of notes, scribbled something on paper, and returned to dinner, explaining that he had thought of a possible theme for one of the characters in *Zhivago* and went on to discuss some of his plans for the orchestration once he had completed the score. I think he said something about securing the services of a hundred balalaika players, and I asked where he could find such an aggregation. In the Soviet Union, he said, and since we were engaged in the cold war, he would record with them in a studio in Paris.

I forgot about our dinner until December, when I attended the premiere of *Doctor Zhivago* as Maurice and Dany's guest. The incredible, soaring score featuring "Lara's Theme" sounded somewhat familiar, and I asked Maurice if the notes he had tinkered with the preceding summer had been the genesis of that extraordinary piece of music. He admitted that it had been. Genius sometimes happens when you least expect it.

One last postscript, about Jerry Lewis: In the autumn of 2002, my wife and I were invited to attend Sid Caesar's eightieth birthday party, at the Friars Club in Beverly Hills. A young comic opened his turn by remarking to the largely show-business crowd that "everybody in this room hates Jerry Lewis." This was unfair, he argued. Jerry should be congratulated for his many good works, particularly for his ability to raise funds during the annual muscular dystrophy campaign. In fact, the comic said, Jerry had played an instrumental role in a medical miracle. It seemed that recently a twelve-year-old boy, who had never been able to walk, suddenly stood up from his wheelchair and walked purpose-fully across the room—so he could switch off the telethon Jerry was hosting.

One of the great and lasting highlights of my career has been the opportunity to serve alongside some of the giants among motion picture directors, as a member of the Screen Directors Guild. My foray into this "real" Hollywood began back in 1953, after I had been hired to direct my first film series, *I Married Joan.* That's when I first set foot in the hallowed halls, so to speak, when I was invited to attend the annual gathering of the Guild. It was astounding to find myself in the same auditorium with Frank Capra, George Stevens, William Wyler, and Alfred Hitchcock, to name a few—a glittering array of some of the greatest names in motion picture history.

The union's members had convened to elect a board of directors, as they did each year. From the floor, members nominated twenty-four candidates, their names written on a blackboard, and then sixteen of those were elected to the new board by secret ballot. While the votes were laboriously counted by hand, the Guild's president, George Sidney, conducted routine business, such as hearing the treasurer's report and welcoming new members, and we "new boys" were asked to stand for a round of polite applause. The president then asked for comments from anyone who wished to speak, and certain directors did so briefly. The slow vote counting dragged on, and Mr. Sidney asked if there were any more statements—anybody? Only awkward silence. My days in radio and early television had taught me never to permit dead air, so I raised my hand timidly.

I began my first public utterance as a Guild member by quoting an article printed in *Variety* that week, commenting that the portion of work done by all the Hollywood creative guilds was approaching 50 percent in television. Motion picture production had slowed down, and TV was taking up the slack. What was my point, asked the president. I said, "I am in awe of the twenty-four names written on the stage blackboard. I am honored just to sit in the same room as Josef von Sternberg, King Vidor, John Ford, and the other incredibly famous men who have been nominated for the new board. But I don't believe any of these illustrious people have ever worked in television."

There was a palpable silence in the auditorium. Finally, Sidney "thanked" me for the comment, and said the union would "look into it." The next day I received a phone call from Joe Youngerman, the Guild's executive secretary, who told me I had been selected as an alternate member of the new board; I suppose that, like the proverbial camel, they preferred to have me inside the tent rather than outside making trouble. So began my service to the Guild as an appointed—then elected, then reelected—board member, and later, secretary-treasurer, second vice president, first vice president, and founding member of the Directors Guild of America–Producers Pension Plan. Except for a short period when I was otherwise occupied with work, I have served on every National Board and every Directors Council from that day on, with great pride and affection for the many men and women with whom I have worked.

Several years later, an interesting union-related problem arose while I was on the set of the Walter Slezak show—a problem that ended up having a huge impact on the Screen Directors Guild. In rehearsal one day, I was visited by a representative of the Radio and Television Directors Guild (RTDG), who demanded payment from me for five years of arrears dues. While I had been an RTDG member, and indeed, an early supporter of that New York union, I pointed out to the rep that I was on honorable withdrawal, and now worked under a Screen Directors Guild agreement. He said I owed the money because I was working in New York. I argued that the RTDG had jurisdiction over live or electronically recorded broadcasts, but because I was directing a film, I was covered worldwide by the Hollywood guild. I told him I would not pay, and the RTDG eventually gave up trying to collect, but the incident stuck with me when I returned home to California.

Soon thereafter, at a meeting of the Screen Directors Guild, I related my story, and also told of a demonstration I had attended at Bing Crosby Productions of a new miracle, Ampex videotape, and said

I thought the two incidents were related. When the Guild's president, George Sidney, asked what I was driving at, I said I thought it would behoove us to consider taking in the RTDG membership, because they had contracts with the three networks. These companies dealt with electronic broadcasting and would soon have access to videotape, whereas our agreements covered only film studios.

Sidney was not impressed, especially when I kept bringing the matter up again in subsequent meetings. He began to refer to me as John "Tape" Rich, and he did not mean it as a compliment. Finally, to shut me up I think, he appointed me as a committee of one to investigate the situation. Soon, I asked for a meeting with Stu Phelps, president of the L.A. chapter of RTDG. For some reason Phelps didn't want to be seen entering our headquarters, so we met in a coffee shop. I outlined a proposal for a merger that would benefit his members, but he seemed uncertain, and as long as he remained president nothing happened. Fortunately, the next man elected president of the RTDG was Jack Shea, who happened to be my best friend from my New York stage-managing days. With a sympathetic RTDG president on board, I began to lobby Screen Directors Guild officers before board meetings and found willing support from Frank Capra, George Stevens, and a few others. These meetings began a long friendship for Stevens and me, in particular, a relationship I cherished until his untimely death. After I reported my one-man committee findings, George Sidney, who seemed opposed to the whole idea, wearily called for a ballot on the merger proposition. He was astounded when the count revealed that I had won a majority. Thus was born the Directors Guild of America, today the most powerful creative union in the entertainment world.

One little footnote about the genesis of the DGA: Some years later, I found myself sitting next to Josef von Sternberg, who usually said very little at board meetings. During a lull in the business, von Sternberg said he wanted to thank me. "For what?" I asked. He explained that before my presentations, he had never heard of videotape, but thanks to me and my unwitting stock tip, he had made a killing accumulating shares of Ampex.

The Screen Directors Guild, and later the DGA, operated as smoothly as it did because of the incredible service provided by our executive secretary, Joseph C. Youngerman. Joe had been a prop man for legendary directors such as Cecil B. DeMille, whose obedient crews instantly fulfilled their director's every request. It was said, for example, that DeMille never looked around when he decided to sit. As soon as there was an indication that he was on the way down, his personal "chair man" was there to keep the sacred bottom from touching the ground. This may be an apocryphal story, but it has the ring of truth. Years later, when I was a young director working at Paramount, my property master was evidently still so imbued with the DeMille tradition that I never had to ask twice for anything. Youngerman was steeped in this brand of old Hollywood culture, and he served the Guild with a devotion and sagacity that were truly inspiring. As his accent revealed, he was a product of the streets of Chicago, and he had a superb, innovative mind that crackled. I learned the art of negotiation from Joe, not to mention many lessons in simply living that he and his wife, Molly, imparted every day. Joe was justifiably one of the most loved, one could say adored, human beings it has ever been my privilege to know.

An example of his brilliance: I learned one day from Joe that the Guild had donated $500 to the estate of the pioneer director D. W. Griffith. Credited as the father of motion picture directors, Griffith had died penniless, and the money was earmarked to provide a headstone for his grave in Kentucky. Youngerman went on to say that many one-time successful film artists had expired in similar straits, because of the industry's woefully inadequate pension plan. Directors got lumped into the same plan that covered camera operators, grips, make-up people, and so on. The problem with this arrangement was that "credits" were earned only by hours actually spent shooting a film. Directors' work included months of preparation, and many more months of postproduction editing, scoring, and dubbing, for which they earned no credit toward their pensions. It was time to create a separate plan for directors and their assistants, Joe said, but the studios would have none of it.

Joe's genius was to link the need for a director's pension plan to another thorny issue, the broadcasting of feature films on television. During negotiations in the late 1940s and 1950s, talks began about compensating actors, writers, and directors with residual payments on films released to TV. At first, it was deemed impossible to determine the financial impact such broadcasts would have, so it was agreed to invoke a "moratorium" on all films made since 1948. The studios would not sell such pictures to TV until a residual formula was established. If a production company violated the agreement, members of the three talent guilds could withhold services from the offending producer. This compromise was ratified routinely in every labor negotiation until 1960. By then, hundreds of millions of potential dollars were tied up in "moratorium" films that hadn't aired on TV, and the temptation proved too much for Republic Studios. The owner of that studio, Herb Yates, announced one day that Republic was selling its backlog to television. Immediately, the Screen Actors Guild (SAG), the Writers Guild of America (WGA), and the Screen Directors Guild announced they would no longer allow their members to work at Republic. "Go ahead and strike," Yates said. "I don't need your members because Republic is no longer making films. We are now a distribution company!"

This was a thunderbolt, and Youngerman reasoned that it was only a matter of time before the major studios—Fox, Paramount, Columbia, et al.—would follow suit. Unfortunately, the leaders of the actors' and writers' guilds did not view the situation to be as dangerous as it was. In a year when new contracts were scheduled to be negotiated, the SAG and WGA led off the bargaining. SDG would not come up for six or seven months. Incredibly, to us, both the actors' and writers' unions stalled in their negotiations and decided to strike the major studios for the compensation their memberships would have earned on films released to TV from 1948 to 1960.

I recall a meeting in Youngerman's office where the discussion turned to the political and financial realities of the situation. Joe made the point that Twentieth Century Fox shares were trading on the stock market that day for about $18. In liquidation, if the studio adopted the "Republic formula," the stock would sell for four times as much. Can you imagine Wall Street opposing such a conclusion? It was clear, Joe said, that all the studios were going to reorganize as distribution centers and start new production arms under new names, without regard for former contractual agreements. Breaking the silence that ensued, Joe said he had come up with a new idea to turn apparent chaos into a win-win situation: releasing the moratorium backlog to the studios in exchange for a meaningful pension and health plan.

Joe's notion was to create a two-tier system, a defined benefits plan and a defined contribution plan. Employers would contribute 5 percent of salaries earned. Part of this new money would be credited to the individual (a Supplemental, or defined contribution, fund), and part would go to a fund for all participants (a Basic, or defined benefit, fund). This scheme would allow high-income earners to defer collecting their supplemental money until some time in the future, which gave them certain tax benefits. At the same time, their contributions to the Basic plan would provide payouts for all classes of earners, so that lower-salaried members would benefit from the assistance of larger-earning directors: the "Robin Hood" Plan. Joe also proposed that each participant have 2.5 percent of his salary credited to his own individual Supplemental plan, thus creating a savings program while making those funds available for use in a large investment pool.

The concept was breathtaking, but what interest would the production companies have in agreeing to those expenditures? The studios, Youngerman said, would immediately benefit from some $100 million in TV sales, and as the plan was implemented the cost of funding it would be tax-deductible for them. Some of our lawyers were skeptical, and our accountants thought the scheme would never clear the Internal Revenue Service, so a study was authorized to test the program's validity. Surprising everybody—except Youngerman—our legal and financial experts eventually concluded that there was no reason to prohibit the complex scheme. Although initially the writers' and actors' unions expressed no interest in the plan, the directors guild made it a priority at our bargaining session with the studios, who immediately adopted it.

The plan, known today as the Directors Guild of America–Producer Pension Plan, began in 1960, with the studios providing the first million dollars to pay small pensions to members who had already retired. The pension plan is a separate entity from the DGA, administered by a board of trustees consisting of thirty-six members, half provided by the Guild, half by the employing companies. I became one of the founding members of the plan, and I have been proud to serve on its board until this day. By 2006 we had paid out over $1 billion in retirement funds and provided a generous health plan for the use of all members. The Supplemental and Basic Plans are today worth more than $2 billion. And we are growing stronger by the day, thanks to the genius of

Joe Youngerman, whose name is proudly displayed at the top of the Pension Building, on Third Street in West Hollywood.

Incidentally, when it was announced that SDG had made a deal with the studios, wiser heads prevailed at WGA and SAG headquarters, and they, too, agreed to pension plans for their respective memberships. However, their programs have no "Robin Hood" features. High-income people can keep all the money credited to their individual accounts, while those on the bottom end of the food chain must fend for themselves. In other words, lower-earning writers and actors did not have a Joe Youngerman to represent them.

Many of the famous directors I encountered through the Guild had been described as "tough," "uncompromising," even "cruel and savage." I never watched any of them at work on a set, but at board meetings they were models of decorum. Smoking was de rigueur. The air was so filled with clouds of pipe and cigar emanations that the meeting room could have doubled as a set for Victorian London. The only known defense for a new boy was to take up smoking himself. Despite serving in the Air Force during World War II, I had never taken so much as a puff on a cigarette, but social pressure soon had me smoking large cigars on a daily basis. I could not afford the kind of cigars my colleagues indulged in, though. They bought the finest Cuban exports, hardly something a TV director could afford.

In a way, cigars were what introduced me to George Burns. One year Burns's production company had hired me to direct a pilot starring Alan Young and William Bendix. Burns visited the set one day and watched me rehearse a scene with the principal actors. As we were setting lights for filming, he approached and said, "Hey kid, that was a nice piece of directing." I thanked him, and he went on, "I noticed you were smoking a cigar. Here, have one of mine." He handed me a Santa Fe Fairmont, a very inexpensive brand. As I accepted it, I said, "I hope you don't mind answering a question." He nodded okay, and I continued, "I happen to live next to Sue Chadwick, who represents the Cigar Institute of America, and she once told me that because of the positive image you've created in your act, you can have any cigar they make without charge." That was true, Burns said.

"In that case," I said, "may I ask why you're smoking a fifteen-cent cigar?"

Flicking ashes, Burns said, "You know, you're the second guy that's asked me that. I once gave one of my cigars to Milton Berle, and Milton said, 'I can't smoke that. I smoke two-dollar Havanas.'" He paused to take another puff, then said, "I told him, 'Milton, before I'd pay two dollars for a cigar, first I'd want to fuck it, then I'd smoke it.'"

I laughed and said, "You've just tried that out on me, right? It's good, but are you thinking of using it in your act?" Burns said he was going to, but since he never used questionable language on stage, he would change the key word to *kiss*. But he was not above using earthy language in private conversation. The producer Aaron Ruben, who wrote for Burns, later told me an amusing story about the comedian. Burns's manager, Irving Fein, reminded his client that he was scheduled to have lunch with his doctor one afternoon. Burns said, "I'm not going." Fein was amazed. "But you promised. You've got to keep the appointment." Burns repeated, "I'm not going." Fein was appalled, "How can you make a promise, then break it so easily?" Burns said, "When I made that promise, the guy had his finger up my ass. What did you expect me to say?"

As to Burns's real reason for smoking Fairmonts, I learned that, unlike expensive Cubans, which are densely packed and remain lit only as long as they are puffed, cheap cigars do not require constant relighting. Onstage, Burns never had to strike a match to his permanently burning stogie, as he waved it about for emphasis or took a drag during audience laughter.

John Ford was particularly interesting when it came to cigars. He would remove the band from a pristine cigar, open his penknife, and surgically slice the Havana into two equal parts, one of which he would jam into his mouth and proceed to chew into a pulp. I don't think he was trying to cut down; it was just messier and he liked it that way. With his eye patch and ever-present handkerchief that he sucked on when he wasn't occupied with a cigar, Ford always presented a raffish figure. There is a story about some studio lackey arriving on one of Ford's sets one day to announce that unhappy studio executives were complaining that the director was four pages behind schedule. According to legend, Ford picked up his script, tore four pages out of it, and handed them to the messenger, saying, "Tell the front office I'm back on schedule." When Ford spoke, everybody listened, and there was always a point being made under the salty language. One of his comments concerned the offensive editing practices of early television. One night he growled to Delmer Daves, who had directed *Broken Arrow,* a film about Native Americans in the Old West, "Del, I saw your picture on TV last night. They cut it so bad, I didn't see one fucking Indian in the thing."

Another director who served on one of our early boards was Henry Hathaway. Hathaway appeared to be a gentleman at meetings, but stories were rampant about his short fuse while shooting. Lucien Ballard, the brilliant cinematographer with whom I worked on four films, had also worked on several pictures with Hathaway. One day on location in Mexico, Lucien told me, Hathaway's best boy (or chief electrician) was getting the attention of the local crew on the catwalks by saying, *"Por favor,"* and then indicating with hand signals how to move a lamp or clamp a shade. Hathaway would have none of this slow routine. He suffered a while, and then screamed, "Cut out that *por favor* shit and move the goddamn lamp." He was colorful, to say the least.

Many of the directors left little doubt who was in charge while shooting. William Wyler, an extraordinary filmmaker who spoke almost in a whisper, had this to say about the way a director should approach his work: "You must avoid all temptation to be a good fellow." Richard Brooks once observed, "We live in a democracy until you step onto my set." Alfred Hitchcock was frequently quoted as having said, "All actors are cattle." Hitchcock bristled at this, saying, "I would never make such a rude, unthinking comment. What I actually said was, 'All actors should be *treated* as cattle.'"

Michael Curtiz, the talented director of classic films such as *Casablanca,* spoke English with a decidedly Eastern European accent. Peter Ustinov once said, "Michael Curtiz forgot every word of his native Hungarian without taking the trouble of replacing it with another language." In the early days of Hollywood, before the advent of powerful unions, lunch was not a mandatory event. It was left to the humanity (or lack thereof) of the all-powerful director to call a break or not, as he saw fit. Curtiz made many movies with Errol Flynn, and at one point he encouraged his star to be more aggressive in the swordfight they were shooting. Curtiz said, "No, no, Errol, you've got to lunch with the rapier: Lunch! Lunch!" He meant "lunge," of course, but by the time the mistake was translated, the entire crew had broken for a meal.

Curtiz was something of a ladies' man and frequently had company in his on-set dressing room. With an amorous visitor ministering to the great director one day, he was approaching a rapturous moment when he chanced to look up. Having forgotten that stage "dressing rooms" are often nothing but an assemblage of flats with no ceilings, he was horrified to find an attentive group of grips and electricians peering down from the hanging walkways above. Curtiz tried valiantly, but I don't think he was very convincing when he addressed the lady thusly: "Get away from me, you dirty girl! How did you get in here?"

Like all successful directors, Cecile B. DeMille was a stickler for details. On one occasion, while filming a long shot of a neighborhood street, he observed an extra who appeared to be aimlessly approaching each house, where he would ring the doorbell, leave without waiting for a response, then repeat the same business, going from house to house without any apparent purpose. From his high perch atop a camera crane, DeMille shouted, "You there, why are you doing that?" The extra looked up and replied, "I'm the village idiot." I don't think C. B. was amused.

During one term, Mel Brooks was elected to the board and became a welcome, if slightly off-the-wall, comic addition to our deliberations. Out of the blue, Mel stood up one day and announced, "Nowhere in the Bible is there a mention of anyone named Satchmo." This was followed by, "The battleship *Bismarck* was once known as Kurt and Otto's Boat." As Mel himself once explained, "I would lie on the bottom of the Yangtze River and breathe through a reed to get a laugh."

The directors' rapiers really came out during negotiations with the producing companies. One year, we were treated to a wry opening speech made by Ben Kahane, an extremely bright, urbane attorney who was chairman of the Motion Picture Producers Association. While plying his trade as a lawyer, Kahane would often "out-actor" the best in Hollywood. At the start of contract talks one day, he welcomed us to the negotiating table and, affecting a faulty memory, remarked, "Did I hear the name of Samuel Gompers?" He hadn't. "Samuel Gompers," he went on, "wasn't he the labor leader who once said, 'Anyone making more than $100 a week has no right belonging to a union'?" Without looking up from the note pad on which he was doodling, George Stevens replied, "No, it was Jefferson Davis." Gompers actually had made the remark (in the late nineteenth century), but with his quip,

Stevens restored the balance of power in the room and stole the floor away from Kahane.

On another occasion, negotiations had almost broken down when the chief of Paramount Pictures, Y. Frank Freeman, asked if our committee could meet with him in his studio office. Freeman had suffered a heart attack and his doctor would allow him to spend only a limited amount of time meeting with our group. We agreed to this reasonable request (even though one of our wags remarked, "Y. Frank Freeman? That's a good question"). Earlier than the others, I drove my Chevrolet through the DeMille Gate, parked, and waited outside Freeman's office, where my vantage point allowed me to view the arrival of the union contingent. Eventually "labor" arrived, driving a Rolls Royce, a Duesenberg, a Bentley, a Mercedes, and the like. Gathering in Freeman's office, we noted a stone tablet bearing the Ten Commandments as we were each served a bottle of Coca-Cola—obligatory when meeting with Freeman, who, I soon learned, came from Atlanta and was the principal owner of Coca-Cola stock. When Freeman entered, we all stood out of respect, and he began the meeting in his heavy southern accent. But there was no mistaking the intellect behind the drawl.

Freeman began with an attempt at disarming humor. "I noticed as I came in here," he said, "that some of y'all were looking at that prop from *The Ten Commandments*. I think it would be appropriate to observe, on an occasion such as this, that one of those commandments is 'Thou shalt not covet thy neighbor's property.'" George Seaton promptly cut through Freeman's plantation chuckle: "There's another commandment, Mr. Freeman: 'Thou shalt not steal.'"

Another impressive display of negotiating prowess occurred in the first collective bargaining session in New York City by the newly formed Directors Guild of America. The year was 1960 and as a junior member of the neotiating committee, I watched an astounding performance by our chairman, Frank Capra, Joe Youngerman, George Stevens, and George Sidney as we sat down opposite the labor relations representatives of the three networks in the CBS building at 485 Madison Avenue.

The network bargaining team was accustomed to pushing around the relatively weak representatives of the former Radio and Television Directors Guild, but they soon found they were dealing with a new set of adversaries now. In setting the ground rules for the meetings, the network tri-opoly tried to impose an impossible condition for the directors' committee. They argued that this was to be solely a network agreement. If we wanted to bargain with network owned and operated stations around the country, our team would have to fly to each city where the stations were based. Since each network owned seven local stations, this would necessitate flying our group to twenty-one different locations.

Capra objected, saying we were all working directors and could not agree to such an impossible schedule. Besides, he pointed out, what if we made a better deal in Detroit, for example, than we had with the network? Would ABC's management ratify such an agreement? This suggestion elicited laughter from the other side, with one of the network attorneys indicating they would make short work of that local management. The comment proved the point, Capra argued. Ultimately, all contracts would have to be approved in New York. Nevertheless, the network bargainers insisted this would cause financial hardship to their side, since local managers would have to be flown into New York, provided hotel rooms, and paid per diem.

Here Capra fired a masterful stroke. "How much would it cost," he asked, "to bring these twenty-one bargainers and their staffs to New York?" When someone mentioned a ballpark estimate of many thousands of dollars, Capra replied instantly, "The Directors Guild will pay to bring those people here." This offer caused an intake of breath from the opposition bargainers. "Of course," he went on, "it might look strange in the press to see labor paying for management's presence at the bargaining table." The networks quickly retracted their gambit. Capra knew his bluff would succeed. He had forced the other side into having to defend a ludicrous position.

Learning from this and other examples of keen bargaining helped me win one of my earliest victories while negotiating. For years, network directors were denied the right to attend casting sessions in New York. When we tried to install a contract provision calling for director participation in casting dramas, network lawyers objected, saying they had never granted such a right and weren't about to start now. I pointed out that film directors had this right, and that any reasonable person would conclude that TV directors' participating could only improve production values for the network. Dick Freund, chief negotiator for ABC responded, "Well, we at ABC reserve the right to be bad." I couldn't believe my ears.

Grabbing a legal pad, I repeated loudly, as I wrote slowly, "We at ABC . . . reserve the right . . . to be bad." I looked at Freund and asked, "Did you really just say this?" Smugly, the lawyer said he had. I said, "and do you stand by this statement?" "I certainly do," he said.

By happy coincidence, as the owner of a modest hundred shares of the company, I knew that ABC stockholders were gathering for their annual meeting the following day. I shared this information with Freund and said, "Since you stand by your strange comment, I guess you won't object if I read this sentence to the assemblage tomorrow. I'm certain my fellow shareholders will be interested to hear how their chief negotiator feels about quality broadcasting."

Freund flushed and croaked, "Please don't do that."

I said, "I'd be happy to say nothing if you retract your outrageous statement and agree to have a meaningful dialogue about the casting question." Thanks to Capra and the other gifted negotiators who taught us, we eventually won the point.

One other key contractual provision came out of those early Guild negotiations, and we almost lost the argument because of one member's carelessness. Screen Directors contracts called for first-class seats on airline flights, on the reasonable assumption that if star performers, for example, traveled first class, it would be unthinkable for the director to fly in the "back of the bus." This was so important a consideration, Joe Youngerman would argue, that the Guild always flew its members the same way when they traveled on union business. The RTDG had never had such a right, and the networks routinely forced that union's members to fly economy class. The broadcasters claimed that all their executives flew coach, even David Sarnoff, founder of RCA-NBC. The argument became so heated it was agreed to table the issue until all other points had been resolved.

With the travel discussion at an impasse, we adjourned one Friday night, with negotiations to resume the following Tuesday. I was involved in weekend editing at the time, and so I went to the airport ready to board a flight to Los Angeles. There I encountered one of our younger members and asked if he were on the same flight. He was, he said, but he was returning in a coach seat. Horrified, I asked, "Didn't the Guild issue you a first class ticket?" It had, he said, but he had taken a side trip to New England and had turned in his ticket for an economy seat. "Don't worry," he said, "I'll return the difference in cost."

Money wasn't the issue, I told him. "What would happen to our presentation about the Guild providing first-class travel if the opposition sees you in a coach seat?" I said. "Turn in that ticket immediately and change it to first class!" We were soon seated in the front section of the aircraft, when I noticed someone I knew stopping at a seat ahead of us. I nudged my colleague as I said to Hank Guillotte, CBS's West Coast vice president and negotiator, "Hi, Hank, how you doing?" He responded with a friendly wave until I said, "Are you lost? I thought all you executives always flew economy. I guess we can settle first-class transportation next Tuesday, right?" Hank nodded glumly as my Guild companion sank lower in his seat. I muttered to him, "That could just as easily have gone the wrong way if you had been seen in coach." Guillotte and his fellow bargainers gave up the dispute, and directors have flown first-class ever since.

As fate would have it, I also played a small role in a landmark clash between the worlds of television and feature films. During the mid-1960s, George Stevens filed a lawsuit against NBC when the network planned to televise *A Place in the Sun,* Stevens's brilliant film adaptation of Theodore Dreiser's *An American Tragedy.* Stevens contended that inasmuch as he had earned the right to final cut, the network would damage the film by interrupting the narrative with a series of commercials. George and his attorney, a former mayor of Beverly Hills named George Slaff, both thought that because of my television credits, I could be useful as an expert witness. I agreed, and shortly found myself on the witness stand.

I pointed out that the picture was designed not to be broken up by a series of "act curtains" but with the intention of being seen in an orderly, linear fashion without interruption. The NBC attorneys grilled me as to whether I had the privilege of final cut while making features for Hal Wallis. I admitted I did not, but that my directorial career couldn't compare to George Stevens's prominence and thus his ability to secure such rights. One of the defense lawyers pursued with me the notion that commercials actually benefited people watching the film, allowing them time to stretch and "relieve themselves," just as intermissions do for those viewing live theater. I argued that theatrical plays are presented with designed act breaks, and Mr. Stevens's film was not.

The "relief" line of questioning came to haunt me some weeks later, when the judge in the case decided he wanted to watch the movie from start to finish. Since the technology of the time did not permit home viewing, court was convened at an NBC viewing room. During that session, this relatively small space became the courtroom, with plaintiffs, defendants, witnesses, and the official court reporter in attendance. As the film began, I alternated between watching the movie and the judge, hoping to read his reactions, but he remained impassive.

About halfway through the screening, I began to sense a familiar sensation in my urinary tract. I ignored it at first, but as the film ground on, it took on increasing urgency. At the same time, to my dismay, the attorney who had grilled me on the witness stand caught my eye and nodded hello. Remembering his suggestion in court about the benefits of commercial breaks, I think I began to hallucinate. Was he staring at me? Could he read my mind? Could he take comfort from my body language? What if I had to excuse myself? Would I lose the case for my friend George?

Aside from this very real concern, all I could think of was the old Henny Youngman joke:

PATIENT: Doctor, I can't control my bladder. What should I do?
DOCTOR: First thing, get off my rug!

Somehow I survived the ordeal until court was adjourned. While I didn't cause havoc that day, if memory serves, George ultimately won a Pyrrhic victory, as the court ruled that his deal with Paramount did, indeed, give him final cut on his film. However, this only entitled him to receive one dollar in compensation. Meanwhile, NBC was granted the right to televise his work with commercial interruptions.

During the trial, the person I felt the most compassion for was Howard Koch, a fellow member of the Directors Guild Board of Directors who was also chief of production for Paramount Pictures, the studio that had released A Place in the Sun. Paramount was a codefendant, along with NBC, in the lawsuit George Stevens had filed; and

Howard was in the unenviable position of having to carry the corporate banner while attacking Stevens, a colleague on the board. During his testimony, with Joe Youngerman and a phalanx of other directors sitting in the courtroom, it was clear that Koch was suffering, compelled to testify in favor of the studio at the expense of his friends. Several times during his sweaty appearance on the stand, Howard requested water, and he once asked the judge if he could have a moment to swallow some aspirin.

On a much happier occasion, Koch was honored by the Friar's Club in Beverly Hills, and I attended his "roast"—not the tame sort that used to appear on network television from time to time, but the real thing: an all-male, raunchy, no-holds-barred, comic attack on the evening's target. The roast-master of the evening was Pat Buttram, who began in his slow, drawling, country-boy delivery, introducing the honoree: "Tonight we honor a man who has just returned from a trip up north, where he won second prize in the annual Montana sheep-fucking contest. Gentlemen, I am honored to present Howard W. Koch." Buttram pronounced "Koch" not with the conventional *ch* sound, but as "Howard W. Cock." He went on, "Now as you all know, Howard Cock is head of production at Paramount Pictures, the studio founded by Adolph Zukor. Howard has always dreamed of working with Mr. Zukor so the screen credit could read, 'This is a Cock-Zukor production.'"

This was pretty standard fare for a Friar's Club roast. Once before, I had attended one honoring Jim Backus. As the evening began, the emcee mentioned Backus's wife, Henny, to the no-women-allowed audience: "There's a rumor going around that Henny Backus is somewhere in the audience disguised as a man, so I want everyone to reach to his right and squeeze the balls of the guy sitting next to you. You may not find Henny, but you could make a new friend." During times when I served on DGA negotiating committees, there were frequent lulls while the management team caucused in another room. Inevitably, as we whiled away the tedious hours, someone would start a round of jokes. No one could top Howard Storm when it came to spinning a tension-breaking comic story. Howard was a stand-up comedian before he took up honest work as a TV director, so his delivery was always sharp and focused. Howard and his frequently unemployed fellow comics had often hung out together in New York, and one of his favorite stories involved his friend Jack Zero, who arrived one day with a full plaster cast on his leg. When asked what had happened, Zero replied, "What happened? I kicked my agent in the heart."

One night Howard told us a classic negotiation story. He and other small-time comics were often booked by a colorful character who operated out of somewhere in Florida, offering three- or four-day gigs to the eager stand-ups, who would snatch hungrily at almost any job offer. The agent, whose name was Nico Kavera, operated on such a meager budget that he always employed a scam on the telephone company when contacting performers. In the days before AT&T wised up, Kavera would phone one of his comics person-to-person. The operator would keep an open line during the call, so the comedian in New York and the agent in Florida could hear each other while a message was being delivered. If the dialogue was encoded in a simple system known to both participants, long-distance charges would not apply. According to Howard, a call from Kavera would go something like this.

Kavera to the operator: "I want to make a person-to-person call to Johnny Jones in New York." The phone rings, someone answers, and when the operator announces, "Mr. Nico Kavera calling from Florida for Mr. Johnny Jones," the comic would know to say, "Mr. Jones isn't here, but I can take a message."

With both parties hearing each other clearly, Kavera would say, "When Mr. Jones comes in, have him phone Nico Kavera in Jacksonville, Florida." According to the prearranged code, Jacksonville was the city where the comic would perform. The agent would go on, "Tell Mr. Jones to call the Roosevelt Hotel," the site of the booking. "Tell him to call at exactly three o'clock," meant that it was a three-day job, and the final instruction, "Tell Mr. Jones to phone Mr. Kavera in Room 175," meant that it would pay $175.

One day, the booking agent phoned a comic named Allan Kent. When Kavera got to the part about the salary, "Room 175," Allan said to the operator, "Ask Mr. Kavera if Mr. Kent could call him back in Room 200." In irritation, Kavera barked angrily at the operator, "Tell him he's lucky to be in Room 175!"

In addition to tough negotiations, my involvement with the Guild has also brought some very cordial moments indeed. In 1964, at the height of the cold war, an arrangement was made with the U.S. Department of

State to allow a delegation of Soviet filmmakers to visit Hollywood. The Directors Guild was asked to host a reception and lunch. Coincidentally, at the same time the Guild was featuring an exhibition of art loaned by some of our most prominent directors. These paintings displayed in the halls of our building had earned appreciative glances by our guests as cocktails were offered. To me, our visitors appeared somewhat subdued, avoiding the alcoholic drinks offered and opting for glasses of orange or tomato juice instead.

Seats had been removed in our theater and a sumptuous lunch had been provided by the famous restaurant Chasen's. The long banquet table gleamed with all the appropriate linen, goblets, and silverware; and as we took our assigned places we were joined by three English-speaking interpreters. One of these men was seated next to me because I was the Guild's vice president. All seemed to be going well, but after a few moments I became aware that most conversations had ceased, with the Soviets retreating into an uncomfortable silence.

It occurred to me that the group may have felt uncomfortable because the news had broken from Moscow that their head of state, Nikita Khrushchev, had been deposed. Apparently this information had reached the Russian delegation while they were on the plane approaching Los Angeles. I ventured to share this notion with my interpreter.

He assured me that the political situation did not concern our guests. With the silence continuing around the table, I pressed for an answer. I said, "Has anyone of us done or said something to cause upset? We have invited you here in collegial friendship, so please be candid. Whatever it was that might have given offense, I'm certain the situation can be repaired."

Again, the interpreter demurred, but his denial sounded a bit hesitant. I tried once more, insisting that we wanted a free flow of conversation, and promising I would do all in my power to rid the table of tension. Finally, with a soft smile, my lunch companion said shyly, "Well, in our country it is customary to have the spirits placed on the table during lunch." I couldn't believe the situation could be resolved so easily. Apparently, we had unwittingly committed a cultural gaffe by cutting off the flow of hard liquor in favor of the wine to come.

Immediately, I called to Ronnie, Chasen's dining room captain, and said, "Please put all the liquor on the table." He was horrified. "Just the bottles?" When I said, "Please," waiters descended on us in a swarm, placing bottle after bottle in front of our guests, who instantly became animated and friendly.

At the opposite end of the table, Mark Donskoi, the well-known Soviet director who headed the delegation, stood up, walked toward me, and opened a small flight bag bearing the Aeroflot Airlines insignia from which he extracted two bottles of vodka. He placed one of them in front of me and said, "I have noticed what you did. And because of your sensitivity and kind friendship, I will drink a toast with American vodka and you will drink Russian."

I was then introduced to a generous serving of Stolichnaya vodka, while Mr. Donskoi returned to his seat and poured himself a tumbler full of Smirnoff. A toast was proposed, and Donskoi swallowed his Smirnoff while I downed the Stoli. I'm sure I had the better of the deal, because my new Russian friend sputtered and choked as he managed to ingest the American stuff, while I experienced the pleasure of down-ing a drink that went down smoothly, with no discomfort. On a count of about eight, however, the liquor hit home and a pleasant flush rushed through my body, revealing the power of a beverage that has become a staple in our home since that day.

Our luncheon proved to be a big success, in part because of a ques-tion posed about the making of a scene in the film *The Cranes Are Flying*. The shot in question had baffled many of us when it had been seen at first. It went like this: We are on a bus with the camera focused on the heroine, who is desperately trying to see her fiancé before he reports for military service. A close-up on her anxious face also reveals a huge crowd, seen in background through the windows of the bus, as the vehicle approaches Red Square. There is no process plate, and this is forty years before animation or computer imaging could create a throng of people. The bus is really moving; the massive crowd is really there.

As the bus slows to a stop, the girl gets up and runs toward the front exit, the camera preceding her all the way. Continuing without a cut, we see her step down from the bus as the camera incorporates the folding doors, and then the exterior of the vehicle. The young woman charges into the enormous crowd, the camera never losing sight of her. Incredibly, we are moving along with her through the mass of people, when the camera suddenly elevates and follows her through the multitude until she reaches her lover's side. It is an incredible piece of movie making.

When our Soviet friends were asked how the shot was made, they smiled and explained that a "very strong and daring operator" held the camera as he backed out of the bus. Bear in mind that he was not using the Steadicams of today; he was carrying a full-scale camera. Walking backward, descending out of the bus, and never losing the girl, he stepped onto the platform of a grounded crane. This is harder than it sounds. When in use, a crane must be completely balanced by counterweights to accommodate the camera and the combined weight of everyone on the device. So as a cameraman steps onto the platform, someone of equal weight must leave. If this balance is not achieved with extraordinary timing, the crane cannot elevate and the shot cannot continue.

I asked how the camera was kept in focus, and they explained that the assistant operator used a remote device attached to the camera by a long wire. Similarly, when I asked how they photographed in the low light of the bus and then successfully switched to the sunlight outside, one of the group made the sign of "wrangling the shutter" to explain how the F-stop was manipulated. Again, this was evidently done by the wire attached to the camera. For its time, it was a miraculous accomplishment and our visitors were justly proud.

I enjoyed this encounter with the Russians, a group with whom we found much in common. We all shared similar problems and triumphs in the worldwide brotherhood of film. Many toasts were offered at that memorable luncheon, and peer pressure may have forced me to swallow glass after glass of a smooth and tasty liquor hitherto unknown to me. While it wasn't easy for me to make such a meaningful contribution to improving Soviet-American relations, I realized that somebody had to become the afternoon's designated drinker. Heroically, I was a willing volunteer, sacrificing myself for the greater good of my fellow man by giddily knocking back multiple shots of Russian ambrosia, for a noble cause: to help bring about global peace and harmony.

At least that's what I thought I was doing, before being struck down the following morning by the mother of all hangovers.

I Married Joan (1952–55) with Joan Davis

John Rich with Gale Gordon and Eve Arden on the set of
Our Miss Brooks (1952–56)

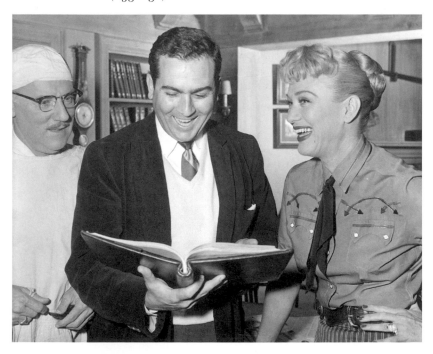

Dick Van Dyke, John Rich, and Mary Tyler Moore on the set of
The Dick Van Dyke Show (1961–63)

Dick Van Dyke and John Rich at a surprise farewell party for *The Dick Van Dyke Show*, 1963

John Rich and Carl Reiner winning an Emmy for *The Dick Van Dyke Show*, 1963

Barbara Stanwyck, John Rich, and Elvis Presley at a location carnival for
Roustabout, 1964

John Rich with Frank Sutton and Jim Nabors of *Gomer Pyle USMC* (1964–69)

Ted Bessell, Marlo Thomas, and John Rich on the set of *That Girl* (1966–71)

John Rich and Lucille Ball in *Make Room for Granddaddy* (1971)

All in the Family (1971–79) script run-through on stage with Carroll O'Connor, Jean Stapleton, Norman Lear, John Rich, and the script supervisor

All in the Family cast shot with Sammy Davis, Jr.

There's a story I've heard about the vice president of a TV network who was ordered to testify in a famous entertainment lawsuit. Raising his right hand as the bailiff asked, "Do you swear to tell the truth, the whole truth, and nothing but the truth, so help you God?" the network man replied, "Can I get back to you on that?" The story may be apocryphal, but in my experience there's a lot of truth to it.

There is probably no better example of certain network executives' inability to function in the real world than an episode that occurred in 1964. I received a call that year from Sherwood Schwartz, one of the finest, most decent men I have been privileged to work with (and a man dubbed by the comic genius Hal Kanter as "Robin Hood's rabbi"). I had first met Sherwood in 1953 when I was directing the situation comedy *I Married Joan*. Sherwood was part of a trio of writers, which also included Jesse Goldstein and Phil Sharp, whom Jim Backus affectionately called "the Habima Scribes," referring to the Hebrew word for "stage" and the well-known troupe of Israelis known as the "Habima Players." Jim liked to tease them for their occasional first-draft lapses into Bronx or Brooklyn rhythms; his favorite invented sample of their writing, which they of course never actually wrote, included the sentence, "Come in, State Senator, sit down, have a piece fruit."

When I was preparing to direct my second feature film, *The New Interns*, Sherwood telephoned and asked if I could meet him for coffee one day. When we met, he told me the premise of a new television series he was about to produce, called *Gilligan's Island*. As he went on, I confessed that I was not that interested. My feature film career was on track, I told him, and the timing couldn't be worse in terms of my schedule. He expressed disappointment and ended up signing Rod Amateau to direct the pilot.

Some months later, Sherwood called again and asked me to view the finished pilot. He told me he was re-editing what they had shot, and would I be interested in directing a substitute pilot with significant changes in the cast? Again, I tried to beg off, but since I had some time, I said I would be happy to assist him any way I could in the process of recasting, or any other area. After extensive auditions, Jim Backus and Natalie Schaeffer were selected to join the new cast, along with the star, Bob Denver, and his partner, Alan Hale, Jr. Also signed at this time were Dawn Wells as Mary Ann, Russ Johnson as "the professor," and Tina Louise as the movie star, Ginger.

One day, Herb Jaffe, a vice president at United Artists who had a financial interest in *Gilligan,* asked me if he could come to my office at Columbia Pictures, where I was editing my film. He told me he needed me to act as coproducer and director of Schwartz's revamped pilot. I was happy to help Sherwood any way I could, I explained, but I couldn't sign on in any official capacity. I would assist in editing, in consultation, anything, as long as I received no credit and no compensation. I would simply be helping a friend. Mr. Jaffe asked for another meeting, this time with my agent, Bill Meiklejohn, who joined us later that week. I repeated my reluctance to join the project by binding contract, and Jaffe excused himself to consult his colleagues on the East Coast. He went into my inner office, made a phone call, and returned, saying, "New York says they must have a written agreement." I then asked him to level with me and explain why I was considered so important to the pilot. Reluctantly, he told me that Procter & Gamble, a sponsor of the series, wasn't sure about Sherwood's ability to deliver. They had liked my work directing *The Dick Van Dyke Show* for three years and would trust me to guarantee success. I thanked him for the compliment, told him I was positive Sherwood could handle everything superbly, and repeated my offer to help without compensation. After another phone call, Jaffe returned and said, "New York says to offer you more!"

After a brief caucus with my agent, with me begging him to come up with a plan that would get me out of this deal politely, he suggested writing a contract so heavily weighted in my favor that they would have to refuse. The agreement we drafted included fees for producing and directing that were far above industry standards, and included, for the hell of it, 10 percent ownership of the series. I didn't even have to show up if I was working on a film or directing another pilot. I was allowed to name a surrogate; my friend Hal Cooper, who had just arrived from New York, was looking for work, and was eminently qualified to take charge. To our amazement, Herb Jaffe said, "You've got a deal."

After reshooting the pilot, I was asked to join Sherwood Schwartz in a meeting at CBS with the executive in charge, Jim Aubrey, known in the industry as "the Smiling Cobra." The conference was held in the CBS dining room early one morning, with representatives of United Artists, agents for Phil Silvers's company—Silvers had a financial stake in the series as well—various CBS executives, Schwartz the producer and writer, and Rich the director. Two uniformed waiters stood at the coffee urns, but only Mr. Aubrey was served, and his coffee cup was periodically replenished. Nobody else was offered a sip. This gratuitous insult amazed me, but it was clearly intentional, which became evident when Aubrey launched into a tirade about Sherwood's production. He hated it—despised the premise, excoriated the writing, and frothed at the mouth about how he would love to keep it off CBS. But apparently test audiences had given it such a high approval rating that he "had to buy it" despite his "repugnance." He wasn't finished. Aubrey thought the opening song that introduced the backstory of the series was "stupid." He demanded that Sherwood sing it for him. There was an audible gasp in the room, but Sherwood gamely went along.

As we returned to our cars in the parking lot, I was seething, and I asked Sherwood how he could have done it. I would have spit in Aubrey's eyes rather than humiliate myself like that. My friend calmly remarked, "At least I've sold the series." My hat is off to him. I couldn't have done it.

As a producer on *Gilligan's Island*, I was given office space and a secretary at CBS in the San Fernando Valley, and I spent as much time as I could reading scripts with Sherwood and checking out the physical layout of the lot in preparation to shoot the series. On one inspection, I was horrified to note that, surrounded by tropical vegetation, a pond had been constructed. This was to be the home island where the castaways, it was hoped, would spend the next several years. The problem as I saw it, was that the shoreline described a complete circle; you could plainly see the opposite shore. "How" I asked, "were these people tossed ashore from the sea?"

No one had considered this. But plainly, the solution was to create an additional patch of water that led, presumably, to the open ocean. Trees and plants would mask the entrances and exits, creating the illusion that the ocean lay just out of sight. This suggestion initially met with complaints from the CBS executive suite, because crews had buried electrical cables under the proposed water extension and the fix would be expensive. I argued that one couldn't do the series without such an escape route, and besides, with a change of vegetation the location could be used for Western dramas to help amortize the cost. Years later, in fact, I personally shot this location for episodes of *Gunsmoke*.

My insistence on practicality began to be noticed at CBS headquarters by Hunt Stromberg, Jr., the executive in charge of new programming. This latest inheritor of the defective network-executive gene had a "brilliant" notion for an episode on the island. With great enthusiasm, he described a big helicopter coming to rescue the abandoned group: "We create a quicksand pond, see. And the helicopter tries to land but it hits the ground and, get this"—he began laughing as he anticipated the punchline—"the blades of the helicopter screw the plane into the ooze until it disappears under the quicksand!" After a moment of silence, I asked quietly, "What do we do if we have to shoot take two?" Stromberg replied, "That's your problem."

But Mr. Stromberg was not yet finished with me. On a trip to New York, I was telephoned by my secretary, Ginger Grigg, who seemed upset. She told me that the lobby board featuring my name and title had been removed, and that people were preparing to move into our office suite. Furthermore, my parking space—always at a premium in film studios— had been relocated far from our building. I told her not to worry, that I would be back in a couple of days and straighten everything out.

On my return, I called the studio manager and asked what was going on. His nervous answer reminded me of Don Knotts on *The Andy Griffith Show*. "Don't you know?" he stammered. I assured him I didn't, and asked if this were his idea, or was he under orders? The answer was, "You'd better talk to Hunt Stromberg at CBS headquarters on Fairfax Avenue." Baffled, I phoned Stromberg and asked for a meeting, which was quickly set up. Stromberg wasted no time as he launched into a tirade. "We"—meaning CBS—"have just acquired *Gilligan's Island* from United Artists and we have read your contract. We can't live with it, and we're going to remove you as producer and director!"

"On what grounds?"

"On the grounds that the contract is ridiculously constructed in your favor—not to mention that we can't talk to this Hal Cooper. He can only report to you! And you don't even have to show up for work!!"

I chuckled as I told Stromberg about the "negotiation" that had led to a contract I didn't really want—that I had offered to help out without credit and without compensation, but United Artists had forced me to accept a clearly overwrought agreement. Stromberg's features softened as he said, "Great, then we don't have a problem."

"I think you do," I said. "If you had called me as a gentleman and told me of your concerns, I would have agreed instantly. But you took a bully's position. You terrified my secretary and you committed the cardinal sin of moving my parking place. This is going to cost you."

"We'll sue you," Stromberg shouted, "and you'll never work in this town again!"

I said calmly, "When it comes to being hired, I'll be at work long after you're dead." (Fate, as it happened, would prove this prediction accurate.) "As to being sued," I went on, "there's no way you can win, because to be in contractual compliance, all I have to do is *not show up for work.*"

There was a long silence as Stromberg digested this information. Finally, through clenched teeth, he grumbled, "What will it take for us to get rid of you?" I answered, "You will pay my full producer's compensation for thirteen weeks." "No!" he screamed.

I told him I wasn't finished. "You will also pay Hal Cooper his full agreed-upon salary for thirteen weeks." Another choked reaction. "In return, you can regain the title of producer."

"What about this ridiculous 10-percent-ownership business?"

I said, "I don't think it likely that there will be any eventual profit from this series, but I'm going to keep the percentage for rooting interest." (That prediction happily proved incorrect: I've earned more revenue from *Gilligan* than any other series except *All in the Family.*)

Stromberg grunted a muffled assent, and I turned to leave. "One more thing," he said. "Will you direct the first six episodes?"

This startled me. "What happened to 'You'll never work in this town again'?"

He was a master of network-speak. "Oh," he said airily, "that was *then*."

It's easy to pick out the schmucks in our business, because they are so plentiful. Producers, or producer/writers, can be a pain in the butt or, on the other hand, exceptionally helpful to a conscientious director trying to do his job properly. But there have also been truly wonderful ones, including John Mantley of *Gunsmoke* and David Dortort of *Bonanza*. These men were always prepared, always ready to answer a question, always providing a script early enough to allow a director time to pre-pare. Aaron Ruben, who had written and produced *The Andy Griffith Show* and *Gomer Pyle,* was another of the gifted ones.

Aaron was a producer in the Sheldon Leonard mold, working at Motion Picture Center. As with his contemporaries who had served the Danny Thomas–Sheldon Leonard enterprise, Mr. Ruben was respectful of the contributions of others, and I cannot recall a single instance of bitter dispute with this gentle man. I was never assigned to the Griffith show, but I did work for Aaron and directed Andy much later in a new series entitled *Headmaster*. However, I was fortunate enough to do about thirty episodes of *Gomer Pyle*. Jim Nabors as Gomer, and Frank Sutton as the beleaguered Sergeant Carter, were marvelous to work with; and Aaron provided a tight, comedically workable script week after week.

Aaron had come from the world of Sergeant Bilko, starring Phil Silvers, and had worked with the extraordinary writer, Nat Hiken. I enjoyed Mr. Ruben's polite manner of running Gomer, but it wasn't until many years later that I discovered what an incredible "mensch" he was. This word, in the Yiddish vernacular, was designed to denote a special kind of "man," a humanitarian, a superior human being who had gone out of his way to perform wonderful deeds for his community.

Anonymously, Aaron had quietly served abused children in Los Angeles as an "advocate ad litum," appearing in court on behalf of the friendless, and sometimes even providing full university educations to underprivileged and emotionally beaten kids. Aaron's wife, Maureen Arthur, a gifted actress, is also known for her great charity work for the Variety Clubs of America. This is a formidable couple whose contributions to society make them standout citizens in every respect, and my wife, Pat, and I are happy to regard them as close personal friends.

In the 1960s, in the period between my long tenures with *Van Dyke* and *All in the Family*, I directed episodes of several popular shows, and even after I had been working in television for well over a decade, at times I still came across things that surprised or even shocked me. That occurred once during a lunch break on the set of *Hogan's Heroes*. I had directed several episodes of that series, even though I always had a bit of trouble with its trivialization of a Nazi prisoner-of-war camp. The comedy was well written and extremely well cast, but I was always somewhat perturbed at having to play the Nazi commandant and his minions as stupid and inept. This feeling was magnified one day when I sat next to Robert Clary, who portrayed a young French prisoner in Colonel Hogan's barracks. Lunch was served outdoors, and since it was a hot day, Robert was wearing a sleeveless shirt.

As I reached for something on the table, I noticed a numbered tattoo on Clary's arm. I was astonished. "Forgive me for asking," I said to him, "but do those numbers mean what I think they do?"

Clary responded without hesitation. "Yes, I was a prisoner in Auschwitz."

A chilling thought came into my mind. "How can you play an inmate," I asked, "even though it's a prisoner-of-war situation, and face those horrible symbols of Nazi authority? How do you interact with swastikas and all the other paraphernalia of a system that condemned you to an extermination camp?"

"It's a job," Clary said with a shrug, "you get over it."

It was hard to believe his cool response, and years later, when I ran into him at a screening, he admitted it had been more than a little difficult.

I could never understand actors' fetishes about their "better sides" for the camera. I suspect the idea came about early in the movie business, when certain cameramen ingratiated themselves with stars by convincing them that one side photographed better than the other. I'm probably wrong about this, since the idea seems to have infected so many performers. But to me it's all a giant waste of time: sets constructed with entrances and exits to accommodate the stars; free movement inhibited during the blocking of a scene.

Like so many others, Marlo Thomas, the lovely actress who starred in *That Girl*, felt that one side of her face was more attractive than the other. If memory serves, unlike Eve Arden and Gene Barry, she preferred the right side of her face to be photographed, although I thought Marlo looked terrific any way she turned.

She was also very bright and very talented, and we got along famously, although she drove me crazy sometimes because she did a complete makeup and hair comb after practically every scene. It was reasonable to do this after a "master shot" had been printed, and Marlo had a fresh makeup designed for her close-up work. But I had always been trained to shoot efficiently to stay on budget, so at first it was maddening to spend so much time waiting. She owned the production company, though, so who could tell her to do otherwise?

Half-hour episodes using single-camera technique normally required three days to complete a show, but I had heard that Marlo sometimes shot for four or five days, with directors earning their negotiated fees but no excess payments, regardless of how much time it took to finish a program. When I was approached to direct some episodes, I told Business Affairs that since I had no need to prove my ability to bring in a show in three days, if they wanted to engage me they would have to pay a pro-rata percentage of my established price for every day we shot beyond the customary three. Screams of indignation came from my old *Van Dyke* friends Persky and Denoff, who were producing *That Girl*, but I stuck to my position. Running overtime, I argued, even if it was no fault of mine, could affect my established price in the market, to say nothing of potentially interfering with other commitments I might have to forgo.

When Marlo heard of the negotiation, she insisted that she wanted me for the series despite my unusual requirements, which meant I got paid a considerable amount of money to read novels on the set, while waiting for make-up and hair to finish fussing over her. When she was ready to work, though, Marlo would come through like the champion she is—always performing with great skill and taste.

I first met another familiar face in classic TV when Florence Henderson won the role of the mother on *The Brady Bunch*, which

Sherwood Schwartz both wrote and produced. I had seen Florence in the stage musical *The Sound of Music* and loved her singing as well as her acting. In life, she was as sweet as she seemed when playing the role of Maria von Trapp—beautiful, cooperative, and marvelous to work with. So was Ann B. Davis, who portrayed Alice, the housekeeper. I had seen Ann B. as "Schultzie" on *The Bob Cummings Show,* in which she had been a major hit. But I had also known her many years before as a fellow student at the University of Michigan. As a matter of fact, we both remembered taking a class in play production at Ann Arbor; she had been cast as an actress in the first scene I had ever directed. She proved to be a delightful addition to our cast throughout the series's long run. After dozens of auditions, Sherwood and I cast all the children's roles, and they too were excellent troupers.

The series' one fly in the ointment turned out to be Robert Reed, whom I had admired greatly when he played a young attorney in the wonderful series *The Defenders,* starring E. G. Marshall. While we were shooting the complex pilot, Reed was as cooperative as Florence and the others. He performed with skill and intelligence, and surprisingly with great élan in some of the comedic scenes, even willingly falling face first into an elaborate wedding cake. When the network picked up the series, though, he exhibited some grumpiness when we first started to shoot. I felt part of his attitude was justified, because at the start I wasn't too happy myself. Having agreed to direct the first six episodes, I was dismayed to learn that Florence Henderson was completing another assignment and wouldn't be available for the first five weeks. This meant that to make air-date, we had to start production without Mrs. Brady, filming all the scenes that didn't require her presence and then taking on the ticklish job of weaving her later performances into the material already shot. This caused enormous difficulty in scheduling, as did the limited number of hours we were permitted to work with children. Child labor laws required them to attend school on the lot for four hours daily, as well as mandating an hour for lunch and an hour for recreation. With the other mandatory breaks, we could shoot with the six "Brady kids" for about three hours a day. It was a massive jigsaw puzzle, and I had some difficult moments myself, so I wasn't too surprised by Reed's sulkiness.

Later, though, I learned that shooting around Florence and the crazy schedule was not Reed's only beef. As Sherwood Schwartz recounted, Reed had become less and less enchanted with the writing, demanding straighter material to the exclusion of much of the comedy. Eventually, the feud reached epic proportions, with Robert sometimes refusing to accept a call for work. I am sorry that such a talented man felt he was wasted in a series that became an American icon for so many people. As for Florence Henderson, I can't offer enough praise for this elegant lady, who must have endured much stress from her costar's frequent complaints.

Another one of my favorite people in the profession was Rod Serling, the brilliant creator of *The Twilight Zone*. While directing a couple of episodes in the early 1960s, I had great fun working with this innovative writer, who probably enjoyed playing host, introducing each episode, more than anything else he did as producer. I think Rod was inordinately pleased with the efficient way he recorded these thirty-second intros, so he looked surprised when we advised him one night that he had run over the allotted time. His first take had run thirty-seven seconds, I told him and would have to be done quicker.

"No problem," Serling said, and proceeded to consume forty seconds on the next take. He looked startled, but agreed to my suggestion to cut a sentence from his lines. His next effort took thirty-five seconds, and by now he seemed rattled. Somewhat self-consciously, he asked me while tugging his suit coat, which was supplied weekly by the Kuppenheimer clothing company, "John, how does the Kuppenheimer look?"

I said, "Your Kuppenheimer runneth over." Rod burst out laughing, and did the next take perfectly.

I knew Danny Thomas from way back. He occupied the stage next to mine at the old Motion Picture Center Studios on Cahuenga Boulevard, where I spent a lot of time early in my television career. This film lot, which later became Desilu Studios, housed *Our Miss Brooks*; *December Bride*; Danny's classic series *Make Room for Daddy*; *The Ray Bolger Show* (aka *Where's Raymond?*), which I directed in 1954; and later such classics as *The Dick Van Dyke Show* and *Gomer Pyle, USMC*. It was a lively lot, with some of the best comedic talents along with a cadre of gifted comedy writers and directors. Lunch was often a riot of laughter as we gathered in the studio commissary. The proprietor was a man named Hal who wore a once-white apron, seldom if ever washed, and featuring streaks and stains so deeply embedded that Garry Marshall once said that "Hal's apron started out in life as the groundcloth for a cockfight in Tijuana."

Danny was the fourth member of Calvada Productions, the company that produced *The Dick Van Dyke Show,* along with Sheldon Leonard, Carl Reiner, and Dick himself. "Calvada" was an amalgamation of parts of the principals' names: *Ca* for Carl, *l* for Leonard, *va* for Van Dyke, *da* for Danny. I had also directed Danny in a cameo appearance on *That Girl,* playing a priest. I had kidded Danny, a devout Catholic who made no secret of his religious beliefs, that we would save money on his costume because he had his own vestments at home.

On another occasion in the late 1960s, I was asked to direct an episode of *Make Room for Granddaddy,* a limited-run program that briefly aired as a sequel to his earlier series. Gathering for our first reading of the script, I had taken my normal position at the head of the table, with Danny sitting immediately to my left. To my surprise, he was chewing tobacco as we read, and had brought along an empty coffee can to use as a cuspidor, sitting just a few inches from my left leg. Some ten or fifteen expectorations later, I began to fear an errant spray might irrigate my trousers. So I asked Danny if he would mind moving the coffee can a little further away. In response, he reached into his briefcase and pulled out a revolver.

He placed the pistol on the table in what he meant to be—or so I thought—a comedic moment. He said, "I keep this handy so I don't have to move anything."

I laughed and said, "By the way, is that gun loaded?"

"Of course it is. What good is an unloaded gun?"

I stared at the weapon and said, "Danny, I was in the Air Force and fired all kinds of firearms when it was appropriate, but here I have to say it makes me uncomfortable. Do me a favor and put the gun away."

Danny said, "You're kidding, right?"

"No, I'm serious, and if you must keep this weapon on the table, I'm going to have to leave." I actually stood up and started toward the door before he agreed, returning the gun to its case while muttering under his breath.

Some time later, while I was in New York, I came upon an item in the newspaper reporting that Danny had lost part of one of his fingers.

According to the article, a car door had accidentally slammed shut on Danny's hand.

It could have happened that way.

I have always disliked weapons, particularly handguns, which cause so much misery in our country today. Even when directing *Gunsmoke*, I tried to avoid the classic street shootout whenever I could, preferring to have the protagonist solve problems by thinking rather than drawing his pistol.

Years later, in the 1980s, when I was one of the executive producers of the *MacGyver* adventure series, I decided after seeing Richard Dean Anderson fire an automatic weapon in the pilot that his character would forever put aside guns. From then on, he never used one in the seven years we were on the air, although we did allow him to use a revolver once. Having disarmed the bad guy while on the roof of an atomic plant, MacGyver had only minutes to turn off a valve and prevent a nuclear explosion. Lacking a pipe wrench, our hero picked up the fallen weapon, knocked out the revolving portion of the gun, and used the metal frame as a wrench to save the day once more.

My feelings about guns were well known, and they extended even to the use of blanks. Many people don't know that even a "blank" cartridge contains a wad of paper that could injure someone, if fired too close; in fact, one young actor lost his life in exactly this fashion when someone discharged a blank too close to his chest. Many years ago, I had occasion to fire a blank pistol as an offstage cue to coincide with the action on stage. I cautioned everyone that I was firing a "full load," and even though I would point the gun straight up into the air, I wanted all the crew to stand well away. Camera rolled, the moment arrived, and I fired straight up toward the catwalks. To my horror, scraps of burnt clothing came raining down on me. My God, I thought, I've killed an electrician! Only when the crew burst out laughing at my stunned expression did I realize I had been had. One of the prop men had carefully ascended into the flies, marked my position, and after I fired, let loose a cascade of cloth.

The subject of firearms reminds me of the old tale about the soldier who carries a Bible in his shirt pocket. A bullet fired at him lodges miraculously in the Holy Book, saving his life. I think it was Woody Allen who reversed the scenario: A crazed evangelist hurls a Bible at a soldier, and the souvenir bullet in his pocket saves him from death.

A round 1974, during the fourth season of *All in the Family*, I received a letter from a viewer who wrote: "I've been watching your show since it began . . . and I've always enjoyed it, except last night you want too far—you tried to tell us that a black man is smarter than Archie Bunker."

This was an interesting comment, to say the least, since it had been our rule from the inception of the series that all black people, as well as anyone else whom Archie's bigotry had assaulted, would triumph in the end. From day one, it had been a basic premise: Bunker loses, the maligned minorities win. After getting this letter, I frequently shared it with our studio audiences, who always reacted in derision. But it gave me pause. Had we perhaps been playing to an audience of viewers who didn't really get it? The thought haunted me from time to time, but I concluded, on balance, that most of the world picked up on our intent while they were being entertained.

Three years earlier, though, the nature of the series had made the casting process tricky at times. One decision, in particular, still eluded us before taping began on the pilot episode. Norman Lear, the producer, and I agreed completely about setting Rob Reiner and Sally Struthers in their respective roles, but we had a slight disagreement when it came to settling on an actor to play Lionel, Mike and Gloria's young black friend who lived next door. I think there must have been some unconscious harmonic at work in me that insisted we cast an actor who came across as completely nonthreatening, to convincingly present a black man teasing Archie Bunker and getting away with it. I felt that America in 1971 would already have to make a huge leap to accept some of the bigoted language that would be flying around. Adding any hint of fear to such a delicate equation could doom the production instantly. Norman had practically made up his mind that the role should go to Cleavon Little, a wonderful performer but who seemed to me to be dead wrong for the part. I had always admired Cleavon's work, but I felt he would be too threatening for 1970s America and a bit too old as Lionel.

When I made my argument to Norman, he astutely suggested I go ahead and find someone better than Cleavon, but it had to happen soon because our first week of taping was only a month away. I called our wonderful casting lady, Jane Murray, and asked if she had read any prospects. Apparently there were many, but she had stopped looking when Norman decided to put a "hold" on Cleavon. I asked her to issue a series of call-backs on some of the more promising candidates, and I interviewed and read aloud about forty applicants over four or five long days. None of these actors matched the image I had in my head, so I asked Jane to call back some who didn't have the same credits as the first group. This led to another series of frustrated readings, and I found no one, with Norman asking me practically every day, "What about Cleavon?"

It's worth mentioning something here about the business of casting. Actors who come in to read for a part sometimes feel that the process is adversarial. Quite the contrary. I have said to many a performer that the director or producer of a show would give anything for an actor to come in and hit a home run in his or her reading. We want them to succeed, possibly more than they do themselves. If an actor reads well, that part is cast and we can go on to other things.

In the middle of another fruitless day of interviewing, I was beginning to despair about my search for the ideal Lionel when a young applicant entered. My heart probably skipped a beat. Could this fresh-faced man just out of his teens, sporting a neat Afro—could he be it? This was the image I was looking for! But could he act?

The young hopeful told me his name, and I asked about his performing credits. None to speak of. He said he was attending Los Angeles City College. "Looking for a degree in . . . ?" I prompted. "Planning an acting career," he said.

"Good, I said. "So what plays have you been in during your time in college?"

"I haven't been in any plays yet."

"Ah. So what's your ambition?"

"Right now, to be in a college play."

"O-kay . . . What high school plays have you been in?"

None.

"Elementary school, church groups, any stage experience of any kind?"

None.

In desperation, thinking "Who knows, maybe he's a natural," I gave him the script to read. It would be wonderful to say he jumped into the role and gave a splendid reading. The truth is, he was awful. Not yet willing to throw in the towel, I gave him a few suggestions about the meaning of the words he was speaking, and asked him to try again. He did only marginally better, which only deepened my disappointment. Curious how he had gotten an audition, I asked, "How did you get here?" His answer floored me: "I was hitchhiking on Western Avenue and an actor gave me a ride. He told me he was coming here to read for you and I came with him. You saw him just before I came in."

There was no way this untrained person could stand the rigors of a live television show, so with great reluctance—because he certainly looked the part—I thanked him for coming and tossed his name and number into the bottom drawer of my desk. Another ten days of wading through thirty more hopeless auditions left me depressed. Still—

Suspecting I had gone completely berserk, I asked Jane Murray to call the young student back. He read for me one more time, and again I was disappointed. What did I expect? His attack was still no good, and yet he seemed poised and impervious to nerves—possibly a hopeful sign. I coached him again. Perhaps I was deluding myself, but he seemed to catch on a little better. Clearly, he was bright, and this was somewhat promising. I threw caution to the winds and phoned Norman Lear to tell him I had a candidate.

In Lear's office, I asked the young man to read again, and he stumbled through the lines once more. Norman looked at me quizzically. I reminded the novice "actor" of some of the things we had discussed regarding interpretation, and this time he was slightly better. I asked him to wait outside for a moment. Lear stared at me for a long time before asking, "Are you seriously thinking of hiring this kid?"

I said I was basing everything on the young man's look. "He's bright, good-looking, and most of all nonthreatening. In a week of rehearsal I can get him to do the words okay. If he's a real bomb, you can replace him next week with Cleavon as his brother, and we can continue the series without him. But if he succeeds, we have found a gold mine."

"Okay," Norman said, "but it's your ass."

With this firm vote of confidence ringing in my ears, I was allowed to cast Mike Evans as Lionel, and he turned out to be everything I wanted and then some. I drilled him mercilessly during the rehearsal week and kept reminding him we would be performing in front of a live audience. I told him that one of the most difficult things for a comedy actor to learn is how to time laughs. I explained over and over the importance of waiting for the laugh to peak before speaking, how our four starring players had the experience and the craft to know how to do this. I emphasized how urgent it was for Mike to be patient, to wait for the crest of the laughter, to speak only when his next line could be heard clearly, and on and on.

On the night of our opening episode, every one of our incredibly talented family managed to step slightly into a laugh. Only Mike Evans performed flawlessly that night. He went on to become an integral part of our series.

It was always Norman Lear's intention to keep George Jefferson completely offstage for the life of the series. George became almost a mythic character in the scripts; instead of showing up himself, he would send his brother Henry over to the Bunkers when it became necessary to interact with "whitey." Played magnificently by Mel Stewart, Henry was as bigoted a black man as Archie Bunker was a white one.

In an early episode, when Edith invites Mr. and Mrs. Jefferson to a dinner party, Henry shows up with Louise. We learn at the end of the episode that Louise's husband is George Jefferson. Henry is his brother, who explains that George refuses to show his face in a "honky" neighborhood. For four years, Henry carries the fight to Archie, and George is kept out of sight, becoming a more menacing figure by his absence.

One day Mel told me he had an offer to do a pilot at Twentieth Century Fox and asked our permission to take the job. Since he was what we called a six-out-of-thirteen-episode player, we could not object, although his absence would cause us some problems. I reminded Mel that because Fox was offering him a leading role in the new series, he would be compelled to sign with them exclusively, and so we could not bring him back to *Family*. I told him how much we would miss his presence, and he thanked me but said this would be a big break for him. Because Mel was leaving, we would now have to introduce the unseen George Jefferson into our series. Our writers, Don Nicholl, Mickey Ross, and Bernie West, went to work fashioning a script to introduce the character we had hoped to keep in the closet.

Ninety-eight percent of the time, Norman Lear and I agreed on casting decisions, so it was surprising, one day to have him inform me, apologetically, that while he was in New York he had to move fast to secure a particular actor to play George Jefferson. He didn't have time to consult me before making the deal, but he hoped I would understand. What was the name of his selection, I asked. "Avon Long."

I was astonished. "Avon Long—the dancer?" I sputtered. I asked Norman if that was the same man who had played the part of Sportin' Life in *Porgy and Bess* on Broadway.

"That's the one."

I think I may have raised my voice a bit. "I was in high school when I saw that production! He must be ancient now!"

Not to worry, Norman said, I would love the man. He was right, to a point. Avon was a sweet old man, easy to like. As we gathered around the table for our Wednesday read-through, however, his hesitant reading of the text gave me pause. He was awkward and slow, showing none of the feisty spirit required to take on Archie Bunker. "He'll be fine," Norman said, "let's see how he does when the cast is on its feet." Our walk-through rehearsals were no better, and I told Norman this at the end of the first day. He was convinced Avon would improve and asked me to keep working with him. On Friday night, when the cast did a complete rehearsal-hall run-through for Norman and the writers, it was painfully clear that Avon would not cut it, and Norman finally agreed. I said, "You told me that I'd love this man and you were right. He's been sweet, gentle, and cooperative, but unable to keep up. Since you cast him, you're going to have to let him go, but it will come as no surprise. He knew he wasn't getting it."

After telling the rest of the cast to take a break, I turned to Norman and said, "For four years we have built up a mystery neighbor who refuses to show his face to the Bunkers. It's now Friday night at 8 PM, and Tuesday we shoot a script introducing George Jefferson to the world. Only we don't have an actor to play the role!"

Lear swallowed and said, "Let's call Jane Murray." Discussing the situation with Jane, I asked if she had listed other actors as potential George Jeffersons. She had not, since Norman had set Avon Long, stopping the search. I told Jane I would prefer someone with stage experience, if possible, but clearly we were in no position to dictate too many conditions. While waiting for her to produce a miracle, Norman and I decided to call the cast in for an unusual Saturday and Sunday rehearsal.

I don't know how she did it, but within the hour, Jane had found a touring company of the play *Purlie Victorious* in San Francisco, and we could make an offer to one of the performers. With no knowledge whatsoever as to what we were buying, Norman authorized a deal, requiring the actor to report for rehearsal the following morning in Los Angeles.

As the company gathered together on Saturday in our windowless CBS rehearsal hall, the place seemed bleaker than ever. While I tried to shake my disappointment at the turn of events, I was approached by Isabel Sanford, who played Louise Jefferson. She took me aside and said, "John, I just rode up in the elevator with some stranger. Is that little runt going to be my husband?" I smiled and said, "I haven't met the man yet, but if he's as small as you say, that might make a pretty funny contrast. Let's just hope he can give us some presence on stage."

I sought out the "stranger," introduced myself, and presented him to the rest of the cast. He was small, and seemed a bit intimidated, so I took a moment to share a cup of coffee and chat with him for a while before our table reading of the script. I had no idea what to expect, and his early attack on the character was less than awe inspiring. During the blocking, however, his work improved considerably, and on the night of the show, he delivered a blockbuster performance. Sherman Hemsley was a smash, not only an instant success on our show but also a star (with Isabel) of the series we spun off from *All in the Family,* called *The Jeffersons,* a giant hit in its own right. Applause, applause, applause for Jane Murray, who found this funny, feisty character in the nick of time.

In addition to the hunches that helped us out in casting, hunches and instinct also led us to suggestions that sometimes led to core behavior for a character. For instance, during our first rehearsal for *All in the Family,* when Rob Reiner (as "Meathead") started to sit in Archie Bunker's chair, I remember shouting, "Don't do that!" The startled actors stared at me. I said, "Nobody sits in that chair but Archie."

I'm certain this outburst was prompted by an old memory of my father, who occupied his living room "throne" to the exclusion of all others. In any event, it became part of Archie's surly order, "Get out of the chair!" anytime Mike dared to violate this sacred position of authority. Only two actors other than Carroll O'Connor ever managed to occupy the master's seat: Bea Arthur, playing Cousin Maude, to torment Archie during a political argument; and Sammy Davis, Jr., who was invited to sit in the place of honor, with great ceremony, by Archie himself.

Another character's trademark habit came about almost by accident. The first time we visited the Jefferson home during an episode of *All in the Family,* George had come home for lunch, and while Louise prepared a sandwich, the script indicated George would be reading a newspaper. When I walked onto the set, I noticed a copy of the *New York Daily News* there. Immediately, I told the prop master to remove the tabloid, which was always seen as Archie's paper. Asked what I had in mind as a substitute, I replied, thinking aloud, "I don't know, exactly, but as opposed to Bunker, this guy is an investor who's moving up in the world." After a moment, I told the prop man, "Get him the *Wall Street Journal.*"

It seemed like a trivial request at the time, but that small choice injected an attitude that stayed with George Jefferson throughout his existence on two different series. In fact, that idea crystallized into the wonderful Marilyn and Alan Bergman theme song for *The Jeffersons* during that series's long run: "Movin' on Up."

One of the most enjoyable aspects of directing and producing *All in the Family* was seeing inspirations for storylines come from unexpected sources. One great example of this illustrated the point that perception is a purely subjective phenomenon, a theme that was brilliantly explored in Kurosawa's great production of *Rashomon.* In that film, three people have experienced the same incident, yet express vastly different viewpoints when asked to report what happened.

During my tenure as producer of the series, a writer had submitted a story involving the refrigerator breaking down in the Bunker household. The notion appealed to me, but I felt it was too thin to fill an entire half-hour program. Nevertheless, I thought the idea would function well as a subplot, so I paid the writer "story money," intending to combine the notion with another theme. For many weeks, the idea languished in my desk drawer while I struggled to find a suitable script to blend with the refrigerator tale. Up until this point, I had been extremely frugal in purchasing only scripts that actually ended up in production, but in this case I was becoming resigned to wasting the money I had authorized on the refrigerator idea. I mentioned my concern to our head writer, Don Nicholl, and as he had so many times before, he came through magnificently.

Don suggested we use the thin story in a *Rashomon*-like fashion, with Mike and Archie each relating what happened with the refrigerator in terms that reflected their biased thinking. In the episode, we see the same incident played out in different flashbacks that varied according to each observer's account. Archie claims the plumber's black assistant had menaced him with an enormous switchblade, describing the helper as a menacing "Mau Mau" with an African dashiki and a huge Afro. Mike argues that the man was an "Uncle Tom" who had no knife at all, viewing him as a shiftless worker in the Stepin Fetchit mold. Ultimately, Edith proves them both wrong when she produces a tiny penknife that the serviceman had dropped and failed to retrieve. Edith saw him as he actually was: well dressed, polite, and capable. With Ken Lynch and Ron Glass beautifully playing the repairmen in the flashbacks, the episode turned out to be one of our best productions.

Another one of my favorite moments from the series demonstrated to me one of the surprising benefits of a liberal arts education: something one has learned can be filed away for years, then brought to the forefront of his thinking in unexpected ways. It was only years after we shot the episode, when I was talking to a film class at the University of Michigan on the subject of expanding a scene and using a script as a springboard to deeper investigation, that it dawned on me: our comic bit had come straight out of *Hamlet*. In the episode, Mike has agreed to go fishing with his father-in-law early in the morning, but, typically, he has overslept, as Archie enters the bedroom:

ARCHIE Oh, geez, look at this. Rip van Meathead. Get up! Get outta the bed!

MIKE *[Opens his eyes groggily]* I'm up . . .

ARCHIE *[Grabs Mike's pants off chair and throws them at him]* C'mon. Here's your pants. Get 'em on you, huh.

MIKE Ssssshhh! *[Starts putting pants on over pajamas]*

ARCHIE I can never depend on you for the—hold it. What're you doin'? You're puttin' your pants on over your pajamas!

MIKE *[Speaking softly]* Sssshh. It's all right. It'll be cold on the boat and I don't have any long underwear.

ARCHIE Just hurry it up!

MIKE Sssssshh!

ARCHIE Why are you shushin' me?

MIKE *[Quietly]* I don't want to wake up Gloria.

ARCHIE Gloria ain't here. She's downstairs.

MIKE What's she doin' downstairs?

ARCHIE She's sittin' in a chair down there. She's all right.

MIKE How do you know?

ARCHIE She told me.

MIKE What did she say?

ARCHIE She said, "I'm all right." Will you hurry it up, please?

MIKE *[As he gets socks]* I was worried about her. Last night she wouldn't talk to me. It was like there was a pane of glass between us. *[He has one sock on.]*

ARCHIE D'you know if we don't catch that fishin' boat there ain't gonna be no deep sea fishin'. We'll have to stay on the dock with the old people—hold it—hold it! *[Mike has started to put on a shoe. Archie looks at him incredulously.]* Hold it! What are you doin' here?

MIKE What?

ARCHIE What about the other foot? There ain't no sock on it.

MIKE I'll get to it.

ARCHIE Don't you know that the whole world puts on a sock and a sock, and a shoe and a shoe?

MIKE I like to take care of one foot at a time.

ARCHIE That's the dumbest thing I ever heard of in my life.

MIKE It's just as quick my way.

ARCHIE That ain't the point. Wait a minute! *[waving arms and flailing at Mike, stopping his action]* Don't be doin' that. Suppose there's a fire in the house and you gotta run for your life? Your way, all you got on is one shoe and a sock. My way, you got on a sock and a sock. You see, they're even.

MIKE *[Caught up in this craziness]* Suppose it's raining or snowing outside. Your way with a sock on each foot, my feet would get wet. My way, with a sock and a shoe on one foot I can hop around and stay dry.

ARCHIE I think you been hoppin' around on your head. Wait a minute! *[Archie grabs Mike's sock]* Listen to me! Supposin' the other sock's got a hole in it.

MIKE It doesn't have a hole in it.

ARCHIE I said supposin' it's got a hole in it.

MIKE All right, suppose it has a hole—

ARCHIE All right, it's got a hole—so you ain't got another matchin' pair . . . so what're you gonna do? Your way, you gotta take off a whole shoe and a sock—my way, all you gotta do's take off one sock!

MIKE All right. If it'll make you happy *[beginning to take off shoe]* I'll start all over again.

ARCHIE *[Stopping him]* Don't do that now. You're halfway through now. Geez, get on with it. We're in a hurry. You can start doin' it the right way tomorrow morning—and do it that way for the rest of your life! *[He exits.]*

Our writers, Mickey Ross and Bernie West, came up with this brilliant concept, and it remained largely intact, with much improvisation and line changes that made it easier and funnier. Also, in rehearsal we found a series of physical bits to go along with the central idea. It turned out to be a happy collaboration.

Years later, during my presentation to the drama class, it hit me that the "shoes and socks" bit we had created was almost pure Shakespeare. My professor at Ann Arbor, H. T. Price, had asked my class if Polonius had been a wise man in presenting a "few precepts" to Laertes as the young man was about to embark for England. Many of us thought the words were wisdom personified, until it was pointed out that the old man's speech went on far too long and could have caused his son to miss departing on time. Shakespeare well knew that in the days of sail, he who missed the turning of the tide in the River Thames was compelled to wait another day. So when Polonius comes upon his son and urges him to "get going," he defeats his own purpose.

"Yet here Laertes? Aboard, aboard for shame! The wind sits in the shoulder of your sail, and you are stayed for. There—my blessing with thee. [He lays his hand on Laertes' head.] And these few precepts in thy memory . . ." He then goes on with a lengthy oration, carrying on endlessly, offering words that appear sensible but endangering Laertes' chances of embarking punctually. Archie Bunker did the same thing, less elegantly, certainly, but just as stupidly. The moral of the tale, I suppose: If you want to become a comedy director, study Shakespeare.

I know that after his initial anxiety about the series, the president of CBS, Bob Wood, was delighted with *All in the Family*, because of its splendid ratings and its contributions to the corporate bottom line. But I'm equally convinced he didn't really understand what the show was about. For example in 1973, we shot an episode entitled "The Saga of Cousin Oscar." The theme of the episode had come about when Norman and I were interviewing writers who were pitching notions for scripts to be developed that season. Every comedy writer in town, it seemed, offered some variation on the tired theme of Archie and Edith buying a burial plot. At the end of a long day, Norman remarked, "Death seems to be in the air," and after a moment's thought added, "Why don't we do a story about a distant relative, disliked by everybody, who dies while visiting the Bunkers?" This was certainly novel in 1973, and I jumped on it enthusiastically, thinking we could take on the funeral industry and the high cost of dying in this country. We could fold some pointed commentary into the comedy.

When it came time to cast the role of Whitehead, the funeral director, I thought back to Cornelius Burke, the slightly built but theatrical Pennsylvania warden I interviewed while starting out on *Wanted*. Trying to cast far away from the expected lugubrious undertaker type, Norman and I agreed on Jackie Grimes, who played wonderfully without resorting to any of the clichés normally associated with such a role. One of our running themes involved Archie trying to bargain with Whitehead to get a cheaper casket for Archie's deadbeat relative.

ARCHIE Whitehead, it's time for a little plain talk. Can a guy buy somethin' such as used?

WHITEHEAD Used?

ARCHIE Used. You got any floor models, demonstrators, fleet jobs . . . whatever.

WHITEHEAD What you want, then, is something modestly priced?

ARCHIE Cheap, Whitehead. Dirt cheap. [*The doorbell rings. After the interruption Archie crosses back.*]

ARCHIE Go ahead—shoot, Whitehead.

WHITEHEAD Archie, I got an item here on page eight. Now, it's the lowest one we got—number 101-P, ninety-seven fifty, but there's no guarantee against warping.

ARCHIE Sold.

WHITEHEAD Let's see what it comes to with the other essentials. There's the burial plot—want it restricted, Archie? Costs a little more.

ARCHIE Are you kiddin'? If it's cheaper, you can slip him in between a couple o' coons.

The audience responded to Bunker's insensitivity with a huge laugh, and Bob Wood sought us out the following day. He'd been in New York when we shot the episode but someone had told him about the outrageous "coons" line. When Lear asked him if he'd heard anything else about that show, Wood replied, "What more do you need? Keep up the great work. 'Slip him in . . .'" He walked off, chuckling. Lear and I looked at one another and, speaking almost simultaneously, we both said, "We ought to cut the line." If a single line was upstaging the underlying message about dying, it had to go.

The day after the show aired, a disappointed Bob Wood found Norman and me at the CBS commissary and told us he had waited "all night" for his favorite line, which never materialized. What happened? We thought he had enjoyed it too much, we told him, which made us think it was overpowering the rest of the episode. Wood stared at us blankly and admitted that he didn't know what made us tick.

On another occasion, when I was producing the show and interviewing freelance writers for the upcoming season, one pitch began with a swastika painted crudely on the Bunker's front door. I felt the script went nowhere after that; the writer went down a path that led not to neo-Nazis, but to American Indian steelworkers. I knew about these "high iron men" who built many New York skyscrapers, and I was vaguely aware that the Nazi symbol might have traced its ancestry to a Native Indian design. But I didn't think the script was right for us. I told the writer, though, that I would buy the *idea* of the swastika itself if the front door of the Bunker's house swung inward, so the audience would instantly see the hateful symbol. In fact, I asked the writer to accompany me to the stage, where I found that the door did open inward into the set. That would allow the story to touch on anti-Semitism, and in a larger sense, the Arab-Israeli conflict that held the world's attention in the early 1970s.

The episode began, as it turned out, on a Sunday morning, with Archie coming downstairs grouchily, looking for his newspaper, and shouting to Edith. She answers from offstage that the paper is still outside; he mutters about how he has to do everything himself in this uncooperative household. Bunker flings open the front door and exits, without seeing the crudely painted swastika. As the audience digests this moment and waits for a reaction, Archie reappears, engrossed in the paper, slamming the door closed but not yet noticing anything amiss. Only after he reaches center stage does Archie look up from the paper, a quizzical look on his face, as it dawns on him that he may have observed something peripherally. He returns to the door, pulls it open, sees the painted symbol, and shouts, "Edith!" in a tone that suggests it's her fault.

As the story develops, we are visited by Paul Benjamin, a member of the "Hebrew Defense Association" who tells the Bunkers that the swastika was meant for a Jewish family nearby and inadvertently applied to the wrong house by his group's enemies, a gang of violent skinheads. The young militant swears he and his buddies will extract revenge for the incident, and his warlike attitude delights Archie. Mike and Gloria are opposed to this kind of eye-for-an-eye thinking, and argue strenuously that violence only begets more violence.

[Doorbell rings.]

PAUL I'll get it. *[He moves swiftly, looks out the window—opens the door to another H.D.A. man.]*

PAUL It's okay, it's one of my men. Hey, Jerry, what's up?

JERRY This is the wrong house!

PAUL I know that, but they don't.

JERRY They do now. We just got word they're on their way to Bloom's place.

PAUL All right, we'll be ready for 'em. Look, why don't you go on ahead? I'll drive on up and meet ya there.

JERRY Right. *[He exits.]*

PAUL Well, I guess you folks are off the hook! So long, everybody. Shalom. *[He waves and exits.]*

EDITH "Shalom"? What does that mean?

MIKE Believe it or not, Ma, it means "peace."

GLORIA Jewish people also use it to say "hello" or "goodbye."

EDITH But how do you know which one they mean?

ARCHIE Why don't you use your common sense, Edith? If a Jewish guy is comin' at ya it's "hello." If he's goin' away from you, it's "goodbye."

EDITH But when does it mean peace?

ARCHIE In between "hello" and "goodbye."

[Suddenly we hear a loud explosion in the street. The family reacts, runs to the door. We see their stricken faces staring past the camera.]

ARCHIE Oh, geez, that's Paul. They blew him up in his car!

At this, I called for a long, slow fade-out on their shocked and horrified faces. Lear and I agreed there should be no closing music. The screen stayed black for several silent seconds, then, quietly, our credits rolled.

Once again, Bob Wood demonstrated his uncanny ability to miss the point. Instead of commenting about the episode's violence—which one could take as a metaphor for the Middle East, or the war in Vietnam—the CBS president was quoted as saying, "I don't understand those guys. You know what they did last night? They blow up a Jew and the credits roll."

Sometime during the airing of our first thirteen episodes, we heard that Sammy Davis, Jr., had appeared on *The Tonight Show* with Johnny Carson, carrying on excitedly about the wonderful new CBS show *All in the Family*. Sammy had remarked to Carson, we were told, what a kick it would be for him to confront Archie. "Imagine a one-eyed colored Jew," he said, "going head-to-head with Bunker." We were pleased to get such wonderful publicity as we struggled to find our audience. But we did not expect to hear from Sammy's agent at the William Morris Agency, as we did one day.

Lear told me Si Marsh had called, wanting to know when we were going to book Sammy on the show. Norman asked what I thought of the idea. "Not much," I said. We both agreed that it wouldn't work. To have a star of Davis's magnitude show up at the Bunker's home would be too unbelievable. Marsh was persistent, saying Sammy could play any part we wanted. But Davis was such a distinctive personality, we insisted, it was clear he could only appear as himself. Besides, we really wanted to avoid the business of guest-star visits, no matter who they might be, and we informed the agent of our decision.

We thought that had laid the suggestion to rest. But Sammy continued to talk it up in interviews, announcing he was going to be on our show. And Si Marsh, ever the tireless agent, relentlessly promoted the idea. Finally, one day Norman told me the pressure to use Davis was mounting, so we talked it over once more. If we were to attempt this unlikely appearance, we agreed, we would have to lay an enormous amount of "pipe" (exposition) to explain Sammy's visit. Accordingly, Norman began to write in a nighttime moonlighting job for Archie, driving "Munson's cab." This was established over the course of several episodes so that eventually Sammy could ride as a passenger in the taxi and inadvertently leave his briefcase in it.

As the story unfolds, we learn that Archie had given the star his address, asking him to mail an autographed picture, and Sammy uses this information to trace Archie's phone number.

ARCHIE *[on phone]* What can I do for ya, Mr. Davis? Oh . . . that fancy briefcase was yours, huh? Well, listen, I turned it in at the cab office . . . Well, how can I help ya get it back? No, wait a minute . . . You say you're goin' out to the airport? That's pretty good 'cause I can have the briefcase delivered over here from the cab office and my house is kinda on the way, off Northern Boulevard. You can stop by here and pick it up? You wanna do that? It'll be an honor, Mr. Davis!

In disbelief, Archie announces to his stunned family, "He's pickin' it up himself! He's coming here!" The entire neighborhood soon learns of the impending visit, and they all go berserk in preparation. The story is solid and believable. Like a team of plumbers, we had laid enough "pipe" to convincingly write in the visit of a superstar.

When I met Sammy, I told him how happy we were to have him, but there were a few rules he had to follow. First, I told him our rehearsal schedule, and that we worked in private. His entourage would have to congregate in the hallway outside the room, and they could visit only during breaks. Also, I mentioned that we never used cue cards, that performers were expected to memorize their lines and work without the crutches normally used on variety shows.

Sammy couldn't have been more affable and willing. But one day he did look up at me, in the tenth hour of a grueling rehearsal day, and say, "Hey, John, you weren't kidding about the work." In the script, he had to deliver almost a full-page monologue, and he had great trouble remembering the words. At one point, he took me aside and pleaded for cue cards. I reminded him of our deal. "Besides," I said, "this isn't a Bob Hope or a Martin and Lewis sketch. You have to be real in this thing, and cue cards are a dead giveaway when an actor is depending on them. Also, you are a great star and I know you can do this. Go home and study."

At the first reading, all had gone quite well until we reached the final page of the script. The stage directions provided that Munson, delivering the briefcase, would take a photograph of the Bunkers' famous visitor with the camera he has brought along. Archie would have none of it, but Sammy says it's okay; he wants to remember this night forever. As we finished the reading and the cast broke for coffee, I remained at the table, deep in thought. Norman approached and asked what I was doing. I told him I thought the script was in fine shape except it had no finish. "There's no snap at the fade-out," I said. "Just having Munson take a picture and have Sammy exit is too lame an ending. Maybe there's some physical action we could come up with. Right now we're ending with a whimper." Suddenly, I broke into a grin and started to chuckle.

"You got something?" said Lear.

"Maybe," I offered. "Just as the photo is flashed, I think Sammy ought to kiss Archie on the cheek."

Norman was silent for a moment. "You think it'll work?"

"It's worth a try."

On the night we shot the show, the moment when Sammy Davis, Jr., kisses Archie Bunker earned us the biggest, longest laugh I have ever experienced. The audience howled and applauded, and kept it up so long we had to shorten the moment for the home audience. Carroll O'Connor's shocked take was awesome, as was Sammy's entire performance. Our adventure into "one in a million" story land had worked superbly. But we vowed never to do it again.

Richard Nixon was never a favorite in my household. In fact, early in 1968 when he moved into the Beverly Hills neighborhood where I was living, paying four to five times as much as my house had cost, I wondered how a man who had never been in private practice could afford such expensive real estate. Nixon had been a congressman, then a senator, and later vice president, at a time when his annual salary, if I'm not mistaken, topped out around $45,000. I could not understand how such modest government pay could generate enough funds to purchase the grand residence into which he was moving.

Naturally, when Nixon was reelected president in 1972, he became a target for discussion in the Bunker household. Archie stoutly defended him and his policies, while Mike and Gloria spoke for the opposition. In one of our early episodes, the script had called for Archie to comment on the "great president, Richard M. Nixon." In rehearsal, I stopped Carroll O'Connor and said, "Since your character is already well known for mangling the language, let's see what we can do for Mr. Nixon." Neither of us was sure where I was headed, but I said something to the effect that perhaps his middle initial should reflect a kind of conservative bias. After much thought, someone suggested that Robert E. Lee represented the past admirably. So Archie would forever refer to his hero as "Richard E. Nixon." It was a small jab, and not everyone got it, but we enjoyed hearing the name misquoted every time Archie said it.

A year or so later, Don Nicholl came up with a wonderful teleplay in which Archie is interviewed at work, praising Nixon on a segment to be aired on the *CBS Evening News*. Archie comes home and tells everyone he's about to appear on national television. With great excitement, the family gathers around the TV set, only to have it blow up minutes before the news comes on. Much of the script is designed to frustrate Archie, as he tries in vain to borrow someone else's television. He dispatches members of the family to canvas the street, and Mike returns with a portable TV. Archie is triumphant, until he discovers the set has no working batteries. Finally, Edith discovers a repairman who has been working in the neighborhood, and she brings the young Mr. Levy into the house. Urged on by a frantic Archie, the technician examines the set and says the problem is minor; it will only take five minutes to fix it. Archie demonstrates great relief, until Levy says he can't do the work until the following Monday. Archie can't believe what he's hearing, and he croaks out a strangled "Why?" The man says he is a practicing Orthodox Jew, and since it is Friday night he must return home before sundown.

Pleading with the serviceman to make an exception, Archie insults him: "Come on, a nice, clean-cut young guy like you is Orthodox?" He then offers to get him a "mispensation." Levy responds gently, "I'm sorry Mr. Bunker, it's against my religion." Archie says, "You're turnin' down money—*that's* against your religion." At this insensitive comment, Levy delivers a line in Yiddish, wishing that Archie "should live in a mansion with a thousand rooms, and you should have heartburn in every one of those rooms!" We never translated the speech for Archie or the audience. When Archie asks what he has just heard, Levy responds, "You'll never know, but believe me, I got even."

In the script, Archie's only remaining option is to go to Kelsey's Bar and try to convince the crowd to watch him on CBS for a few minutes instead of the basketball game that the local barflies are watching. But before we could reach that point, I had to undertake some unusual preparations. I wanted actual footage of Nixon to interrupt Archie's big moment. We asked CBS News if they could provide some innocuous footage of the president for us to use on screen: no way. It seems the news department had a strict rule against sharing any archival footage with the entertainment division, even though we both worked for the same corporation.

We set the script aside for a while, and I asked my associate director, Bob La Hendro, to keep an eye out for Nixon footage anytime he was in the CBS basement. The relatively primitive equipment at the time required the network to use the same two-inch tape machines both for assembling edited masters and for recording the incoming daily news feed from New York. When the time came to receive Walter Cronkite at 4 PM, edit tapes would come down, and raw tapes would be mounted to record the nightly news for broadcast on the West Coast at 7 PM, Pacific time. One day, La Hendro phoned excitedly and said he had taped Nixon off the news tape. I rushed down and viewed the footage, which showed Nixon announcing two Supreme Court nominees, Haynsworth and Carswell. The Senate ultimately rejected both nominations, but that didn't matter. We had our Nixon tape.

To lead into the scene, I recorded an "interviewer" standing in front of a chain-link fence:

INTERVIEWER To round out our report on reaction to the new Nixon economic policies, we sought the views of some average working men.

ARCHIE *[In the bar, addressing disinterested drinkers for whom he has bought a round]* Here it comes. Here I come now!

INTERVIEWER During the lunch break at a plant in Manhattan, we talked to some of the workers who will be among the first to feel the force of those policies. And here is one of those men, Mr. Archie Bunker—*[The picture suddenly changes to show the Presidential Seal]*

STUDIO ANNOUNCER We interrupt this program to bring you a special report from CBS News in Washington, where President Nixon is about to address the nation. Ladies and gentlemen, the president of the United States.

ARCHIE Wait a minute, where am I?

[Nixon's picture appears on screen; I was able to use all of his opening remarks from our tape]

NIXON My fellow Americans, the president of the United States, sitting at this desk, in this historic room—

ARCHIE What's he doing up there? I'm supposed to be on there.

DRINKER Oh, it's something about the Supreme Court.

MIKE I bet he's gonna nominate his buddy, Bebe Rebozo.

ARCHIE Why is he doin' this to me?

EDITH Oh, Archie, he don't know what he's doing.

DRINKER Nobody's listening to this—let's get back to the game.

ARCHIE No, wait! Hold it—they may get back to me any minute.

GLORIA Daddy, I think Nixon's almost finished!

At this point, I cut back to Nixon, delivering his commentary with excruciating slowness:

NIXON . . . throughout this great land of ours. *[For our purposes, Nixon couldn't have done better—with Archie straining in impatience, the president slowly folded his hands, placed them deliberately on his desk, looked at the camera a long moment, and finally resumed speaking]* Thank you—and good night.

[The face of Dan Rather appears on screen. La Hendro had captured this, too; we paid Rather $500 to use his image]

DRINKER Put the ball game on!

ARCHIE Wait a minute—there might just be a piece of me. Who's that guy?

EDITH That's Dan Rather. He's gonna tell everybody what Mr. Nixon just said.

ARCHIE *[Digs in his pocket to pay for the round of drinks]* I'll tell ya, that Nixon's gonna open his mouth once too often, and he ain't gonna have Archie Bunker to kick around no more!

Technically, this episode was extremely difficult to pull off. We had to assemble a basketball game in progress, for which we paid the Los Angeles Lakers and their longtime announcer Chick Hearn, for his play-by-play. We had to incorporate the "interviewer" segment, Nixon's commentary, the studio announcer (a part that I read), and Dan Rather. We had to use two video screens, one in the bar and one offstage, we had to employ several "roll cues" to master control, and we had to guess about the timing of the audience laughs we would earn. Once the tapes rolled, we couldn't stop the sequence. It was daring, but we brought it off, and it remains one of my favorite episodes in the series.

Years after the Watergate scandal had been revealed, people would often say to me that we must have reshot much of our political commentary. We never did. What's on the tapes today, as the show is rerun, is precisely the way the programs were shot and presented during the height of the controversy. We always tried to present Archie's defense of Nixon while Mike and Gloria attacked him. But I must confess, some of our choices of words for Archie may have "accidentally" backfired on him. I remember fondly one particular exchange, during the heat of Watergate:

ARCHIE Lay off President Nixon, huh? In this country we don't kick a man when he's down.

MIKE Archie, it's not Nixon who's down. Remember what he said, he's not wallowing in Watergate? It's the country that's down!

ARCHIE I still got faith in Nixon.

MIKE Which one?

ARCHIE What do you mean, which one?

MIKE The Nixon who knew why we should be in Vietnam?

ARCHIE Yes!

MIKE The Nixon who knew all the reasons why we had to be friends with Russia and China?

ARCHIE Yes!

MIKE The Nixon who knew all the secret reasons we have to keep bombing Cambodia?

ARCHIE You're damn right!

MIKE The Nixon who didn't know a single thing about Watergate??

[The argument continues for some time, then]

ARCHIE The only mistake the White House made was just hirin' a coupla screw-ups.

MIKE "A coupla screw-ups"?

ARCHIE That's right. They shoulda hired Japs instead of all them Krauts.

MIKE What?

ARCHIE In the first place, the Japs are better than the Krauts at electronics. In the second place, if the Japs get caught they do the right thing. They kill themselves!

Another subtle detail that set *All in the Family* apart from so many other sitcoms was how the actors actually put food in their mouths during scenes when their characters were supposed to be eating. This reminds me of an old "Jewish mother" joke. A neglectful son has finally called his mother to ask about her health: "How do you feel, Mom?" She answers in a weary voice, "To tell you the truth, not so good. I haven't had anything to eat for ten days." Anxiously, the son asks, "What's wrong? Why haven't you eaten?" Mournfully she replies, "I didn't want my mouth to be full in case you should call."

When watching television programs, I have always been critical of "eating scenes" in which the actors toy with their meals and push some food around on their plates, as they deliver speeches completely unencumbered by the task of actually swallowing what they are supposedly consuming. It is easy to understand why this happens so often; it's another result of the customarily late delivery of scripts by our friends in the writing business. Most people cannot imagine how difficult it is to eat naturally and deliver dialogue succinctly without getting trapped by an occasional mouthful. Ideally, every bite has to be choreographed, not only to avoid actors choking on screen, but to put them in position to deliver their lines with clarity. Any actor can understand the importance of not having a full mouth when it's time to speak a line.

The first time I ran headlong into this difficulty on *All in the Family*, the villain was a glass of orange juice. All week we had worked on a breakfast scene. During three days of "dry" rehearsal, the actors pantomimed drinking, but on camera day the property master provided real juice. This was served all day Monday and during the run-throughs conducted on Tuesday. While taping the dress rehearsal, however, I noticed some of our group had trouble getting their lines out. During the dinner break, as I was giving notes before the evening performance, all the actors complained about the juice. It seems the prop man had provided clear juice during the day, but had substituted juice containing pulp for the eight o'clock taping. Not a good idea. I learned a great lesson that night, and ordered that no such changes occur again between dress rehearsal and "air show."

Some time later, on another episode, I faced the problem of staging a dinner scene that went on for an entire act. Seeing the cast pecking away at their empty plates, I stopped the work and conducted a short seminar on the subject of eating. I told the group that in order to maintain realism, the family needed to attack their meals with gusto as they spoke their lines. Aware of the actors' need to rehearse the pinpoint timing of chewing, swallowing, and speaking, I asked the property master to provide the same food for rehearsal that we would serve "on the air," and to start bringing it in on Thursdays or Fridays, depending on how well the cast had begun to memorize their lines. (It made no sense to give them actual food in the early stages, when lines might still get rewritten.) We would serve the same menu during Monday and Tuesday's camera blocking.

As it turned out, this system required a little fine-tuning. On the first day of rehearsal-hall work in which we used real food, the prop man had opened several cans of supermarket stew. Carroll O'Connor managed just a couple of bites before he said, "John, I know you're right about rehearsing with food, but I can't eat this stuff." To keep everybody happy, I sent out for stew from Chasen's, and from then on, the cast had no trouble eating with intensity and dedication. The people watching the budget were less pleased, but I convinced them that the money was well spent: some of our best shows featured the family arguing while chowing down.

In another episode, one in which the writing was a bit weaker than usual, I decided to try choreographing an eating scene in which no one said a word for several uninterrupted minutes. This was harder than I had expected, but it came together beautifully—illustrating contention between "Meathead" and Archie as each reached for the same dish, or defiance as Archie poured ketchup over everything, to Edith's great discomfort. The family ate voraciously as they went through the carefully staged business, and the audience howled in appreciation.

Another of my sitcom peeves revolves around TV series's use of perpetual springtime. Nobody wears a coat, it never rains, and doors often remain wide open in winter as actors make entrances and exits. On *Family* this was a serious no-no; I insisted that the actors had to wear weather-appropriate clothing. Archie always entered the house dressed in the same ill-fitting lumber jacket, and there was always the business of hanging up coats or putting them in the closet. Except for summer heat waves, when an actor came onto the set he carefully closed the door against the elements. I think this explains why more than one person was surprised to learn that our program was taped in Hollywood. In our perhaps excessive desire for truthful detail, we made at least some viewers believe we were actually shooting in the borough of Queens.

CHAPTER

10

I am frequently asked why I left Norman Lear's company after having directed or produced almost one hundred episodes of *All in the Family*. It would be easy to say I had burned out, but the truth lies elsewhere. Sometime during the fourth season of our series, Norman approached me one Friday night with a problem. He had hired someone to direct the pilot of *Good Times,* starring Esther Rolle, John Amos, and Jimmie Walker. Lear had fired the director after the first three days of rehearsal, and he was asking me to take over. The schedule called for shooting the following Tuesday, and I pointed out that *All in the Family* was being taped at the same hour. He reminded me that my associate director, Bob La Hendro, could run the cameras, since I had already staged our episode over the last three days.

There was a bigger problem, I said. We would have to call a weekend rehearsal of the pilot and my son, Anthony, was having his sixth birthday party at our home on Saturday, an event I could not miss. Norman looked at me as if I hadn't spoken and said, "He'll have other birthdays." I couldn't believe what I was hearing. "He'll never be six again," I protested—to no avail. Lear persisted, using every ploy in the book, and I finally relented.

"However," I said, "at the end of the *All in the Family* season, I'll be leaving the show." Norman laughed at such a preposterous idea, but to his surprise I kept my word. When he realized I was sincere in my decision, he hosted a lavish going-away party in my honor and we were able to part on friendly terms.

Good Times sold as a series, but at the time I hadn't the wit to ask for further pilot compensation, except for a very small royalty. This followed a pattern that Tandem Productions exploited when it came to compensation for *Maude* and *The Jeffersons*. Since 1972, I had been happily under contract to direct and produce *All in the Family*, but it never occurred to me to request profit participation for the spinoff *Maude*, again settling for a small rerun royalty. When it came to *The Jeffersons*, however, I asked for a participation percentage during a friendly negotiation with Bud Yorkin. I was acting as my own agent at the time and Bud, a co-owner, bargained on behalf of the company. After some discussion, Yorkin granted me the same percentage I had enjoyed on *All in the Family*, and I left the meeting well satisfied.

Unfortunately, when it came time to formalize the deal, I learned to my dismay that a new managing partner had entered the picture. While I was busy working on *All in the Family*, the recent arrival was busy denying the existence of the agreement I had reached with Bud Yorkin. As is customary in the industry, I had provided services for four years without a signed contract. In those days, we relied on a handshake to bind an agreement, leaving the task of formalizing the terms until much later. Months after leaving Lear's employ, when I received final contracts to review, I was shocked to see that the drafted language had omitted my percentage of *The Jeffersons*. I confronted the new manager, reminding him that when he took over the reins at Tandem, we had gone over all the points Yorkin and I had negotiated, and I could point to the bound notebook he had used in our discussions.

When the manager refused to honor my request to provide his notes, I did what I should have done years before. I hired an attorney, preparing to sue. My lawyer, Arnold Burk, one of the wisest people I know, reviewed the record and advised me to forget litigation with respect to *Jeffersons* because it might endanger my participation in *All in the Family*. Since the original series was a known commodity, while *Jeffersons* was just beginning, and didn't appear to have the same potential for success, Burk advised me not to contest the issue and settle for the small royalty Tandem offered.

I followed the advice, and through the years I have earned a most satisfactory return for my work on *Family*. On the other hand, *The Jeffersons* became a giant hit and ran about twelve years. If the company had lived up to the original agreement I made before the advent of the new partner, the profit participation on the spinoff series would have exceeded the compensation I've earned from the show that started it all. As to the other pilots I directed for Norman, I am happy for his multiple successes and forever grateful to him for the opportunity to be part of the *All in the Family* story.

Beyond mere monetary compensation, I derived enormous pleasure from being granted the gift of working with Bea Arthur as Maude. This incredibly talented performer could do more with a tilt of the head than many actresses could accomplish with pages of dialogue. Bea had appeared as a guest on *All in the Family,* playing Edith's cousin Maude, who hated Archie passionately.

"You know what I like about you, Archie?"

"What's that, Maude?"

"Nothing."

Maude was designed to be the left-wing flip side of Archie, and they battled hilariously when she came to Queens to take care of Edith's family when they were all suffering from winter fevers. I believe it was Fred Silverman, then head of programming at CBS, who conceived the idea of having Bea play the character in a spinoff series. I was asked to direct the pilot.

At our first table reading, Bill Macy, playing the part of Maude's husband, Walter, remarked, "Hey, I'm not playing Jewish in this thing."

"That's right," I said. We read on.

Again, Bill spoke up. "My name is Findlay—that's not a Jewish name."

The table grew quiet as I repeated, "Bill, you're not playing a Jewish character, so what?"

He wouldn't be silenced. "I always play Jewish. I am Jewish."

At this point I said, "Carroll O'Connor is a politically liberal Roman Catholic, but he managed to portray Archie Bunker as a bigoted right-wing Protestant with some success. It's called acting. Can we get on with the reading?"

Bill tried again, "But—"

Bea cut in. "Darling, I saw you in *Oh! Calcutta!*"—in 1969, Macy had appeared in the Broadway play, which featured full frontal nudity—"and I didn't know you were Jewish!"

Bea's throaty observation broke up the table. Bill went on to play Walter for a lengthy run.

In the spring of 1974, Henry Fonda appeared on Broadway as the famous trial lawyer Clarence Darrow in a unique one-man show created by playwright David Rintels and directed by John Houseman. The play was presented at the Helen Hayes Theatre, where it earned rave reviews. Shortly after the initial Broadway run, my agent at William Morris, Rowland Perkins, contacted me and explained that Rintels was planning to produce *Darrow* on television and would like to consider me as the director. (Apparently, John Houseman was either unavailable, or felt unprepared to handle a live-on-tape production.) Since my four-year engagement on *All in the Family* had ended, I was ready for something new. The idea of working with Fonda, a brilliant actor I had long admired, was irresistible.

I met with David, read the script, which I thought was absolutely wonderful, and in due course met with the producers, Mike Merrick and his partner Don Gregory. After the meeting, I asked Perkins about the compensation, and he told me they had a limited budget, that they only had room for a modest director's fee and that "everybody" was working for a salary that was ludicrously low for the time and effort that this difficult and ambitious production would require.

With Perkins's assurances I signed on—clearly not for the money— and began lengthy meetings with Rintels to discuss cutting the play to its ninety-minute television format and to decide whether to record the production in an actual theater. I thought a real theater would hamper camera movement, although I felt it was important to perform in front of a theater audience. I then suggested we could simulate a theater at an NBC studio, which would allow me to shoot over the audience and still use a plywood floor, which would allow at least one camera to make tracking moves.

With the help of a talented art director named H. R. Poindexter, we created a "proscenium" with wings, curtains, and various "teasers" and "tormenters" to create the look of a Broadway playhouse. My idea was to use four video cameras to shoot two performances on successive days, and then edit the best takes of the two into one finished product. Rintels agreed to this, and we set to work with Mr. Fonda, who, at sixty-nine, proved to be as gifted as ever. *Darrow* was a one-man show with the actor playing to imaginary people, to nonexistent juries, at times to a lighted chair or a prop. His power of suggestion was so extraordinary that one could easily visualize a witness he was questioning, or a judge he was addressing, even though he was alone onstage for almost two hours. Fonda had a pacemaker, but he never tired of rehearsing and polishing his performance through long periods of work that left others wondering at his stamina.

I was also impressed by his extraordinary ability to remember the cuts that had been made in the text. After all, he had played the original piece on Broadway with different transitions and words that were now in somewhat altered order but still close enough to the original to tax anyone's memory. I had even suggested slightly different attacks on certain phrasing, and Fonda was grateful for the effort to keep everything fresh. I will always remember how gracious he was in accepting these minor changes—as was David Rintels. One moment remains imbedded in my memory.

We were shooting a pick-up that involved a rather tricky camera move. During rehearsal, with Fonda addressing a jury about a young child forced to work in a coal mine, I observed that after an impassioned plea Darrow had become so moved by his argument that incipient tears began to show as he concluded his lengthy speech. To fully realize the moment, I decided it was urgent to wind up with an extreme close-up so that the home audience could easily read the moisture in Henry's eyes. We needed to begin with a long shot and move in slowly until his face filled the screen.

Unfortunately, the move was so difficult for the camera operator that, just as he came to the end of his dolly, the camera would shake, making the previous two or three pages of performance unusable. Only reshooting back from the beginning would give the shot emotional meaning. I apologized to Henry for forcing him to go so far back in order to make the shot. He indicated it would be no problem—even after having to do it over three times. At one point Fonda asked if he could do anything to help! On the fourth attempt—after, fearing for Henry's health, I had almost decided to quit for the night—everything fell into place. The emotion was sustained, and the cameraman performed with great skill under enormous pressure. For me, it was one of the high points of the production, and I will never forget the determination and sheer grit displayed by one of the great icons of the American theater.

One bitter memory remains from this otherwise happy experience. After finishing the live taping, our two producers removed themselves to a Hawaiian vacation, while David Rintels and I were left to edit and finish all the work that normally falls into the laps of those who claimed credit as producers. In a way, it was fortunate not to have any interference from these men, since David and I worked so well together on the final cut. What really bothered me was to learn later that our producers had pocketed inflated fees, while my compensation remained the same as they originally offered under the theory that "everybody" was working for less. When I confronted the partners and complained, I was treated to some fancy double-talk, and I decided not to pursue the matter but to hold on to the happy memory of working with Rintels and Fonda. Those relationships far outweighed the pettiness displayed by people whose devotion to dollars mattered more than being associated with a landmark television event. And the privilege of working with them remains one of the happiest memories in my professional life.

One other, humorous event remains in my memory: We had created the "theater" for *Darrow* on the floor of one of NBC's largest studios. My center of operations was located some twenty feet above the audience. To the right of this control room we had created a space for a VIP audience where Henry Fonda's wife, Shirlee, sat, along with agents, friends, and family members. I had heard that Mrs. Fonda had been a flight attendant before marrying Henry, which made sense when, during one of the tapings, she came into the control room to say, "John, the passengers are complaining it's too cold out there."

"Thanks, Shirlee," I said, "but I'm not the pilot today, and here we call our passengers an audience." Shirlee laughed along with the rest of us, and we warmed up the studio to her satisfaction.

As a footnote, NBC aired *Darrow* to remarkable reviews, prompting the producers to restage the show at the Minskoff Theatre in 1975, where it enjoyed another long run.

After *All in the Family*, I was showered with offers to direct or consult on other series. One such opportunity came when Alan Shayne, who headed Warner Bros. Television at that time, asked me to review a pilot that one of the networks had tentatively selected for inclusion its fall schedule. Mr. Shayne felt there was something inherently wrong with the acting but couldn't put his finger on it. He offered a very large sum for me to look at the work. Frankly, I was embarrassed to accept his offer—it was a pot of gold—and I was fairly sure my comments would not make a huge difference in the life of the production. "Alan," I said, "I can't accept such a bonus for an observation I might make that you already know. It would make me more comfortable if you would agree to pay me nothing until I have viewed the pilot. If I then say something you haven't thought of, I would gamble with you that the series has potential, and I would accept a royalty payment for every episode made."

Shayne thought this was an eminently fair suggestion, and I then ran the pilot of *Alice* with the Warner chief. When it was over I remarked, "I was right to turn down your generous first offer. What I see appears to be so elementary that I feel certain you already know it." He was all ears as I continued, "Everybody in the piece is trying to be funny, including the boss [played by Vic Tayback]. Linda Lavin, a very accomplished actress, is trying to crack jokes around Mel when she should be concentrating on keeping her job. The owner of the café can't appear so lighthearted. He'd better act strong enough and demanding enough to put Linda's character in jeopardy. Suppose she gets fired?" In essence, I told Alan that all the characters must be more real and to allow the situations to provide the laughter.

Shayne admitted he didn't know any of this. Part of the pilot was reshot using some of my notes, and I earned a healthy royalty that far exceeded the original offer, since the series produced 201 episodes. Joe Youngerman, of the old Screen Directors Guild, often said when negotiating industry contracts, "Never make a deal that is too good for one side over the other." He taught me to forgo greed and instant gratification in favor of compromise. Following Joe's example has rewarded me handsomely.

My involvement in another long-lived series began shortly before I directed *Clarence Darrow*, when I got a call from Danny Arnold, a gifted writer and producer. Years earlier, before *All in the Family*, I had directed a series for Danny that lasted only one season called *My World and Welcome to It*, inspired by James Thurber's writings. (NBC, not convinced the show had "legs," had abandoned it, only to see it win multiple Emmys after it had disappeared.) Danny was often fun to be around, but on the phone he sounded depressed when he asked me to look at a pilot he had just completed. It was called *The Life and Times of Captain Barney Miller,* and ABC had just rejected it. He asked me to evaluate the work, and in those pre-videocassette days, he reserved a screening room so I could see it.

I thought the show was great, with one exception. I remarked that a comedy about a Jewish New York policeman should include a wife that suggested Manhattan rather than the Midwest. The actress playing Mrs. Miller was Abby Dalton, well qualified for many roles but in my opinion, clearly wrong for this one. In my view, I said, it should have been—Danny and I both said this at the same time—Nita Talbot, a very funny lady, adept at comedy and more ethnically suited than the blonde and beautiful Miss Dalton. "Those bastards at ABC insisted on casting Abby," Danny shouted in anguish, "while I was begging to use Nita." I told Danny I sympathized with him; I had suffered the same kind of network interference many times. "But what are you going to do?" I said. "That's the business we're in."

I forgot about the incident until I was invited to a lunch meeting with the three top executives of ABC at the Polo Lounge—Jim Backus used to call it the Polio Lounge—in the Beverly Hills Hotel. I had signed a deal to develop new programs for the network, having formed my own production company after leaving *All in the Family,* and my hosts were Marty Starger, the chief, second-in-command Barry Diller, and junior executive Michael Eisner. The dialogue went something like this.

"Well, John, what programs are you going to bring us?"

I smiled and said, "It's only been a few weeks since I completed *Family.* I haven't really had time to think about much, except that I've agreed to direct Henry Fonda in *Clarence Darrow.*"

"Yeah," one of the men said, "but when you're finished with that crap, what kind of comedies are we going to get?"

I said, "I don't think it's crap. I think it's important television and, frankly, I'm looking forward to giving my brain a rest from making people laugh." Another executive said, "Well, have you seen anything that others may have done?"

What a great straight line to put in a plug for Danny Arnold! "I did see something I thought had great potential," I said. "It was *The Life and Times of Barney Miller.*"

"Are you kidding? We passed on that. We thought it was awful."

Here I became mischievous. "The only thing I found wrong with it was the casting of the wife. By the way, you ought to find out who at your network insisted on choosing Abby Dalton. Whoever it was should be hung up by their corporate gonads, because with the proper casting the series could be a big hit." I knew this triumvirate was totally responsible for insisting on Miss Dalton, but their only reaction was a subtle rattle of silverware.

About a week later, Michael Eisner phoned and asked if I really thought *Barney Miller* had potential. When I said yes, he told me they would make a new pilot if I would direct. I told him I wouldn't do it, because Danny Arnold was a good friend who tended to be erratic and excited during production. Eisner persisted, offering a substantial sum. I remember how depressed Danny had been at the screening of his pilot, so I said, "Look, I'll do it out of concern for Danny, and I don't need a percentage." (Was that a cloudy crystal ball!) "Just pay me a small royalty, but don't take it from Danny; let it come from the network. Also, I don't want to shoot on film, I'd rather do it live-on-tape. One more thing: The new script should not include a wife for Barney. I think it's a wonderful gang comedy that can take place completely in the squad room."

I made the pilot and shot another episode, while Danny drove me crazy standing in the control room and yelling, "That camera isn't ready!" I said, "It will be when I need it." And of course it was, driving my friend into further frenzy, because he didn't understand the technique of working live with a studio audience. I prefer that route to a laugh track, because audiences keep you honest. If it's funny they'll laugh. If it's not funny, the writing or the acting is lacking, and no laugh track can obscure this truth.

After I delivered the pilot, Danny proceeded to make cuts that drove me up the wall, so I removed my name from the production credits. However, ABC did pick up the series, and it had a remarkably long run. My two shows had eliminated the wife, but in subsequent episodes they tried again to incorporate Barney's home life by casting Barbara Barrie, a very talented lady. Ultimately, however, it was decided to concentrate on the police station. The series made millions for Danny, and, ironically, Ted Flicker, who shared screen credit on the first *filmed* show (entitled "The Life and Times of Captain Barney Miller")—the version that ABC hated and never aired. I have never begrudged Danny one cent of his take. He put enormous work into the production during all its years on the air, and he deserved everything.

One day in 1974, my agent sent me a script for another pilot from Warner Bros. and suggested I respond to the offer rapidly. I read the material, and despite my representative's ardor for the writing—I think the author was also one of his clients—I said I couldn't direct it. "This is an attempt to create a menage à trois situation," I explained, "but it falls flat because there's no real stake involved." The story was about two friends, one of them in jail, the other living in a house with an unattached female. When the first man gets released from the penitentiary, he joins the others and the three continue to live together. Aside from using jealousy as a continuing motif, I asked, "Where's the jeopardy?" As a courtesy, I met with the Warner people and explained my concerns. They responded that they had purchased a series that had been an enormous hit in England, in hopes of producing an American version. Because it had done so well in Europe, would I not reconsider my decision to pass?

Curious, I asked to read the original British text, and was astounded to find the American writer had left out one small detail. In the English series, called *Thick as Thieves,* the man in jail was *married* to the girl now living with his best friend. After serving his sentence and finding out that his wife and friend had engaged in sexual intercourse while he was gone, he still agrees to move back in with the other two. When I pointed out that the stakes were enormous in the British series, and that's what made it work, my agent and the Warner people expressed shock that I would consider such a plot for U.S. television. Without that element, I said, there was no point in doing a series. It would have no bite.

That was not the end of the matter, though. The craftsmanship of the two writers, Dick Clement and Ian LaFrenais, had so impressed me that I asked my agent if he could contact them for me. At that time I was represented by the William Morris Agency, a global organization that without too much difficulty should have been capable of finding two writers in London. Weeks went by. Every time I asked about the writers, the ten-percenters assured me they were "working on it." Finally, I grew impatient, called London myself, and quickly found the writers (who, by the way, were represented by the London office of William Morris). By happy coincidence, they were just then heading for the United States, and I asked them to bring other samples of their writing. They were brilliant writers, and we had wonderful meetings. They brought along *Porridge, The Likely Lads, Whatever Happened to the Likely Lads?* and *Man About the House,* to name a few. We hit it off so well that we decided to produce an American version of their hit series *Porridge* for ABC, called *On the Rocks.*

I was happy to offer a full partnership to these talented men, who were accustomed to working for the penurious BBC. They were deliriously happy about the compensation but surprised that we had to deliver as many as twenty-four episodes in the first year. Writers in Britain, though not paid all that well, have the power to provide only as many installments of a series as they choose. Fortunately, they could borrow heavily from plots they had already written in England. "Nothing is ever wasted," was their motto.

The two also had some difficulty adapting to the bowdlerized requirements of American television, and the strictures imposed on them by Standards and Practices, that corporate euphemism for censorship. Ian LaFrenais, in particular, frequently groused about the restrictions; "We're producing a prison show," he said, "with all the gritty realism of *Hogan's Heroes.*" Week after week, we received memos dictating largely subjective comments that usually served to weaken something funny the two had written. After a while, I noticed that they were beginning to censor themselves as they wrote, and some of their scripts began to lose bite.

Network executives continue to fascinate me, and our dilemma with *On the Rocks* gave me a delightful chance to watch one up close. ABC had assigned the young suit Michael Eisner to "cover" our show for the network. One day, when Eisner dropped into my office, I complained to him that the ABC standards police were hurting the show, and my writers were beginning to shackle themselves. Eisner's response was, "Do not self-censor, let me fight your battles." He delivered this speech in such a florid tone as he was leaving—and I knew there was nothing he could do or even attempt to do about the censor—that I asked my secretary to have the words made up into a small sign. The sign was printed in Gothic lettering to match the orotund sound of the utterance and identified the author: "Michael Eisner, May 28, 1975." I had it framed and placed on my desk where it could be enjoyed by all.

Months later, Eisner visited me again, viewed the placard, and said, "Did I say that?" When he left, I ordered another sign quoting the latest statement, and dated it "Michael Eisner, Dec. 10, 1975." This was displayed next to the original work, which caused Eisner to say—on March 22, 1976—"I'm not talking. Every time I say something you make up a sign." Of course, I had that one printed too, and after seeing the three signs together he avoided coming to my office. After that, anytime we needed to conduct business, we met on his turf.

During the first season of *On the Rocks*, Fred Silverman, who was then program chief at ABC, was a big supporter of our series as well as *Barney Miller*, since both programs were earning rating shares in the high thirties. (I was particularly proud of these two shows because I had sold Fred Pearce, ABC's president, on the idea of broadcasting the two series back to back: "An hour of cops and robbers," I had suggested, and Mr. Pearce bought it.) Mr. Silverman was devoted to the Nielsen numbers, and he would call, at times in the middle of the night when I was editing, to announce another ratings coup. We enjoyed a mutually friendly relationship, until we neared the end of the first season, when the lead actor of our show began to make my job harder.

I was forced into late-night editing sessions because the star, Jose Perez, thought he was doing a dramatic series and tried to turn every comic line into a speech loaded with social meaning.

When we had started casting the series, I had seen Jose in a production of *Steambath,* and I thought his Puerto Rican character would serve us well in the lead role. He was terrific in the pilot, perhaps because we had more time to rehearse, so Jose could memorize his part with a sense of confidence and security. However, our weekly schedule was far tighter, and Perez frequently had to carry the exposition with long, sometimes florid, speeches. In the original series *Porridge*, Clement and LaFrenais invested all their characters with a stylized form of elevated speech, even though they were small-time felons. The leader of the British group, Ronny Barker, and his fellow miscreants spoke with cockney accents but always made high-flown word choices.

We wanted to translate this notion to the American version by aiming for a Damon Runyon kind of elegance in the dialogue, with the inmates speaking "above" their expected stations, regardless of color, ethnicity, or poverty-stricken origins.

Fortunately, we were blessed with an outstanding supporting cast, all of whom understood comedy. Hal Williams, Rick Hurst, and Bobby Sandler played petty-thief inmates to perfection, and Mel Stewart and Tom Poston delivered marvelous performances as minimum security guards. But as time went on, our lead actor began to object to the highfalutin language being written for him, finding his lines difficult, and he began to demand simpler dialogue. Increasingly, Perez could not keep up, and out of necessity we began giving some of his long speeches to the other players. After taping our performance, when the audience had left the studio, I wound up doing pickup after pickup to maintain the correct flavor of the dialogue. I spent untold numbers of hours in editing, splicing Perez into the episodes week after week. As the series gained popularity, Jose began telling everyone how "things would be different next year," how he was going to assume more control. Evidently, he enjoyed watching his performance in the episodes as much as the audience did, but he had no idea how much labor it took to patch those performances together. My partners and I were certain we would get renewed for another season, but we became more and more convinced that continuing to deal with a militant Perez would make the game not worth the candle.

Accordingly, I approached Fred Silverman and advised him of our problem. We would certainly appreciate getting picked up for a new season, I explained, but we would only accept the order if we could replace Jose. Silverman, of course, had seen no difficulties at all because the show we delivered was first rate. His reaction was no surprise: "Are you mad? Change the star of a hit series?" I argued that we were doing a gang comedy with a very talented group of players, and we could continue happily with any number of performers who could deliver rapid-fire comedic exposition. Silverman was quiet, but promised to think it over.

I hated to do this to Fred—I knew he was counting on us to continue—but I made it clear that the production team would not show up if we were forced to continue suffering Perez's ambition to take control and ruin the show. Fred didn't believe for a moment that we would turn down another year. But when he proposed giving us another season only if we continued with Jose, we passed on the offer. The writers and I had other fish to fry, but I have always felt particularly sad about the wonderful supporting cast that lost out because of one misguided actor and a network executive who didn't understand the dynamics of making our series a long-lasting hit.

Five years later, in 1980, I crossed paths with Fred Silverman again in Hawaii. I had been hired by Witt-Thomas Productions to be executive producer and director for the series *Benson* for ABC, but before we could begin production, we were hit by an occurrence of what I call "the annual writers' and actors' strike." In its entire seventy-year history, the Directors Guild has called one strike, which lasted literally fifteen minutes before getting settled. Actors and writers are clearly a different breed, striking often and lengthily. In any event, during the strike of 1980, I took my family to Hawaii, telling my office to reach me the minute the strike was over.

One day, while I was sunbathing at the Kahala Hilton pool, a momentary eclipse turned my day into night. I opened my eyes and found Fred Silverman standing in front of me, casting a large shadow and nervously fingering a cigarette. I said hello, closed my eyes again, and half-heard Fred make some comment that didn't completely register in my consciousness. Whatever the remark was, it caused some of our friends nearby to laugh, and Fred said, "I got you pretty good just now."

I opened my eyes once more and asked, "Are you trying to play insult comedy with me? Don't try it, because I'll get you back with interest." Fred was also suffering from the industry strike, since as the head of programming at NBC he had ordered into production several major failures, not the least of which was an excruciatingly expensive bomb called *The Train*. At poolside, Fred responded to my warning by remarking, "I'm not worried about you. You're not doing anything at NBC." I shot back instantly: "Neither are you!"

Silverman gasped audibly, and said, "Okay, you win."

Sometimes it's good to be an independent producer.

In the two years I stayed with *Benson*—working for two successful producers who had given me lots of work, Tony Thomas (who is

Marlo's brother and Danny's son) and his partner, Paul Junger Witt—
I sometimes noticed that our star, Robert Guillaume, had a lot of
pressure weighing on him. As a black actor in a starring role, Bob was
often pushed by leaders of the African American community to avoid
stereotypical behavior. This was more push than was necessary, because
Bob's own persona demanded that he portray Benson in the most dig-
nified manner possible. His character was clearly the brightest person
on stage, and he would bring this out with great humor and intellectual
awareness. Still, I had the impression that certain voices were forcing
upon him more baggage than they needed to, because at times he would
become irascible and difficult. Sometimes he would lose his cool over
apparently insignificant details.

For example, one day while we were rehearsing a breakfast scene,
Bob balefully regarded the plate of food set before him and went into a
profound sulk. When I asked what was troubling him, he replied, "You
should know." I was bewildered. Was there something wrong with the
food? I checked with the property master, who said he had served what
the script had described. I reviewed the text, and realized that I had
scarcely noticed the stage direction calling for Benson to eat pancakes.
This seemed innocent at first blush, but I thought deeply about the situation while our star repaired to his dressing room to compose himself.

Suddenly, I had a hunch. I asked Bob, "Does this have anything
to do with Aunt Jemima or Black Sambo?" Bingo. He shouted, "Right!
It's those writers—they should know better!" Quietly, I said, "Bob, can
we fix you some eggs? There's no story point hanging on pancakes." He
nodded okay, but continued to sputter, "Those guys are writing from a
racist point of view. It's got to stop." I managed to calm him down, we
served him scrambled eggs, and the rehearsal continued. But it was a
serious lesson in how the most innocent-seeming prop can disrupt the
performance of a sensitive man who is carrying a banner in his head for
an entire embattled people. I felt supremely sorry for this intense actor
who, during the course of a long series, had to fight demons most of us
never had to encounter.

CHAPTER
11

There is an old joke that was popular some years ago, and it still earns chuckles every time it's told. It seems the Devil has approached a talent agent and offered him the deal of a lifetime. For the next five years, every one of his actor and actress clients will win Academy Awards, every writer and director on his list will win in their respective categories, and every producer he represents will be guaranteed to win Oscars for Best Picture. In return, Satan tells the agent, he must pledge his immortal soul, and the immortal soul of his wife and four children, for eternity. The agent thinks for a moment, then asks, "What's the catch?"

Needless to say, some talent representatives are better than others. In 1985, I was fortunate to have Leonard Hanzer in my corner. Hanzer was a no-nonsense, take-no-prisoners kind of agent. He was short and overweight when I knew him, but he had been a paratrooper and a major in the Army, and in his physical prime he must have been a terror. He named his company Major Talents Agency, at once bestowing a kind of exclusivity on his clients, some of whom may have known nothing about his military rank but enjoyed the implication anyway.

One day, Leonard introduced me to Henry Winkler, another one of his clients, who had been the breakout star of Garry Marshall's long running series *Happy Days*. Hanzer explained that although Henry was a famous actor, he had ambitions to become a producer and director. Leonard revealed that ABC had made a deal guaranteeing two pilots to be made by Winkler's company, Fair Dinkum Productions. My company, John Rich Productions, had made a similar two-pilot commitment. Hanzer suggested that the two of us form a new entity, at which time he could sell our package to Paramount Pictures for a significant sum. The studio would function as our "bank" as we developed new television series, financing any product we would bring to them. Offices, staff, and studio support would be provided for us. Leonard felt that the synergy of Winkler-Rich Productions would work handsomely for us as well as for the studio that backed us, and his instincts proved sound.

Because Henry had the greater name recognition, he would get a larger share of Paramount's advance payment than I would. But once we started production, because of my experience, my fees would be higher, on the assumption that Winkler would learn from me some of the complexities associated with executive-producing and directing. Like the agent in the joke, neither one of us could see a downside, so we formed a partnership that did well from its inception. In our first full season, we made two pilots for Paramount and, miraculously, both sold. One was a half-hour situation comedy named *Mr. Sunshine,* the other a full-hour adventure series titled *MacGyver.*

With respect to the half-hour show, through long experience one learns that the basics of situation-comedy writing demand that the series's protagonist have a problem. He can be trapped in an unsatisfactory job, he can be in deep financial trouble, he can endure a difficult sexual relationship—as long as he has some sort of pressure to try to overcome. After much discussion, we decided to give our lead character in *Mr. Sunshine* an enormous problem: He would be blind. We would also make him a distinguished university professor, so we could avoid the sin of writing down to our audience; we felt it was time to give our viewers some real meat to chew on. These requirements, however, proved beyond the reach of most writers to whom we spoke. We commissioned several pilot scripts, but none came close to fitting the bill. We had a commitment from the network if we delivered by a certain date, but we were so disappointed by the poor scripts that Henry and I decided to pass on that pilot season. No studio likes to adopt this generally dangerous position, believing (usually correctly) that scheduling the proverbial bird in the hand is better than chancing a total wipeout six months down the line. But we didn't want a weak maiden effort, and Paramount executive Richard Weston helpfully agreed to take the risk, supporting us completely in our desire to get it right.

The finest comedy writer in town, David Lloyd, was working so consistently that it was difficult at first even to arrange a meeting with him. We finally did, and even though he didn't say much as we outlined our ideas for the series, I thought I detected in his eyes a glimmer of interest. He is so quick, so bright, and so well read, I felt that the challenge probably intrigued him, particularly the numerous writing roadblocks we were tossing his way. Although David left the meeting having indicated some interest, he had made no commitment. A short time later, to our immense relief, he called and accepted the offer to write a pilot. Within a week, this incredible man delivered a script that was so well crafted, I couldn't wait to get started. Among other attributes, he had endowed our blind professor with an acerbic, don't-pity-me attitude, which kept the situation from falling into a vat of treacle. It was a brilliant stroke. In addition, he had created a cadre of supporting characters who would be terrific if we could find the right people to play the parts.

While I had not yet formed a strong opinion as to what the lead actor should look like, I was certain it was not the bald, full-bearded applicant who came in to read one day. Just out of courtesy, I asked him to read the part aloud. After hearing him attack several speeches, I sat bolt upright and realized we had found our man. Jeffrey Tambor hit every note perfectly and never disappointed us in any of his performances. In fairly short order we found three magnificent women—Barbara Babcock, Nan Martin, and Ceci. Hart—to fill important parts, and their contributions did much to sell the pilot. ABC gave us a thirteen-week on-the-air commitment.

Even though David Lloyd had agreed to stay with our show as long as it ran, we needed other help, and we were extremely fortunate to secure the services of Gene Reynolds as executive producer in charge of the writing staff. Gene had been the producer of *M*A*S*H* during its long run, and he supervised the scribes while I was in charge of production and direction. Reynolds soon added Peter Noah, a young playwright, and Bob Ellison to the group. Barry Kemp, the well-known producer of *Newhart* and *Coach*, has called Ellison "the funniest man in town," and I heartily agree, even though I have played pigeon to some of his antics over the years. In 1993, when the Directors Guild honored me with the Robert Aldrich Award, Bob wrote me a note: "The DGA is giving you an award, and Roman Polanski has to live in exile." (You could almost hear him sigh at the injustice.) David Lloyd was no slouch either when it came to tossing off a quip, particularly if it contained a touch of gallows humor. One time, as he was being wheeled into the operating room for minor surgery, a nurse checked his identification bracelet and asked, "Are you David Lloyd?" He nodded yes. She said, "And do you spell Lloyd with two Ls?" "Yes," David replied, "but I'm here to have one of them removed."

In the same year that *Mr. Sunshine* was accepted, Paramount, Winkler, and I also sold *MacGyver* to ABC. With an hour and a half on network television, we were now, in the words of our attorney Skip Brittenham, "players." Our dual triumph didn't last long. Although *Mr. Sunshine* was achieving moderately good ratings, which were on the rise, the network began to get cold feet. Even though we never went for the cheap blind-man laugh, some of the affiliates apparently felt uncomfortable about presenting a show about a sightless English teacher. Was the material too elevated for most of the country, or was the blindness a genuine concern? We never found out; we simply didn't get renewed for more episodes. It was a great disappointment for us all.

With *MacGyver*, which was in development at the same time as *Mr. Sunshine*, Henry and I knew we had a potentially workable adventure series, but we realized everything depended on casting. During our search for the lead character, every audition seemed to produce hulking actors who sported, in Winkler's observation, "huge belt buckles" along with their Western accents. Disappointing.

One day a tall, good-looking, athletically built actor showed up to audition. He stumbled in reading some of the lines, stopped, and asked if we would mind if he put on his glasses. As he produced a pair of half-lens "granny glasses," we looked at each other hopefully. This honest display of a slight vulnerability was a terrific plus, in our view, and his reading didn't disappoint us. Richard Dean Anderson did everything we demanded of him in the course of shooting almost 150 episodes, and added significant humanity to every scene in which he appeared. Nothing we could invent would slow him down. Immersed in water, buried under snow, hanging by his fingertips from a cliff—he was always cheerful, pleasant, and successful in anything he attempted on the show, with one exception: comedy.

One night, once the series was well established, I was viewing the dailies of the previous day's work when I was stunned to see Richard attacking a scene with the clear intention of getting a laugh. The director on that episode was one of my favorites, a man with a wonderful disposition and great talent as an action director named Charles Correll, Jr. I was certain that Charley had permitted Anderson's sketchy leap into comedy, so I asked the director to join me the next day during a break. Over the years I have learned never to underestimate the usefulness of lousy past experiences, because you never know when the lessons of your darker days might come in handy. With Charley, I began by telling him about my ill-fated attempt, after graduating from Michigan, to take up a career in carpentry with my dad. My father was an expert craftsman, I told him, who could drive ten-penny nails with a few strokes of his hammer using either hand. His strength was awesome. The result, I went on, is that to this day I am a textbook example of reaction formation: I cannot saw a straight line, cannot pick up a piece of lumber without injuring myself, cannot change a light bulb without calling an electrician. Charley wondered what I was driving at.

I reminded him that his father, Charles Correll Sr., had played Andy on the *Amos and Andy* radio show. "Your dad was acknowledged to be a comic genius," I said, "one of the most famous comedy performers of the twentieth century." Charley looked puzzled. I said, "Charley, the point is, certain traits skip a generation. My children are good with tools. Maybe your kids can handle comedy." Charley laughed appreciatively, and he and Richard Dean played it straight from then on.

All that came later, though, long after the series narrowly escaped a premature death. Authorized to deliver a ninety-minute drama to ABC, Winkler and I hired Lee David Zlotoff to write the pilot script and Gerald Freedman to direct. Freedman shot the pilot in Utah, and he delivered some stunning camera angles and pictures shot around the town of Moab. We saw spectacular stunts and exciting action footage in the dailies, so we felt Freedman was using the $2 million budget effectively. We couldn't wait to see his director's cut assembly, and on the appointed day, we gathered in a Paramount projection room to view our mutual creation.

When the lights came up, there was the usual heavy silence that blankets a room when a bomb has just been screened. Breaking the gloom, my first words were, "What's the playing time of this cut?" I was hoping to hear that the show was running extremely long—it certainly played that way—which would permit the slashing of some numbingly boring indoor sequences. The answer was shocking: "The episode is exactly on time."

I turned to our director and asked, "Are you intending to reshape some of this cut?"

"No," he replied casually, "I think it's perfect." With that, he walked out of the room, appearing (I thought) somewhat smug. When everyone else departed, Henry and I were left alone to consider the screening's miserable outcome. Time was running out and we owed the network a look, but there was no way we would attach our names to this abomination. Still, there was nothing to do but show the film to our studio and the network and tell everybody exactly how we felt.

When Winkler and I presented this dreary cut to ABC's executive staff, they reacted as dismally as we had expected. "Look," I offered, "I think we were blindsided by spectacular outdoor footage in the dailies but thought some of the dull interior scenes could be spruced up in editing. Unhappily, there's not enough footage to allow this. However, Henry and I feel that Richard Dean Anderson is, potentially, a break-out star. I know it's a lot to ask when you've expected ninety minutes, but we both feel there is a wonderful sixty-minute show hidden in this material."

I am forever indebted to Ann Daniels, chief of long-form programming for ABC, who could grant or deny my appeal, as well as Henry, who acted as an outstanding salesman in convincing the network to go along. Henry was eloquent in getting Ann on board, and she bravely gave us the okay to proceed, provided the film could be delivered within ten days—a formidable task. Instead of spending an Easter holiday with my family in Palm Springs as planned, I headed for the cutting room.

I attacked the film with ruthless energy, throwing away indoor scenes that dragged and allowing our hero to work his way out of one perilous situation after another. By judicious trimming, we also took out lengthy internal pauses, adding life to sequences that had seemed to run endlessly. I spent many days standing over a hot Movieola with my editor. To my surprise, we were visited on several occasions by the president of Paramount's television division, Mel Harris, who would pop in anxiously and ask how we were doing. I tried to reassure him, but I knew a lot of studio money was at risk, so his calm demeanor impressed me. Though justifiably worried about our eleventh-hour gamble, he remained cheerful and supportive.

I am happy to report we did not disappoint him. When we delivered the film to ABC, the network was ecstatic. The episode moved at breakneck speed, and we were given a thirteen-week commitment that eventually stretched to almost eight years.

The pilot did not please everyone, however. Its writer, Lee David Zlotoff, and director, Gerald Freedman, were both so horrified at the "butchery" I had inflicted on their work that they demanded their names be removed from the credit list. According to Writers Guild protocol, Zlotoff was allowed to make up a fictitious name to substitute for his own. Freedman, on the other hand, was required to petition the Directors Guild in order to use its standard pseudonym, used whenever foul play had allegedly undermined the director's intent. This moniker was the infamous "Allen Smithee."

A bit of historical background: Since its inception in 1936, the Screen Directors Guild's by-laws had stated that whenever work on a film was completed, for better or worse, the director was compelled to accept screen credit. The Guild's founders felt this would prevent tampering with legitimate credits, and so directors lived with this requirement until sometime in the 1960s. By that year, more and more directors were complaining to the Guild and petitioning its board to allow them to employ a pseudonym. Members indicated that studios and networks were increasingly interfering with the creative process by forcing rewrites or reshoots, or indulging in reediting that violated the director's vision for his or her film. We all felt—and I still subscribe to this idea—that the director has a right to complain, and to try to seek redress if his work has been unduly savaged. This would hold true even if one could make an objective case that the alterations had actually improved the movie or TV episode. What counted was the director's intention, and this argument began to gain weight in our deliberations.

Rather than following the Writers Guild formula, discussion around our council table led to the notion that a single pseudonym, used in each occurrence no matter who the aggrieved director was, would send a message to the industry that our director had felt abused by outside interference. As we searched for an appropriate name, I recall reminding everyone that the legitimate theater had used this practice for many years. When an actor is "doubling," or appearing in such a small role that he prefers anonymity, it is common to read in the playbill the notation "played by George Spelvin." Some women who appeared in pornographic films later expanded on this, choosing to hide behind the credit "Georgina Spelvin."

Someone at the table—possibly a member who had signed several hotel ledgers anonymously—suggested that our pseudonym use the name Smith. This was promptly shot down, on the grounds that we already had directors named Smith and more were likely to join in the future. Another member said, "Why not spell the name 'Smyth' and pronounce it that way?" I spoke up and said I thought that too might come confusingly close to real members' names; I have a friend who is a director, for example, named Jack Smight.

Another member said, "Let's go back to Smith, but add an *e* to make it Smithe." I said, "It's still pronounced 'Smith.' But if you love the name Smith so much, why not add two *e*'s and make it 'Smithee.'" I was somewhat surprised to have my idea adopted instantly, with the addition of Allen as first name—sometimes spelled "Alan."

This pseudonym-by-consensus served our guild for many years, until a writer named Joe Eszterhas came up with a script entitled *An Allen Smithee Film*. Eric Idle played the title role, and Arthur Hiller directed the production. Ironically, when Arthur and the writer subsequently fell into a dispute, Mr. Hiller petitioned our council to use the pseudonym, and that's how the film was released—*An Allen Smithee Film* carried the credit "Directed by Allen Smithee."

After this madness, the board decided "Smithee" must go, and a new scheme is being invented even as I write this.

Getting back to the objections over the *MacGyver* pilot, I was present at the DGA Western Council meeting when Gerald Freedman, the disappointed director, made his appearance. As a member of the Council I did not think it proper for me to vote on Freedman's request, and so I recused myself. However, one of the requirements for allowing a petitioner to use this credit is acquiescence by the producer or company representative of the movie in question. As one of the executive producers, I was authorized by Paramount to decide our collective response, and I was happy to approve the waiver request. After the board voted to grant the pseudonymous credit, I asked Freedman, and later Zlotoff, that since the pilot had so badly damaged their reputations, were they also refusing to accept residual and royalty payments that might become payable in the future? Both abandoned their highly principled positions, swallowed their distaste for my insensitive editing, and vehemently refused to give up their monetary participation.

While working on *MacGyver*, we found ourselves on the cutting edge of some changes in production that, for better or worse, have since become commonplace in the industry: electronic editing and the boom in production migrating north to Canada. The first development was, without a doubt, a great leap forward. This came about for us after ABC declined to renew *Mr. Sunshine*. The upside of that disappointment was that I could then devote more time to *MacGyver*, especially since Henry had told me that series was running into the problem of late delivery.

When I visited the cutting rooms, I was dismayed to find at least four teams of editors working overtime just to make air date. They were still cutting in the time-honored fashion, using Movieolas, scissors, and paste to put together each picture. Not only was the work creeping along at a disastrously slow pace, but some of the cutters were at sea, with no guiding hand to keep them in line with the basic concept of the series. Each editor was left to his or her own devices; there was no unifying thread to keep the series on track. Jerry Ludwig, our producer, was so occupied with turning out scripts that he couldn't pay much attention to postproduction. And Henry tried valiantly to help by viewing and commenting on rough cuts, but his limited experience at the time prevented him from taking complete charge. It became clear to me that we were falling so far behind in preparing episodes for delivery to the network that we needed to take drastic action.

I had heard, vaguely, that some companies were using a form of electronic editing, and this led me to Modern Video, a company controlled by an entrepreneur named Moshe Barkat. At his plant, I was shown the Montage system of editing, which linked twenty-eight Beta video recorders to a computerized control board. Once film dailies were loaded into this system, an editor could call up the images at a central location, then edit them electronically (or, more accurately, store them in the computer until calling them back for final assembly). No Movieola, no paste, no scissors. An editor could make trial "cuts" instantaneously, since no literal cuts were ever made. If something didn't work electronically, no one had wasted time scissoring film, glueing the pieces together, and looking at them in a projection room. The press of a button instantly called up the trial edit. Today this all seems commonplace, but back then it was a real breakthrough.

I contacted Paramount executives, who called in their editorial department at my request. They were instantly suspicious, claiming the new techniques would never work—there weren't enough cutters qualified to run the machines. Besides, they argued, how would you prepare a final negative cut to send out to the world? Their objections all had relatively easy answers. There were many qualified editors already working on television productions, and if more were needed, a few weeks in a class would sufficiently train any veteran cutter to run the computer keyboard. As for how to ship a final print, I pointed out that networks transfered all motion pictures to videotape before transmission. Why couldn't we eliminate the middle step and never provide a cut film, but instead send the assembled videotape itself to the broadcaster, all of whom had the correct playback machines? My proposal would save endless hours of cutting time, recoup a small fortune in labor costs, and—most important—guarantee weekly delivery of each episode.

The bottom-line people saw the wisdom of the innovation, and from then on *MacGyver* was edited in this fashion, with me superivising the process at Modern Video. In the seven-year life of the series, we never missed an air date.

After filming *MacGyver* in California for its first two seasons, we moved the headquarters of the production to Vancouver, British Columbia, where Henry and I were fortunate to have Steve Downing as our executive producer. Downing had been deputy chief of police in Los Angeles, and had worked as an adviser to Jack Webb's *Dragnet* before deciding he could write better detective stories himself than those submitted. He used this talent on *MacGyver* to maintain the quality of the writing on location. Moreover, his administrative and people skills were outstanding, and he brought together an outstanding team that operated harmoniously, efficiently, and with good humor. His able assistants included Mike Greenburg, as supervising producer, and John Moranville, who took charge of dubbing and postproduction facilities. After two years, we moved the entire editing process to Canada, where we enjoyed further savings.

Today, our industry is suffering because of "runaway productions" shooting in Canada, aka "Hollywood North," and it's become a serious problem for every craft and guild that services the film world. When Henry and I decided to move *MacGyver* out of state in 1987, it was almost out of desperation; we had run out of "scope" in the Los Angeles area. We needed urgently to expand our ability to shoot colorful locations, since *MacGyver* relied on a different venue every week. But when making the move, we insisted that American crews staff all key departments, including cinematography, assistant directors, editors, stunt supervisors, and a host of others. This provision resulted in many inflated budgets because we had to provide union pay, hotel accommodations, per diem, and so forth. But we were pleased to do it because we had imported the best technical help one could find anywhere. Now, though, unhappily for our industry, our terrific L.A. staffs are no longer welcome "up there," as Canadians have learned how to service Hollywood productions almost too well. In addition, the dollar exchange rate is so favorable to visiting companies, and there are so many provincial tax breaks, that many studios insist on using northern locations despite their desire to maintain a local industry. In recent years, six productions supposedly set in New Orleans have been shot in Canada!

To fight the scourge of runaway production, the directors Taylor Hackford and Paris Barclay have worked tirelessly and some years ago formed a political action committee to address the problem. After learning they could not legally use union funds for this purpose, Taylor and Paris began contacting interested directors and their assistants. With a pledge of $1,200 a year from each member, a Leadership Council was formed to make campaign contributions to various senators and representatives and to invite them to educational lunches. Many legislators, regardless of party affiliation, have attended these meetings; on occasion, for example, more than forty council members articulated the Guild's point of view to Speaker of the House Dennis Hastert, an Illinois Republican who was shocked to discover that the award-winning picture *Chicago* was filmed outside of the country. When the PAC was started, we were prepared to be patient. Recently, however, we were surprised and delighted to see Congress pass legislation favorable to the American film industry in 2005. To date we have entertained lawmakers from Ted Kennedy and Hillary Clinton to Orrin Hatch and David Dreier, discussing a host of issues, including film piracy and copyright protection, from the creators' point of view.

People frequently ask me how we came up with "MacGyverisms," those cleverly improvised mechanisms that enabled Richard Dean Anderson to escape danger week after week—and that, indeed, became synonymous with his character. Some of them sprung from the fertile imaginations of some of our writers. Others, including one I'm particularly fond of, came through the mail.

We had offered monetary incentives to anyone who could write in a usable trick for MacGyver, and even though we had a dedicated staff reading every letter, very few useful suggestions came along. One day, however, I passed the stack of mail being sorted, and out of curiosity plucked out one envelope from the pile. A young fan had written that if MacGyver ever found himself trying to drive a vehicle that had lost all its water through leaks in the cooling system, he could temporarily solve the problem by cracking an egg into the radiator. As it cooked, the egg would harden and plug the hole, allowing the car to start and run for a short time. We tried it, found that it worked, constructed an episode around the trick, and happily paid our devoted viewer for the tip.

Another time, a freelance writer came up with a situation in which a time bomb had been placed in a U.S. Postal Service truck parked near a construction site. According to the script, MacGyver would disarm the device by using a rotating concrete truck to fill the vehicle, rendering the bomb harmless. The question was, how to fill a truck with concrete without having it solidify and destroy a perfectly useful truck. As Morey Amsterdam used to say, we "racked our brains to the white meat" trying to find a substitute for concrete that would look like and pour like, but not set up and harden like, the real thing. Finally, after much research, we decided to use—concrete!

I had often wondered what would happen to a load of the stuff if, on the way to the workplace, a mechanical malfunction caused the huge machine to stop rotating. Would it harden and render the truck forever useless? Posing this question to a concrete delivery company, we learned that the answer was low-tech simple. Apparently, every driver routinely carried a five- or ten-pound container of sugar in the cab of his truck. If a breakdown occurred, he would toss the sugar into the mixture and a chemical reaction would take place to prevent hardening.

Sure enough, when filming the episode, we used real concrete, after dosing the mixture with a healthy shot of the granulated sweet stuff. After pouring in enough to completely cover the bomb, MacGyver stopped the explosion. When the sequence was completed, our crew hosed out the vehicle, causing no damage at all.

It would be remiss to suggest that everything always went smoothly during production of *MacGyver*. There were gaffes and miscues and inaccurate details, as come up in virtually any production at one time or another. I saw this happen time and time again throughout my career.

To direct successfully, I believe, a director should read avidly and observe intensely. I remember, years ago, almost driving an actor crazy when I called "Cut" because of the way he was blessing himself in a church scene. When he asked why I had stopped the action, I said, "You crossed yourself incorrectly. The vertical part was correct, but then you touched your left side first."

Incredulous, he stared at me as if I had lost my mind, and informed me, tight-lipped, "I have been a Roman Catholic all my life. I think I know how to make the sign of the cross."

"The scene we're shooting takes place in a Russian Orthodox Church," I replied, "where the right side of the body is touched first." How did I know that, he asked. I answered truthfully, "From watching Russian movies."

When we were shooting *Wives and Lovers*, my first feature film, in 1963, the back lot of Paramount studios had been transformed into a Broadway street for the opening of a play written by the protagonist, played by Van Johnson. I had ordered a high crane to take in the full expanse of the

New York location at night, and peopled it with well-dressed extras. (This was 1963, when people still dressed appropriately to attend the theater.) We had Yellow Cabs, uniformed NYPD patrolmen, mounted police, and all of the proper "dressing" to simulate a gala opening night. At the left of the camera shot, the theater itself was featured, well lit with an impressive marquee announcing the name of the production as well as "Opening tonight, a new play by William Joseph Austin," the name of Van Johnson's character. I rode the crane to its proper elevation. The street looked spectacularly real, with an authentic Manhattan look.

Yet something bothered me. It's a feeling I can only describe as the way it feels to have a speck of dirt in one's eye—not gravely serious but too irritating to ignore. Something in the shot was out of order. Looking through the camera lens, I began a slow visual scan, quadrant by quadrant, taking more time than I could really afford and still stay on schedule. I read the long side of the theater marquee: "A new play by William Joseph Austin." The short side also seemed fine until I suddenly noticed: "A new play by William *Howard* Austin." I dismounted from the crane and asked the art director to check the signage. Neither of us could figure how the error happened, but a quick correction removed the grit from my eye and kept the glitch from enduring on film forever.

Once I even caught a mistake like that on a film set I had nothing to do with. One day, I happened to drive by Twentieth Century Fox studios, where a superexpensive set of an 1890s New York street had been constructed for the film *Hello Dolly.* This set was so elaborate it featured an elevated railway and numerous period buildings and so massive it could easily be seen as one drove by on Pico Boulevard. To conceal the modern buildings and stages located behind the false street, crews had erected a large billboard at its far end, advertising "Heinz Catsup."

When I reached my office at Paramount, I telephoned Fox and asked to speak to the art director who had created the *Dolly* set. I asked him if he was aware that the Heinz company never made "catsup"; they had always labeled their product "ketchup." (I had noticed, when I moved to California in the 1950s, that Hunt's Catsup seemed to be the favorite local condiment, and I guessed the designer was himself a product of the West Coast.) In any event, someone double-checked, the sign was repainted, and I spared my unknown friend some serious embarrassment.

When reading any sign created for a film, I think it's important to mentally spell out every word and make sure you're not being fooled by the phenomenon of gestalt perception. Once on a studio location, the art department had furnished a sign reading "Medical Bulding." If one reads too quickly, the brain misreads the second word as *building*. Look back to the last sentence; *bulding* has no letter i. Every time I call one of these slips to the attention of a studio artist, he first says, "What's wrong with this? The spelling looks all right to me?" They're always amazed to realize what they inadvertently left out.

Sometimes no one catches the blooper until it's too late. During the 1960s, I was assigned to direct an episode of *Run for Your Life,* starring Ben Gazzara. The producer was cautioning me to carefully scrutinize signs and labels, and he showed me one that slipped through. The scene called for the lead actor to be sitting in a tavern in some Eastern European country, engaged in earnest conversation with an informer. The script referred to a formidable local drink called "Bull's Blood," and a bottle of the stuff sat prominently in the foreground as the two actors drank and carried on a lengthy dialogue. Whenever the "Eastern European" spoke, he used his native tongue, with translated subtitles appearing at the bottom of the screen. It was all very authentic-looking, except for the prop liquor bottle, in sharp foreground focus, with its label reading "Bull's Blood"—in plain English! The illusion of an exotic foreign locale evaporated.

I have not always escaped reprimand from producers who discovered carelessness in my work, and the stinging memory of such rebukes has made me strive, perhaps obsessively, for perfection as I traveled from job to job. One such painful memory goes back to around 1959, when I directed an episode of the detective series *Markham,* starring Ray Milland. A nighttime escape from some "heavies" required the detective to run through dark woods. Shooting at night can be very expensive, so I was ordered to use a process known as "day for night," in which photographic filters create the illusion of darkness even when filming with the sun ablaze. This is not an entirely satisfactory method; real night has a convincing blackness about it that no filters can approximate. Furthermore, television productions that appear too dark for broadcast transmission end up at the mercy of local video technicians, who twist their control knobs to wipe out any semblance of night from exposures that cameramen have taken pains to create. I don't know if it's sardonic, but in the French film industry, "day for night" is known as *la nuit americaine.* In any event, Markham tried to make his escape wearing a light, highly reflective blue shirt, which I had okayed. There was no way he could have escaped notice as he ran, and my producer wasted no time in reaming me out. Even worse, he was right.

Having been on both sides of such encounters, I've found that I'd rather be the producer finding fault than the working stiff trying to do his job under a microscope. I suppose, then, that I could have been more compassionate about one of the men doing second-unit and "insert" work for me during the *MacGyver* years. For those unfamiliar with the term, *inserts* refer to close-up work set aside by the primary crew when they're photographing principal actors. They can be as simple as photographing the face of a watch or a newspaper headline, or as complicated as a second unit supervising the stuntmen taking part in a chase scene. These shots require considerable patience, and it's not economical to have high-salaried performers standing around while the time-consuming inserts are made.

One of our second-unit supervisors on *MacGyver* formed a habit of bringing in footage that had to be reshot, so often that I began to refer to him as "Cimino." This was a form of homage to the director Michael Cimino, who, legendarily, almost brought a studio to its financial knees in running millions of dollars over budget on the motion picture *Heaven's Gate.* Our "Cimino" never came that close to causing bankruptcy, but in terms of a television budget, his constant need for retakes was beginning to give us pause. In one episode, our story found MacGyver attempting to remove an artifact from a museum case when an alarm trips, locking him in a glass enclosure with time and oxygen running out. MacGyver's boss, Pete Thornton, played by Dana Elcar, was in charge of security. Thornton had been called away from the premises, and he had selected the code numbers that could release our hero if only the combination were known. The character Jack Dalton (performed by Bruce McGill) is outside the case with access to the electronic buttons that could lift the glass, but doesn't know the code. After several fruitless pantomime attempts, MacGyver reasons that Thornton could have used his birth date as the code, and he signals this information to Dalton by breathing and writing the numbers in reverse on the fogged glass. His theory works, the buttons are punched, and MacGyver is freed.

It was then left for our insert crew to photograph, in extreme close-up, the digital buttons that permit the escape. When "Cimino" returned with the film he had supervised, the shot read something along the lines of 4–12–34, and I pointed out that digital readouts always employ double numbers; for the month of April, for example, it would read 04–12–34. Since I thought using a zero might be confusing, I advised him to pick a double-digit month, such as October or December. This would call for a 10 or a 12, clear two-digit numerals that wouldn't require the audience to think too much.

Not thinking too much was a hallmark of this person's style. Having shot the retake, he proudly ran the film, showing me the sequence 12–40–34. "Double digits all around," he said. "Just what you ordered, right?" As he left the room, after I had fired him, I still don't think he understood what could possibly be wrong with December 40, 1934.

If it seems harsh to fire a man for such a transgression, it may help to view the situation in the context of his other disasters, not the least of which involved a major stunt in which MacGyver's Jeep had been forced off of a road. As our hero jumped out just in time, the production camera followed the crashing vehicle all the way down the mountainside. The next day, while viewing the dailies, I noticed that the film was abruptly cut just a moment before the Jeep had finished its violent plunge.

"Surely this wasn't shot this way," I said. "Why don't we see the car come to rest?" When I insisted on seeing the entire take, in its precut condition, all became disgustingly clear. When the wreck landed at the bottom of the hill, the Jeep came to a stop and its hood flew open— revealing that the vehicle had no engine!

Rather than reporting the truth, our man had hoped I would overlook the mistake. Instead, we had to reshoot the entire stunt, leaving a significant dent in our budget. "Cimino" was not fired that day, but he came close. I held my temper and gave him more than a dozen chances to redeem himself. On December 40, my patience wore out.

Another production faux pas on *MacGyver* occurred in Vancouver. While watching dailies one night, I was annoyed to find a lapse by the set-decorating department. Our crew had photographed a cargo ship that had just made port after a long ocean voyage, fighting wind, wave, and searing sun. Crates of cargo on deck had been lashed down properly—but they had been built out of brand new wood. I called a meeting and pointed out that such a trip would have aged the boxes considerably, so we needed to paint them in a manner that suggested the crates had been battered by the elements during their time at sea. "Right, chief; gotcha. It won't happen again."

True to their word, in the following episode, which included a burial service, the coffin had been aged to look as though it had weathered an ocean voyage. I sighed, and called another meeting.

Henry Winkler had the gift, or sometimes the curse, of superstardom. He was incredibly popular on the Paramount lot, greeting everyone with a smile and a hearty handshake. Walking with him on the studio street was like trailing behind a small-town mayor running for reelection. As much as I tried to engage him regarding some of our production problems as we walked, it was an impossible task, and any serious talk had to take place in one of our offices. During casting sessions, whenever an actor entered the room to audition, Henry would immediately shake hands with him or her, compelling everyone in the room to do the same. At the close of the reading, he shook hands again, kicking off another round of flesh pressing.

With a director and three producers in attendance, two representatives of the casting department, an occasional writer, and a notetaker, seven or eight people would each stand and ritually shake hands with each hopeful—twice. If we auditioned twenty actors in a session (and sometimes we did more), we were shaking hands almost two hundred times a day! Not only did this waste an inordinate amount of time, but it also helped transmit many colds. Hoping to avoid any hard feelings, I at first made no mention of my growing irritation with this process. In my increasing fear of contamination—especially when an actor punctuated his arrival by sneezing violently—I would beg forgiveness of the applicant by not gripping his hand and indicate that I was suffering from a cold, in hopes that Henry would catch on. He never got the message. Something evidently made an impression, though, because he frequently described me to others as "the most idiosyncratic person" he had ever known.

After listening to a reading, Henry would go into a paroxysm of praise for the performance, gripping the actor in a farewell handshake and expressing how "terrific" his reading had been. After the candidate had left the room, someone would ask Henry, "Did you really think that was a good reading?" His answer was, "No, I thought it wasn't very good." I would follow up with the natural question, "Then why did you praise his reading so effusively?" His reply: "I wanted him to feel good."

Some time later, in a private conversation, I attempted to teach Henry certain standards of behavior an executive producer should adhere to. "The actor," I explained patiently, "feeling considerably pumped up by your congratulatory handshake, is going to call his agent immediately and tell him you loved him so much, he's a cinch to get the part. When he isn't cast, because his reading was below par, two things will happen. First, he will feel far worse, after listening to your praise in the room, than if you had been noncommittal."

"You said two things would happen," Henry said. "What else will?"

I said, "Since there were only two executive producers in the room, that actor is going to say, 'Henry thought I was great—so it must be that other bastard, John Rich, who turned me down!'"

At this time, I also unloaded my feelings about the handshake ritual, but Henry insisted on continuing the practice. We managed to work out a compromise, to the relief of all the other attendees on our side of the auditions: In the waiting room, someone from the casting department would explain to each actor that our group didn't mean to be rude, but in the interest of conserving time, Mr. Winkler would shake hands for all of us.

Henry has all the instincts of a polished politician, which continues to be a great asset for our company. His enthusiasm and generally upbeat attitude when making a sale has stood us in good stead throughout the years. But when people refer to our partnership as "good cop, bad cop," who do you think gets the reputation as the evil one?

When it comes to producers, in contrast to the Sheldon Leonard or Carl Reiner or Norman Lear method of operation, one occasionally runs into the likes of Ed. Weinberger—usually referred to as "E-D period," because that's the way his screen credit reads (ED. Weinberger). I had heard about E-D from shellshocked directors who had worked under him, and some of the stories seemed almost too weird to be true. Apparently he possessed an innovative comic mind, even if his frequent lapses into bizarre behavior kept everyone off balance. He had earned his spurs as a successful writer, coming out out of the Jim Brooks school of writing on *The Mary Tyler Moore Show* and later on the hit series *Taxi*. As a producer, he was evidently less gifted, engaging in off-the-wall antics that often made him difficult to understand, as well as being extremely uncommunicative.

I had heard all these comments before meeting the man, so when Paramount asked me to direct *Dear John*, a Weinberger-produced series that had begun to flounder, I was hesitant to get into the frying pan with a show runner who came with so much negative baggage. But Paramount was my partner in two shows I had on the air at the time, so I accepted the commitment. Since I had my own reputation for being outspoken, people held their collective breath, expecting a clash of personalities. In fact, the arrangement worked productively, and we managed to get along well enough to keep the series going. I enjoyed the pleasure of working with Judd Hirsch, Jere Burns, Isabella Hoffman, Harry Groener, and Jane Carr—a superior cast. E-D was frequently irascible, but as long as his irrational outbursts were directed elsewhere, I didn't mind.

After my stint at *Dear John*, a film series, Weinberger asked me to direct a new pilot called *Honor Bound*, starring Ray Sharkey. This was to be shot on tape, using electronic cameras, and I would direct from a control room. I had heard that E-D would customarily stand behind his director and scream comments during the production, and I asked him if this were so. While he denied screaming, he said that's how he worked. There was no way I could permit this, I told him; his outbursts would be heard throughout our internal communication system and confuse the camera operators. I expected a tirade, but instead he asked mildly where he could watch the show. I said we'd set up a special room for him containing a TV set and a telephone, if he would agree never to ring the control booth while we were taping, but to call only after a scene had been completed; at that time I would be happy to listen to his comments. It surprised me that he accepted this without a murmur of complaint. Once again, we worked together amicably and produced a pilot that sold the series, which was later retitled *Man of the Family.*

In casting the show, Weinberger and I had agreed on a particular actress to play the role of the mother. One day he came to me and said he thought we should engage someone different for the part. I thought about it and said, "If we use the woman you're suggesting, you're going to have to rewrite everything and make the character much tougher."

"It'll be easy," he said. "I'll model her after my own mother."

I was surprised. "Is your mother that difficult?"

"Let me put it this way" he said. "I once took her to visit the Sistine Chapel in Rome, and she said the floor was dirty."

A man doesn't become E-D Weinberger all by himself.

In the early 1990s, I had occasion to work with another famous TV personality when my agent called and asked if I'd like to direct an episode of *Murphy Brown,* starring Candice Bergen. The show had been running for a few years by then, so I wondered, Why me now? The answer was that Candice's husband, the famous director Louis Malle, would be appearing as himself in the episode, and Garry Marshall had been cast as the network president. The idea was to have someone with experience guide these two directors through the performance. I was honored to do the job and had a good time doing it.

Mr. Malle was not available for the first two days of rehearsal, and Candice exhibited some nerves on behalf of her spouse. When he finally arrived, he seemed a bit ill at ease as we began rehearsals but gradually fell comfortably into the part, although our leading lady watched his every move with apprehension.

During one run-through, I noticed that Candice's lips were mouthing Louis's lines as he was saying them. I took her aside, and told her what I had observed. She admitted doing it unconsciously out of concern, but she promised to be on guard. Later, I noticed the same behavior again, and remarked, "It must be genetic. Your father [the great ventriloquist Edgar Bergen] also moved his lips when throwing the voice of his dummy Charley McCarthy." Candice laughed and moved her lips no more.

Sometime after that, against all odds, my turn arrived to stand on the other side of the camera. Ed Sherin, a good friend at the DGA National Board, asked me one day if I'd like to appear on *Law and Order*, the hit show on which Ed was executive producer; he thought I'd make an excellent judge. I demurred, explaining that in all the years I had directed, I had made a point of never appearing on camera. Ed was insistent enough for me to ask how much time it would take. In view of my four or five lines, he said, no more than three days. With this assurance, and with some degree of excitement, I agreed.

A week or so later, an assistant director on the series advised me that Julia Roberts had been signed to play the lead role in that episode, and so the shooting board had been revised to concentrate primarily on her schedule. This meant that my bit was now extended to eight days. The good news was that I was now entitled to receive compensation at "top of the show" and costar billing, which put me in a class with Ms. Roberts. I grumbled a bit but salved my annoyance at being hijacked for extra days by saying to anyone who would listen that Julia Roberts and I were now receiving the top salary available on *Law and Order*. By extension, I was fond of telling my friends, this meant that I could now quote my price for acting as the same as Ms. Roberts's—$20 million a picture! Few who heard this news, however, were impressed.

Among the new group of talented and considerate writer/producers, one must include the names of Judd Pillott and John Peaslee. In the 1990s, I worked for these gentlemen on several episodes of a series called *Something So Right*, starring Jere Burns, whom I had known from our days together on *Dear John*. Not only were Pillott and Peaslee skillful writers, but in their style of producing they demonstrated incredibly nimble footwork. They amazed me constantly in the delicate way they handled network and studio "notes"; they actually listened to some of the nonsense thrown at them. It seems they could always come up with acceptable compromises without giving up the store.

Their most astonishing tap dance occurred one week when the script revolved around Thanksgiving dinner, which was to be served to the visiting parents played by Shirley Jones and Bob Barker, the famous emcee of *The Price Is Right*. The script was intelligent and funny, so I was looking forward to the week's work. It was also a great plus to have both the network and the studio quiet, for once, about the content of the show. After all, I thought, how could anybody object to something as innocuous as Thanksgiving? The answer arrived shortly after the first reading. Mr. Barker, an avid supporter of animal rights, refused to appear in any show featuring the eating of turkey, or any other comedic reference to it (such as one hilarious scene that took place in a butcher shop). Yes, turkey was off the table for Thanksgiving!

When the writing team filled me in on Barker's ultimatum, I expected them to recast the role. Instead, this exceptional team immediately set to work rewriting the entire episode. The butcher shop disappeared, replaced by a completely different but equally funny scene. A vegetarian dinner appeared in place of the reprieved turkey. The visiting players were enthusiastically helpful, and Jere Burns delivered his customarily brilliant performance, giving us one of the best episodes of our series.

I had the privilege of working with these talented writers again in 1999, on a series entitled *Payne,* starring John Larroquette and JoBeth Williams. In my opinion, it was one of the best comedy series I have ever directed, and it deserves to be on the air to this day. Unfortunately, CBS deemed the series too highbrow for its audience. The dumbing-down of America had struck again.

Time for a confession. During my years as a director, I may have displayed outbursts of temper that might have actually frightened some people. Naturally, I have always thought of these alarums and excursions as a result of my perfectionist desire to bring in the best program possible. But I know it's pointless to offer this as an excuse for displays of anger. At this stage of my life, I cannot dispute the perception that, during the last half century, I have stepped on some toes. I have mellowed considerably in my later years, but when I was younger, more than one group regarded me as something of a terror. A psychiatrist once told me, "You have a great ability to draw blood. It's as if you're wearing a sharkskin glove on your hand."

Wow!

While I'm in a public confessional mood, I suppose it's appropriate to relate some old tales. Once, when directing *Benson,* using electronic cameras with an audience in attendance, I had been shooting a scene using a long lens on one of the cameras. Unaware that the camera was positioned far back, a network still photographer unwittingly wandered in front of the shot, ruining the scene. In a rage, I called "Cut!" I demanded to know who had screwed up. Doug Smart, my associate director, said, "It's someone from ABC." I frothed, "ABC is a series of letters! I want a name, I want a face, I want a throat I can choke!"

It was then that Doug came up with the line that he frequently used on me whenever I threatened to slip my tether. He said, "John, it's time to hose out your enclosure." Doug's humor saved me from making things worse, and I always laughed when he uttered those words.

Doug had worked with Lawrence Welk for many years before teaming up with me, and he was a font of stories from those days. Welk always worked "live" and never edited anything after the fact, even if the show had been taped. During one broadcast, the director passed the word that the show was running long. Lawrence would have to make some cuts, so the control room suggested perhaps eliminating one song. Welk approached his lead singer, Johnny, during a commercial and said, in his unique accent, "Chonny, I want you to pee on your toes, because I may have to jerk you off later."

On another occasion, Welk looked at a cue card with the line "A medley of songs from World War I." He announced it on air this way: "And now, a medley of songs from a World War Eye." At Christmastime, Welk was fond of introducing members of his family, starting with a grandson: "Here he is, Lawrence Welk the turd." And on a location shoot for a Midwestern meat-packing company, with his female singer in the audience about to perform a song for the corporation's president, Mr. Welk offered some advice: "Be nice to him, Fern, and he may slip you a nice fat sausage."

After working together on *Benson,* Doug and I also collaborated on the Bob Newhart pilot that featured the actor as the owner of a Vermont inn. Barry Kemp and Sheldon Bull wrote and produced, and it was a great pleasure to direct their excellent script with such a wonderful comedic performer. But we were in for a surprise in the control room. Most of the time, Doug and I had been accustomed to rapid-fire readings that required hundreds of cuts in a half-hour production, which required a constant state of alertness. Newhart's brilliant comic delivery, on the other hand, was so deliberate, so slow, that we could sit on one shot for as long as a minute at a time. In the middle of our on-air taping, I leaned back in my chair, looked at my associate director, and said, "Does this make you think we're stealing the money?"

Unfortunately, Doug Smart had not been there to remind me to hose out my enclosure when I was in rehearsal one day on *All in the Family.* For some reason, Sally Struthers did not respond to the stage manager's call to join the rest of us at the other end of the hall. She continued to sit at the table and read, paying no attention to anybody. I called over, "Sally, we're waiting for you." She was clearly going through some private problem and went on ignoring us. I repeated my invitation for her to join the rest of the cast. As we all waited for some response, she maintained an apparently arrogant disregard of our call to work. This was too much. In frustration, I kicked at a folding chair standing near my podium. I caught it on its bottom rung, and the chair flew through the air and hit the opposite wall. As with a home run ball, I am told that the distance of the flight was later measured, earning me the distinction of having drop-kicked a chair further than anyone had ever done before in a CBS rehearsal room.

I walked to the door and said with as much authority as I could muster, "When you're ready to rehearse, please call me. I will be in my office." With great dignity, I exited the room, slamming the door behind me. Had a camera been stationed in the hallway as I entered that space, it would have caught me grabbing my foot in agony and exhibiting a "pain take" that would have matched any ever performed by Dick Van Dyke or Sid Caesar. Then I limped to my office and called an orthopedist. Rehearsal was over for me that morning.

At the doctor's office, X-ray studies showed no break but a severe strain that required a short plaster cast. When the physician asked how the injury had come about, I told him, and he remarked, "That wasn't too bright. However it's not as bad as the patient I treated one time who put his fist through a door. He could have bled to death if he had sliced the right blood vessels." He shook his head. "Some people are really stupid."

"No kidding," I said. "I did that once." He just stared at me.

After lunch, when I returned to rehearsal, Sally apologized and everyone had a good laugh, including me. We never did find out what was bothering her that day.

Reflecting on the incident, I consoled myself that I had least maintained my dignity by standing at the door of the rehearsal room and delivering my exit speech without revealing that I was in pain. It put me in mind of a story involving the British actor Christopher Lee, who often portrayed Frankenstein's monster in England. He had gone into a tantrum about something and said, to the entire stage, "When you have finally decided that I am correct in this matter, you may call me in my dressing room." Unfortunately, he had delivered this ultimatum while standing in the center of the studio, still in his monster makeup and costume. So when he turned to storm off in a dramatic exit, his lead boots allowed him to take only one clanking step at a time as he made an excruciatingly slow departure.

In an odd coincidence, I received a Golden Globe Award the same week of my injury, and I was compelled to attend the ceremony wearing both a tuxedo and a cast on my right foot. When I rose to accept the honor and limped toward the podium, my dear friend Florence Henderson, who was presenting the award, noticed the plaster-adorned shoeless foot and started to laugh. As the audience applauded, I whispered I would explain later. It was extremely embarrassing to be photographed in this manner, but later I learned to my relief that the director in charge of the national telecast had thoughtfully ordered the cameras to photograph me above the ankles.

During one of my periodic rants, my dear wife, Pat, put me in my place with her ready wit. At a National Board meeting of the DGA in New York, my old friend Arthur Penn asked if I might be interested in directing a theatrical play under the auspices of the Actors Studio in Manhattan. I read the script, *Lighting Up the Two-Year Old* by Benji Aeronson, and liked the writing very much. It was a dark piece, based on the custom of killing racehorses by electrocution in order to defraud insurance companies. This was to be a free-theater exercise, limited to a four-week run, and I was delighted to accept the challenge. It was a labor of love, and I enjoyed every minute of working with Benji and a talented threesome of actors, Robert Hogan, Peter Ashton Wise, and Brad Beyer. One night, I invited Benji, the cast, and their wives, to join my wife and me for dinner at a nearby restaurant. At the start of the evening, one of the wives asked me what plays I had seen since taking up residence in Manhattan some three months earlier.

"None," I answered truthfully, "by design."

Why? she asked.

I said, "Any town that will support *Miss Saigon* for nine years is not a serious theatrical community." I earned a laugh and went on, "Besides, I worked in Manhattan in the early 1950s and I was fortunate enough to see the original *South Pacific*, the original *Guys and Dolls*, the original *My Fair Lady*—"

Unable to resist this down-the-middle-of-the-plate straight line, Pat cut in, adding, "The original *Our American Cousin*"—the play Lincoln was viewing when he was assassinated.

There are times, however, when I think some anger and disappointment are justified. Something I wrote several years ago will help explain what I mean. In 1994, I received a call from someone representing the Society of Stage Directors and Choreographers in New York City. This person wondered if I'd be willing to write a piece for the group's magazine focusing on the demands facing legitimate directors who might consider jumping into the unknown world of television. They were particularly interested in my views about the apparent decline in the quality of TV programming. My first thought was to remember Fred Allen's famous comment on his radio program: "The reason television is called a medium is because nothing is well done." Without sharing the joke, I agreed to the request, and my comments ran in the winter edition of their journal. What I said then still applies today:

What's wrong with televsion today? In my opinion, what's primarily wrong is this business of the daily rewrite—the hourly rewrite, if you will. As directors you will be driven to distraction as some writer or some executive producer/writer arrives on your set bearing the rewrite du jour. As you attempt to smile and maintain cordial relations, your rehearsal will be stopped by "Hold it—do it this way." Your visitor will hand you a restructured line, not necessarily better, just different enough to demonstrate complete disregard for the actor's process. The harried performer now has to incorporate new words to go with his previously rehearsed action.

This kind of "lateral" writing, particularly when it comes late in the day, is positively destructive to the orderly conduct of rehearsal, and ultimately the final product suffers because of it.

I go back to an earlier time; the days of Carl Reiner and Sheldon Leonard and Norman Lear, exemplary producers who used to encourage their directors to direct. For example, it was unheard of, in our day, to have a "run-through" on the first day for the benefit of the writing staff. Run-through of what? The cast is holding book and barely stumbling through a reading of the text.

In that long-ago lost time you would have three uninterrupted days of rehearsal before showing your wares to the producer. It was wonderful. You and your cast would have the luxury and the excitement of finding things together; you'd be able to experiment, to discover nuances, and even to fail, while trying something that wasn't necessarily in the original text. In the early stages of rehearsal I would often put down the script and just listen to the spoken dialogue. More than once I'd be able to say to an actor, "You've just spoken a line that isn't totally responsive to the previous speech—as the character, what other response could be appropriate?" We'd have an inventive improvisation for a moment, and often gold would come out of it. Sometimes it wouldn't be so great, and you'd throw it away, but the rehearsal would be enriched for the effort. This method of working enables the director to present a play in miniature instead of a series of poorly rehearsed vignettes.

Examine an early *Dick Van Dyke* or *All in the Family* episode. Most of the time the action would take place within the confines of one or two sets and the scenes would be long and uninterrupted. Look at today's situation comedies—a series of hit-and-run twenty-second bits utilizing multiple set changes. Some of these shows are simply photographed radio plays. Many are quite well scripted, have excellent word gags carefully honed, but they are usually delivered in close-up after close-up (inserted after countless "takes" until the actor got it right) long after the audience has departed. In the current fashion, what you don't get is the ensemble playing of an acting company that has been well rehearsed. Instead we are treated to regiments of performers who appear to be in a daze, delivering readings untrue to the character they're portraying because they are struggling with the thought, "What's that new line I was just asked to speak?"

Win some, lose some. In my opinion, for every gag line that has been "improved" at the last minute (and it must be allowed there are some), there is a loss suffered by other parts of the production because the actor's process has not been considered by writers who are unconsciously writing for radio, where the last-minute rewrite can be accurately read from the scripted page. I did not have a large writing staff on *All in the Family,* which was one of the last major hits to rehearse in the manner I employed. Three talented men, Don Nicholl, Mickey Ross, and Bernie West (in addition to Norman Lear), either wrote or rewrote every word of the nearly one hundred episodes I directed or produced during the first four years. Nicholl, Ross, and West went on to write and produce *Three's Company,* and then retired.

The Mary Tyler Moore Show writers came out of a different discipline, and their staffs have gone on to many other series, continuing the same method of operation.

Don't get me wrong. I'm not knocking the *Mary* show or some of its "offspring." With writers such as Jim Brooks and Allan Burns, David Lloyd, and Bob Ellison, they were bound to enjoy enormous success. The problem is, they were so good at what they did that they spawned a system that encourages junior writers to behave in the same manner.

When you have inexperienced writers suddenly running shows as if they were Jim Brooks, the effect is to eliminate the productive rehearsal in favor of the hourly rewrite, and the inevitable consequence of this behavior is to subordinate the director (particularly the young director) to a staff of relatively ineffective writers/producers.

In the early days of television, some network bosses such as Pat Weaver of NBC and William Paley at CBS followed their gut instincts when buying programs. These men had the courage to enlist the expertise of producers, writers, and directors and allow them to do their work without interference once a series was scheduled. In those long-lost days, the networks acted as distribution services, leaving production in the hands of skilled showmen. This happy state of affairs ground to a shuddering halt sometime during the late 1960s, when the notion of "testing" pilots came into vogue.

Without regard for anything resembling scientific sampling, networks began sending recruiters into the streets with orders to entice audiences into attending a newly minted program's first screening. These so-called average viewers would be asked to sit in judgment of our work. And since their conclusions could affect a network's decision to accept or pass on our offerings, I attended one of these bloodbaths early on.

A small screening room had been outfitted with "like" and "don't like" dials to indicate moment-to-moment audience reaction as a film was projected. After watching dials in the control room indicating whether we were seeing a successful screening or enduring a bomb, I decided there was little to learn from this adventure and left early. It occurred to me then—and remains my conclusion to this day—that something familiar would appeal to the audience, and something novel or seriously different from the norm would suffer. How else do you explain why *All in the Family* scored abysmally low on these "tests," as did *Mary Tyler Moore, Cheers, Seinfeld,* and a host of others? Conversely, pilots that scored well often appeared on the schedules only to have the ensuing series fail miserably and get canceled after three or four weeks.

I have often asked why, to my knowledge, no one has ever conducted studies to gauge predictions of success or failure based on audience "research." I have never heard a satisfactory response to this question, probably because we might learn the awful truth that the system doesn't work and never has. Yet the madness continues, probably because testing gives an insecure programmer reason to pass on or accept a concept. The "research" gives them cover. In the case of a number of major hit shows that managed to emerge after receiving extremely low test scores, their success can be attributed to some fluke of circumstance or to the insistence of some brave network chief such as Brandon Tartikoff or Grant Tinker to ignore the scoring and go with their instincts.

I write about this phenomenon because one day in the late 1970s, I found myself in New York City with time on my hands. Idly window shopping, admiring an exhibit of expensive pipes in Dunhill's Fifth Avenue shop, I was greeted by a young man with a sheaf of tickets in his hand. He asked me if I would like to help judge a new television show at CBS. I waved him off, thinking I had no business participating in such an adventure. However, as he continued to solicit passersby, I began to think, Why shouldn't I? I view television as part of a mass audience just as others do. Besides, I had nothing to do until my dinner meeting. The clincher was, it was starting to rain.

I approached the free-ticket man and accepted his invitation to report to CBS within the next half hour. Feeling a little self-conscious as I joined the queue outside a building I had entered many times before under different auspices, I hugged the wall and made myself as inconspicuous as possible, fearing I might be seen by show business acquaintances. When the line moved into the familiar lobby, I continued to seek anonymity as I listened to a CBS guide explain what we were doing here. The first thing that struck me was a ludicrous statement by our host: "You people are about to do something very important. You will decide if a new program is going to be scheduled by the network or not. Some years ago, another group like yours rated *All in the Family* and *The Mary Tyler Moore Show* so high that they were selected."

Obviously, no one had told this person that the two shows he mentioned had scored at the bottom of the test audience heap. Oh, well.

In due course, we were escorted into an elevator and subsequently ushered into a long room featuring a TV monitor and several rows of chairs lined up at *right angles* to the screen. At each chair, the familiar "like" and "don't like" dials were positioned. Having noticed there were more people than available electronic devices, I chose a chair at the back of the room, where I was told I would have a written form to express my opinions rather than comment with an instantaneous selector. This suited me fine since I was soon to discover that the pilot in question was a Twentieth Century Fox entry. At the time, I had an office on the Fox lot and a development deal with the studio, so I decided not to vote but simply to observe the process.

The "master of ceremonies" of the test advised us again of our importance, and added something that really stuck in my throat. We were told—and told again—"You don't have to like what you see. If something bothers you on the screen, be sure to say you think it's bad." I thought this was laying it on a bit thick—prejudicing the jury in favor of a conviction. Also, two things struck me instantly. Because of the rain that had fallen as we gathered, respondents in the room were trying to balance coats and umbrellas and still manipulate their dials in a meaningful fashion. It was impossible to do so. Items of clothing, purses, and shopping bags fell with alarming frequency. All this commotion added to a general sense of discomfort. The configuration of the room caused viewers to crane their necks over their left or right shoulders. Furthermore, the TV at the end of the room was far too small to register important details.

As I recall, the pilot episode was something about nurses and starred Adrienne Barbeau, the lovely and talented costar of the Bea Arthur series *Maude*. Alas, her many charms were lost on the tiny screen, which had to be viewed obliquely at the end of the long, narrow room. The pilot never saw the light of day.

If randomly chosen audience members arbitrarily twirling dials hasn't turned out to be an accurate predictor of a series's prospects, many times the highly paid network executives do little better. Lou Ehrlich was chief program executive at ABC when he was offered Bill Cosby as the star of a new series. Ehrlich turned the show down twice after it was brought to him by independent producers Marcy Carsey and Tom Werner, former ABC executives themselves. Lou's well-publicized rationale for passing on Cosby was his oft-quoted line, "Comedy is dead." Denied a slot at their former home, Carsey-Werner sold the show to NBC, where it flourished, along with other hit series they produced for the network.

In the late 1980s and 1990s, I was still in the business of making pilots for ABC, and so found myself one day playing the network game of bringing talent to Century City to be reviewed by the "suits." Casting a pilot was once the exclusive province of a producer and director, and often the writer, with no assistance from outside sources. Network executives saw the selected actors on film or tape only after the pilot was delivered. This antediluvian formula, good enough to create years of classic television shows, was apparently unacceptable to the new breed of program chiefs, who insisted on "helping" production companies with their "suggestions" for casting not only actors but directors and writers as well.

"Suggestions" now have the force of law in TV. You want X to play a role? The network will tell you if you can employ that person. Today, a production company is asked to provide two or three of their best choices out of the many who have answered a casting call, and these finalists are brought "to network," where the poor actor undergoes an intimidating appearance before a tribunal that seldom laughs or responds in any other way to the audition. All networks now follow this procedure.

For the person auditioning, the setting at ABC is truly terrifying. An auditorium with many raised rows of seats, dimly illuminated, looms over a brightly lit space below. I have always thought of the arrangement as an execution chamber, and no matter how many times I have warned performers not to exhibit fear when they enter, the best of them have been known to resemble Jell-O when asked to read under these conditions. It's my custom to sit in the very lowest seat closest to the "stage" in order to show a friendly face, and actors have thanked me for this support. But more than one player has told me that the auditorium's oppressive atmosphere never allows them to show off their best stuff. Accordingly, whenever possible, I've tried to lighten the mood in the room by telling a joke or making some "smart" remark while waiting for the next candidate to be led in.

On one such occasion, Lou Ehrlich himself provided the straight line for me. Having been the butt of many industry jokes regarding his failure to buy the Cosby show, he was now offering self-deprecating comments himself, such as, "And I'm the guy who turned down Cosby," after which he would slap himself smartly in the face. This usually earned a polite laugh from his staff.

Hearing and seeing this, I turned from my downstage seat and addressed Mr. Ehrlich, who was ensconced on the highest tier. "Lou, I don't always agree with you, but I think you did the right thing by turning down Cosby."

"What are you saying?" he ground out.

"Well, look where they are in the ratings."

Ehrlich sputtered, "They're number one, for Chrissake."

"My point exactly," I replied. "How long can it last? Five years? Ten years? You're going to be vindicated!"

Ehrlich laughed heartily, then answered my attempt at levity with a "There you go again, Rommel!" When he really liked something I said, he called me "Patton."

On the subject of network bosses, I'm reminded of an incident that occurred during one of my "closed set" rehearsal days. I think the show was either *Walter and Emily*, starring Cloris Leachman and Brian Keith, or *Benson*. I am sure the episode was for ABC, and that my assistant was Doug Smart. While running a scene at one part of the stage, I noticed a small group of strangers clustered at the other end of the building. Instantly, I called a five-minute break for the actors and glanced at Doug, who picked up my meaning at once. I watched him approach the uninvited visitors, and I was surprised to see him walk back to me while the strangers remained nearby.

"Why aren't they leaving?" I asked.

Doug's answer was, "It's Buffy Thermopolous and her guests, and she wants to watch you work." I had never heard of Buffy, but her last name struck a familiar note—Tony Thermopolous was president of the network. I told Doug to invite the young woman and her friends to return on any Monday or Tuesday. They would be most welcome on camera days, but unfortunately, the set is closed to everybody during the first three days of rehearsal.

"You want me to say this to the president's daughter?" Doug asked, looking skeptical.

"Tell her I wish I could accommodate her group, but I'm afraid I can't make exceptions. Be polite."

Doug left, talked to the visitors briefly, and watched them exit the stage. He returned shortly, shaking his head. "That is one angry girl," he reported.

I went back to work and forgot about the incident until the stage phone rang. "It's for you, Mr. Rich," the page on duty said. "Tony Thermopolous is calling from New York."

I sighed and said I'd take the call, aware that everyone on the stage would be listening. Taking the phone, I said, without pausing to take a breath, "Tony, I'm so glad you called. I was going to phone you later and ask a favor. I don't know if you remember my two boys, Anthony and Robert. Anthony is now twelve and Robert is ten, and we're going to be in New York next week, and my boys are real interested in how a network executive conducts business. They're both extremely well behaved, and I promise they'll cause you no trouble, so will it be all right with you if they stand quietly in a corner of your office and watch you conduct business? *Will that be okay with you, Tony?*"

There was a long silence. Then I said, "By the way, why did you call me?" Mr. Thermopolous's answer was gratifying: "No reason. I just wanted to know how things are going."

The crew, at least, enjoyed my end of the conversation.

I encountered another shining example of network thinking in the late 1970s. The William Morris office, which was representing me at the time, arranged for me to meet with another of their clients, Jean Shepherd, a well-known radio personality and author of several prize-winning books. Shepherd had a mordant wit and a talent for wringing comedy from nostalgic situations that either he had lived or that sprang fully formed from his wildly imaginative brain. After several meetings, we decided to use one of his famous short stories as the basis of a pilot we would present to ABC. The network seemed enthusiastic, and Brandon Stoddard, ABC's executive in charge of long-form television, gave us a "Go."

Following some discussion, Jean and I selected one of his classic tales, "Ollie Hopnoodle's Haven of Bliss," which appeared in his book *Wanda Hickey's Night of Golden Memories*. The script Shepherd delivered was a faithful adaptation of his short story, which featured the family setting off for their annual two-week summer vacation at an Indiana lake. The trip is a nightmare trek, with everything going wrong that could go wrong—carsickness, frequent restroom stops, getting stuck behind a chicken truck "spraying feathers and a dark-brown aroma over the countryside." The comedy arose from multiple frustrations, capped by the family's arrival at the lake, where they were greeted by a torrential rainstorm that promised to last the entire two weeks.

I thought the script was wonderful, so one day when I was in New York, I was happy to receive an enthusiastic phone call from one of Brandon Stoddard's lieutenants. I had never met the man, who introduced himself as Cliff Alsberg, a messenger bringing good news. He reported that all the executives on Stoddard's staff thought the script was terrific. "Wonderful," I said. "Thanks for letting me know." Alsberg went on, "I have just a few notes for you, if you have the time." I sat down heavily on the hotel bed. I had heard those ominous words before, and it usually spelled trouble, but I never expected to hear what came next.

"Everybody loves the idea of the vacation show," Alsberg reported, "but could we dispense with all that driving stuff and get to what happens when the family reaches the lake?"

I thought I had lost my hearing. "Get rid of the driving stuff? The driving stuff is what the comedy is all about. *Nothing* happens when they get to the lake. It's raining, the vacation is ruined, it's what you call irony!" I must have sputtered to a stop because my caller then said, "Mr. Stoddard wants to start the show at the camp."

I tried to be patient. I explained that the story had won literary prizes for excellence, and I wasn't about to go back to the author and force him to destroy his own creation. I went on, "I can understand if you don't want to do the script that's been written. Shepherd has many other stories, and I'm sure we can agree on one of them, but you'll have to compensate him for a brand new pilot script."

Alsberg was palpably relieved. "I'll have to check with Hollywood, but I'm sure we'll figure out a way to make Jean happy. I'm glad we had our little chat." This concluded the "few notes" session, and after returning to Los Angeles, we structured another deal with Shepherd and delivered a new script that apparently met with everyone's satisfaction. Everything seemed to be nicely on track as production began on the Twentieth Century Fox lot. We started shooting "night for night," and I was extremely satisfied with the work, feeling everything had gone off without a hitch. Little did I know I was about to be blindsided once more.

The second night found me on location, filming a 1950s-style used-car lot. In the days before cell phones, it was awkward and time consuming to be summoned to a public telephone while shooting, so it was disturbing to have a studio messenger tell me that Mr. Stoddard insisted on speaking with me at once. This delay would cause a serious crimp in my shooting schedule, but there was nothing to do but respond to the call. I had a Teamster drive me to the nearest pay phone (which wasn't all that near) and in a relatively foul mood I reached the ABC chief, who began to shout at me, "You have done something terrible to Richard Venture" (the actor playing the protagonist's dad). "How could you let wardrobe costume him like that? He looks like an accountant!!"

I reflected on his words for a moment, then said in a voice as controlled as I could manage, "He *is* an accountant."

The receiver spat out, "Well, what about the steel mill?"

I held back my inclination to say "Read the script," and remained relatively calm. "The *son* works in a steel mill; the father is an accountant who works someplace else. The steel mill work will be shot a few weeks from now on location at Inland Steel in Indiana." Brandon Stoddard hated me from that day forward and saw to it that ABC never picked up the pilot.

As a matter of fact, I learned some time later that the film I had directed was sold in Europe as a small feature. Since the work we had delivered was not long enough for a theatrical release, the network had arbitrarily glued pieces of outtakes together to create a thoroughly botched presentation. I heard about this abomination just in time to request, and receive, permission to—irony of ironies—remove my name from the credits and substitute the DGA pseudonym, Allen Smithee.

The whole affair reminded me of Sheldon Leonard's experience after he directed the pilot of *Gomer Pyle, USMC*. Leonard delivered his film to a network executive, who liked the action but hated the "phony set that looked nothing like a real Marine Corps facility." Sheldon quietly informed the man, "The pilot was shot at the Marine Corps base in San Diego."

The Morris office arranged one more meeting for me in New York. I was staying at the Pierre Hotel on Fifth Avenue when I was asked if I would like to meet their client David Mamet. I was happy to do so, because I had just seen one of his brilliantly written plays on

Broadway, *American Buffalo*. Mamet came up to the suite, flanked by several agents, and I soon learned they had brought him to me with the idea of forming a partnership for television production. Surprised, I asked Mamet if this were something he really wanted to do. He looked unsure when trying to answer my question, so I said, "You have such a distinctive voice in your plays that if I were you I'd be very careful about jumping into TV land. I think it would be a big mistake for you to abandon the theater in favor of a world that will not accept the wonderfully colorful dialogue you provide on stage."

The Morris boys were beside themselves, frantically signaling me to take another tack, but I ignored them and went on in the same vein. Mamet looked relieved. I like to think that I helped shelter a major talent from the seductive grasp of an industry that would have surely destroyed this important contributor to the American theater. My agents were not thrilled with me.

CHAPTER

13

Certain colorful phrases used throughout our industry have always amused me. The call "This shot is going to be M.O.S." confused me in my early work until someone explained that when those letters were called, sound would not have to roll; the camera would be recording a silent scene. "Okay," I said, "but what do those initials stand for?" When I was told M.O.S. stood for "mit out sound." I thought my leg was being pulled, but when I was directing *Our Miss Brooks*, I learned who had first used the phrase. My cameraman for that series was Karl Freund, who had been a director and cameraman at UFA studios in Berlin during the 1920s and had never lost his German accent. Whenever he referred to silent shooting, it was always "mit out sound," and the initials are used today wherever films are made.

Another well-understood announcement that's used worldwide is, "Okay, everybody, this is the Abby Singer shot." This generally means the company is about to shoot the penultimate scene of the day. Abby Singer was (and still is) a fine assistant director who was fond of saying to his crew, "Okay, everybody, this shot and one more." Of course, "one more" sometimes became a few more, but the cry "Abby Singer" made everyone begin to think about shutting down for the day—or at least get ready for the "martini shot," which would be the final scene of the day.

My wonderful director of photography for five feature films was Lucien Ballard, who had invented the "O.B.," a special lamp placed over the camera. When I asked, "Why isn't it called an O.C.?" I learned that Lucien had once been married to the famous actress Merle Oberon, and he had invented the unique lamp placement when photographing the star. Her initials are still used today.

One of my favorite phrases—"Panic Peak"—applied to the frantic attempt to film one last close-up as the sun was sinking. This was in use during the days when we shot Western locations without the benefit of artificial light. Electrical generators and studio lamps never accompanied us when shooting on location. If the crew decided we needed supplemental lighting, that was achieved by using "shiny boards"—large squares of reflective aluminum placed on stands that could be tilted to catch sunlight. Customarily, we would travel in the dark hours of the early morning in order to arrive at a location by sunup. Except for a half-hour lunch, photography would go on until the end of "magic hour," that time of day when the light was golden and suffused. At the end of this idyllic time, with the sun threatening to disappear behind the nearest mountain, a director would shout, as he ran for high ground, "Follow me to Panic Peak." The entire company, lugging camera, sound gear, and shiny boards, would race for some modest hill nearby to take advantage of the sun's dying rays. Another coinage I often heard on Western locations was someone excusing themselves to "bleed the lizard," that is, leave the set briefly to urinate.

The "owl shot" is an expression describing a close-up of the heroine watching her hero fighting the bad guys, or indeed it could apply to any bystander who is not actively engaged in punching someone. For editing purposes, it's important to cut to a player on the scene reacting to the violence, in order to substitute a stunt man for the protagonist or to cut away from an awkward moment, such as a clearly observable "miss" during a fight, when a misdirected fist collides with nothing but air. The origin of this interesting locution goes back to the days of cheaply made suspense films at Republic Pictures. Given little raw film stock to make the movie, directors would be forced to forgo expensive coverage of a scene. They would grind off footage of a "dark and stormy night" involving a mysterious or otherwise ominous location. During editing, when a scene required shortening, Republic used an old stock shot of an owl in a tree. There was usually a moon and some scudding clouds behind the bird, lending an air of mystery to the proceeding. I can actually remember sitting in my neighborhood theater as a child, during many a Saturday matinee, wondering why the same bird seemed to show up in so many different movies.

In 1957, while directing an episode of *Gunsmoke* on location, I finished shooting the first scene and called, "Cut . . . Print." Behind me I heard an older member of the crew shout, "Release the pigeon!" I had no idea what he meant. When I inquired about it, he told me, "It means you've okayed the first shot." According to the grizzled crewman, long before the advent of cell phones or radio communications, in order to keep the studio informed as to the company's progress, a homing pigeon was brought to the location. When the first shot was printed, a crew member would attach a note with the time of day to its leg and set the bird free to bring the news to headquarters.

Many years later, while shooting another Western, I wrapped a scene and heard the assistant director call out, "Warm up the snake." I knew the schedule called for filming a rattlesnake, but since I had never heard this particular order before, I asked what it meant. Because we were shooting very early in the day, I was told, the snake was lying in a torpid state. Rattlers will not move until their bodies have been heated by the sun. If one wants to shoot when it's cold, the snake is placed in a secure box, a high-powered lamp is directed into the enclosure, and the viper is soon ready to do his stuff for the camera.

Shooting on location meant lengthy days for everyone, but for the director there would frequently be a conference with assistants regarding the following day's work. Exhausted, many of us would get our best sleep in the transportation the studio provided for the long ride back. A short night in bed would be interrupted by an insistent alarm clock ringing well before dawn, and we would repeat the process all over again. If it was raining hard, the company would use a "cover" set to shoot indoor scenes that had been predetermined for just such an occasion. If it was just cold, causing a freezing drizzle, outdoor shooting went on regardless. When facing a particularly tough shot in such conditions, a camera operator with whom I worked frequently named Harry Webb would always say, "If this was easy everybody would be making pictures." It's a phrase that should be imprinted on the brain of everyone who ever worked in, or will work in, our industry.

The weather is one of a host of problems that must be solved daily when making a film. Two valuable members of the directorial team get to contend with this variable over which there is absolutely no control: the unit production manager and the first assistant director.

Any outdoor location shooting is scheduled first, so that in the event of inclement weather the company can retreat inside, do some of the work that would normally be scheduled for later, and return outside when the weather clears. It's frequently a difficult call to make, and assistant directors and unit production managers keep in close touch, sometimes hourly, with the weather bureau regarding the local forecast. If it appears the weather will be fine, the company remains on schedule for location work; if not, someone has to make the decision to "run for cover" or remain in the field and wait out a passing storm. Making such a call correctly can easily save a company thousands of production dollars. A bad call can jeopardize the entire budget.

Some years ago, on a Western being shot in a remote part of Utah, one assistant thought he had found the ideal solution to the problem of handicapping the weather. Local lore spoke of a character who was reputed to be an incredibly gifted forecaster. The AD sought out the reclusive old-timer, who lived alone halfway up a nearby mountain, and made a deal offering to pay him ten dollars as a test to see if he could accurately predict the next day's weather. The old hermit agreed and said for openers, "All day tomorrow is gonna be fine." The AD scheduled the work accordingly and the forecast proved correct. After a few more successful trial runs, the assistant offered to pay ten dollars every day for the rest of the shoot.

For the next three days, the hermit continued to call each day's fair weather correctly, but on the fourth day predicted, "Tomorrow it's gonna rain all day." Even though the night appeared fine, the assistant took a chance and scheduled indoor work. Sure enough, the forecast was accurate. The delighted AD reveled in his good fortune until, climbing up to the seer's cabin one day, he opened his wallet and asked, "How's the weather look for tomorrow?" "Sorry," the old prophet said, "I can't tell ya."

The shocked assistant couldn't believe his ears. "What? What did you say?" "I said I can't tell ya. My radio's broken."

Assistant directors and unit production managers are fond of another story that has been circulating recently: A man in a hot-air balloon realizes he is lost. Reducing altitude, he spots someone below, descends a bit more, and shouts, "Hey, you! Excuse me, but can you help me? I promised a friend I would meet him an hour ago, but I don't know where I am."

The man on the ground replies, "You're in a hot-air balloon hovering approximately thirty feet above me. You're between forty and forty-one degrees North latitude and between fifty-nine and sixty degrees West longitude."

The balloonist says, "You must be a unit production manager."

"I am," the man replies, "but how did you know?"

"Well," answers the balloonist, "everything you told me is technically correct, but I have no idea what to make of your information, and I'm still lost. Frankly, you haven't been much help."

The man below responds, "You must be a producer."

"I am," replies the surprised balloonist. "But how did you know that?"

"Well," says the UPM, "You don't know where you are or where you're going. You have risen to your position due to a large quantity of hot air. You've made a promise which you have no idea how to keep, and you expect me to solve your problem. You're in exactly the same position you were in before we met, but somehow now it's my fault."

The great English actor Edmund Kean (1789–1833), unrivaled in his day as a Shakespearean tragedian—he starred as Shylock, Hamlet, Othello, Iago, Macbeth, Lear, and Richard III—is said to have coined a famous death-bed utterance. As he lay dying, a friend asked him, "Is it hard, Edmund?" The actor is reputed to have answered, "No, dying is easy. Comedy is hard."

Along those same lines, I have been reminded many times of the sage advice Mack Sennett gave me decades ago. As I noted earlier, when I met the legendary creator of the Keystone Kops he offered me a great gift with a wise observation. "The audience will not laugh," the motion picture icon told me, "if it is mystified." In other words, if the situation for a joke is unclear to the listener, there is no way a laugh will be forthcoming; the setup makes the joke. The talented Rose Marie, with whom I worked on *The Dick Van Dyke Show* and other programs, was one of the greatest "fast-talking straight women" in the history of our business. When she laid out a straight line, it was child's play for the comic or "top banana" to swing from the heels with the punchline. On the other hand, if the straight line is muddled, the comedian can deliver punchlines with all his might, but to no avail.

In talking to university drama classes, I have frequently used an old New York joke to illustrate Sennett's point: Sam, the owner of a candy store, is sweeping his back room when he discovers an ancient lamp. As he rubs it clean, a genie appears and announces that he is the slave of the lamp and will grant the owner any wish. Sam muses that he has always wanted a holiday in the Catskills but wonders to himself: If I go to the mountains, who will watch the store? Without hesitation the genie says, "I will watch the store for you." With that, Sam makes his wish, the genie gestures, and the happy proprietor is whisked off to his holiday. The following morning, the genie, now wearing an apron, opens the shop for business. A regular customer appears and asks where Sam is. "Sam is on vacation," the genie responds. "I, the genie, am here to grant your wish." The customer responds, "Okay, make me a malted." The genie gestures toward the man and says, "All right, you're a malted!"

Without the proper straight line, the punchline obviously doesn't fly. I once heard an old friend of mine attempt to tell this joke, only he has the customer who walks in say, "Okay, I'd like a chocolate soda." The genie, of course, is comedically incapable of granting this request. The setup line is the most important part of the gag. Otherwise, the audience is mystified.

My wife and I returned recently from the University of Michigan, where we attended a series of seminars at the Institute for the Humanities. One of the lecturers was Ted Cohen, an extremely interesting professor of philosophy from the University of Chicago, who spoke of a book he had written entitled *Jokes—Philosophical Thoughts on Joking Matters*. I bought the book at once and was fascinated to find some curious treatment of several jokes with which I was familiar. One that Cohen recounted went like this: "Early one morning a man awoke in a state of terrible anxiety because of the dream he had been having. He immediately called his psychiatrist, and, after making a special plea because of his distress, he was granted an appointment that morning— even though it was not the day for seeing his psychiatrist. When he arrived in the doctor's office, he said, 'I had the most awful dream you can imagine. In it I raped my mother, killed my wife, and seduced my daughter, and more things worse than those. I woke up shaking and sweating, and I called you immediately. Then I had a quick piece of toast and some coffee, and ran down here to see you.' '"What?' said the psychiatrist. 'You call that a breakfast?'"

Professor Cohen went on to write, "For this, one needs to know only two things, although one other thing deepens the joke. One needs to know the exceptionally high proportion of Jews among psychiatrists and to know the commonplace belief about Jewish mothers that they are excessively concerned, especially about food. The joke is deeper for those who believe it an occupational hazard of psychiatry that its practitioners tend to look for deep and convoluted explanations when simple and direct ones would do, and, conversely, that they tend to look only at the surface in the few cases in which something hidden is at work."

What would Mack Sennett have said about this? I believe he would find, as I do, that the joke is burdened by unnecessary information. Not only that, the Professor's conclusions about the things "one needs to know" are not required if the joke is told in this manner: A young man wakes up anxious to report a curious dream to his analyst. He races to the doctor's office drinking a Coke as he runs. Breathlessly, he says "In the dream you were my mother, my mother was you, the two of you morphing back and forth interchangeably. I couldn't wait to get here so I grabbed a Coke for breakfast and got here as fast as I could." The doctor looks at him disapprovingly: "A Coke? What kind of breakfast is that?" In my opinion, brevity and clarity win the day.

Another basic tenet of comedy: It's easier to get a laugh if the audience is primed a little. Morey Amsterdam would frequently "warm up" our *Dick Van Dyke Show* studio audience by suggesting, "Everybody hold hands and the guy on the end stick your finger into the electric socket." Redd Foxx was famous for using "blue" material from his nightclub act to break in studio audiences for *Sanford and Son.* Aaron Ruben, the producer of the series, would plead with Redd to stay away from the risqué stuff, pointing out, correctly, that the huge laughs he was getting would seriously impact the milder material that would be heard during the scripted episode. Redd wouldn't—or couldn't—go along, arguing that it was important for him to get the biggest laugh he could at any time. One night when I attended the taping as Tandem Productions' representative, Redd warmed up the audience by launching into a routine involving heavy petting with his girlfriend while parked in his car. He became very descriptive, with the girl getting so hot she begged Redd "Kiss me. Kiss me where it smells." There was an audible gasp from the crowd, followed by Redd's punchline: "So I took her to El Segundo."

The script didn't stand a chance that night.

There are times when people are in desperate need of a good laugh. This may be the reason why, at funerals for our departed show-business friends, humor often dominates the proceedings. After Walter Matthau died, the story was told at his memorial service about the time Walter was shooting a film in Germany. He had a day off, and so he and his wife decided to visit the infamous Auschwitz death camp. Driving to the site, Walter and his wife got into a tiff, which escalated into the beginnings of a heated argument, and threatened to become more serious until Mrs. Matthau said, "Why don't we put this aside and talk about something else?" Walter replied, "All right, but I'm telling you right now—you have ruined Auschwitz for me!"

I recall another example of a time when a joke was desperately needed. Some years ago, I was asked to attend a meeting of a group of directors who were stockholders in an organization known as Directors, Inc. This group had been formed as a profit-making arm of the Directors Guild of America, which itself was not permitted to earn taxable dollars since it was a tax-exempt organization. Directors, Inc., had been used briefly in the late 1950s when the Guild had sold a for-profit television series known as *Screen Directors' Playhouse.* Many well-known filmmakers had been asked to donate their time to direct half-hour episodes, and I was once selected to direct a comedy starring Joan Caulfield and Wendell Corey. It was a prestigious assignment, with each director donating his fee to the Guild's Educational and Benevolent Foundation. At Joe Youngerman's request, I became one of the stockholders of Directors, Inc., which is why, many years later, I was summoned to an extraordinary meeting.

Upon assembling, we were advised that legal counsel had decided that the corporation had no further need to continue existing, and our task, therefore, was to disband it. Glancing around the boardroom table, I was slightly dismayed to note that although I had passed the age of 65, I was still the youngest member of the group. Veteran directors in their late seventies and eighties voted to dissolve the corporation, ordering that any remaining funds be donated to the Educational Foundation. It took less than five minutes to accomplish this, and suddenly a sense of gloom came over the group, as it struck us that we were no doubt meeting for the last time ever. I felt as though I was listening to the cherry orchard being demolished in the Chekhov play. A profound silence descended.

I decided to try to break the mood. "It would be terrible to leave this meeting with such a sense of heaviness in the air," I said. "Let me tell you a joke that's going around." An out-of-work ventriloquist, I began, has fallen on such hard times that his agent advises him to follow many of his colleagues and open a séance parlor. "With your skill at throwing voices," the agent says, "it's a cinch you'll make a fortune 'contacting' the dead." At first, the ventriloquist rejects the suggestion, but hunger finally convinces him to try it. Once he opens for business, his first client is Mrs. Goldberg, who asks him to contact her dead husband, Harry. The trickster agrees to do so but says, "First, let me tell you my fee structure: For twenty-five dollars you can talk to Harry. For fifty dollars Harry can talk to you. And for a hundred dollars you can talk to each other while I'm drinking a glass of water!"

The joke earned an appreciative laugh from our group, and the tension was broken. But there always seems to be somebody who doesn't quite get it.

During my recitation, I had noticed that the attorney for the corporation had gathered his papers and left the room. Later in the rest room I ran into the lawyer who apologized for walking out while I was speaking. I told him the joke was kind of "inside material" but he said he really wanted to hear the story. "Would you tell it to me?" I looked around the tiled room. "What, here?" "Please," he said.

If one were casting a film and looking for an actor to nail the image of white-bread Pasadena society, this affable attorney, white-haired and impeccably dressed, would have been a cinch to get the part. He had heard part of the joke, so I scaled the story back and got quickly to the ventriloquist's fee structure.

Upon hearing the punchline (a hundred dollars while I'm drinking a glass of water), the man offered a thin smile and said, "Yes, yes, that's very amusing. I'm going to tell this joke downtown, but I'm going to make the chap an *attorney*."

I would have loved to be a fly on the wall as he delivered this "joke" to his fellow barristers. Mack Sennett was right. In the presence of mystification, no laugh is possible.

I would like to offer a final note on the happy years I have spent with the Directors Guild. In March 2003, I was chosen to receive an Honorary

Life Membership in the Guild. At the awards dinner, because of the lateness of the hour, I had been asked to deliver my acceptance speech in two minutes or less. I was honored to have Rob Reiner make the presentation, and this is what I said on the big night:

> Several years ago, during a National Board of Directors meeting, Sheldon Leonard was notified that he had been selected to receive an Honorary Life Membership award. In expressing his thanks, Sheldon said the following: "Big deal. You give a Life Membership to a guy who's eighty-nine years old." I am fortunate to be considerably younger than Sheldon was at the time, but old enough today to ask the Board to grant me a favor: Could you make this year's award retroactive?
>
> Most acceptance speeches end with the recipient thanking his wife and his family for their support. I want to begin my comments by paying tribute to a remarkably patient, wonderful lady who rightfully shares this prize for having kept me relatively sane for so many years: my dear wife, Pat.
>
> I first joined the Council of the Screen Directors Guild in 1953, and while it doesn't seem possible, as the year 2003 begins, I am entering my fiftieth year as a member of your National Board of Directors. In that span of time, I have had the privilege of working under fourteen DGA presidents: George Sidney, Frank Capra, George Stevens, Delbert Mann, Robert Wise, Robert Aldrich, George Schaefer, Jud Taylor, Gil Cates, Frank Schaffner, Arthur Hiller, Gene Reynolds, Jack Shea, and Martha Coolidge. These extraordinary directors have taught me much through the years—mostly how important it is to keep public speeches short, and when appropriate, to say "Thanks" quickly and abandon the stage to others. So . . . Thanks!

Many people congratulated me that night, mostly, I believe, for getting off in one minute and forty seconds.

I think I have dried up the well of this memoir. Just as in shooting a film, there comes a time when the director is expected to say, "Cut! Print!" I believe I have arrived at that moment. It's time to release the pigeon.

FILMOGRAPHY

Key to abbreviations
 D = Director, Sc = Screenwriter, W = Writer,
 P = Producer, ExP = Executive Producer,
 Cam = cinematographer (features),
 bw = black & white, c = color

FEATURE FILMS

Wives and Lovers (1963)
 D: John Rich. Sc: Edward Anhalt. P: Hal B. Wallis. Cam: Lucien
 Ballard. Cast: Van Johnson, Janet Leigh, Shelley Winters, Ray Walston,
 Martha Hyer, Jeremy Slate, Claire Wilcox, Lee Patrick, Dick Wessel,
 Dave Willock, Marianna Hill, George Bruggeman. In the adaptation
 of Jay Presson Allen's play *The First Wife,* a suddenly successful author
 moves his family to Connecticut, where his wife can stand only so much
 upper-crust fraternizing. Paramount, 103 min. bw.

The New Interns (1964)
 D: John Rich. Sc: Wilton Schiller. P: Robert Cohn. Cam: Lucien
 Ballard. Cast: Michael Callan, Dean Jones, George Segal, Stephanie
 Powers, Barbara Eden, Inger Stevens, Telly Savalas, Kay Stevens, Greg
 Morris, George Furth, Ellie Wood Walker, Lee Patrick, Jimmy Mathers,
 Michael Vandever, Sue Ane Langdon, Dawn Wells, Adam Williams,
 Charles Lane, Rusty Lane, Norman Cole, Gregory Morton, Marianna
 Hill, Alan Reed, Jr., Norman Cole, Beverly Adams. This follow-up to
 The Interns (1962) presents the lives, loves, and travails of a young
 hospital staff. Columbia, 123 min. bw.

Roustabout (1964)
 D: John Rich. Sc: Anthony Lawrence, Allan Weiss. P: Hal B. Wallis.
 Cam: Lucien Ballard. Cast: Elvis Presley, Barbara Stanwyck, Joan
 Freeman, Sue Ane Langdon, Leif Erickson, Pat Buttram, Steve Brodie,

Joan Staley, Dabbs Greer, Jack Albertson, Joel Fluellen, Beverly Adams, Norman Grabowski, Jane Dulo, Wilda Taylor, Billy Barty, Teri Garr, Joy Harman, Marianna Hill, Richard Kiel, Ray Kellogg, Raquel Welch, Red West. Elvis plays a drifter who links up with a carnival and romances the owner's daughter. Paramount, 101 min. c.

Boeing-Boeing (1965)
D: John Rich. Sc: Edward Anhalt. P: Hal B. Wallis. Cam: Lucien Ballard. Cast: Jerry Lewis, Tony Curtis, Dany Saval, Christiane Schmidtmer, Thelma Ritter, Suzanna Leigh, Lomax Study, Joe Grey. Curtis plays an American in Paris whose affairs with three airline stewardesses come into jeopardy when their schedules change and an old friend, played by Lewis, visits him. Based on a Marc Camoletti play. Paramount, 102 min. c.

Easy Come, Easy Go (1967)
D: John Rich. Sc: Allan Weiss, Anthony Lawrence. P: Hal B. Wallis. Cam: William Margulies. Cast: Elvis Presley, Dodie Marshall, Pat Priest, Pat Harrington, Jr., Frank McHugh, Skip Ward, Sandy Kenyon, Elsa Lanchester, Ed Griffith, Read Morgan, Mickey Elley, Eliane Beckett, Shari Nims, Tom Hatten, Diki Lerner, Robert Isenberg. Elvis plays a Navy frogman who believes he has discovered a fortune in sunken treasure. Paramount, 95 min. c.

TELEVISION SHOWS

John Rich directed at least thirty-five television pilots, mostly situation comedies. Although he is most often associated with groundbreaking sitcoms, such as *The Dick Van Dyke Show* and *All in the Family,* Rich has directed installments of drama anthologies, Westerns, musicals, and mysteries. He has also directed episodes of continuing dramas and adventure series as well as special events, such as the first televised Academy Awards. His career has virtually spanned television's history and its genre spectrum. As a stage manager or associate director, Rich worked on *The Kraft Television Theater, All-Star Revue, The Jack Carter Show, The Colgate Comedy Hour,* and other programs. Rich's television involvements as a director are as follows.

The RCA Victor Show (1951–53)
Retitled *The Dennis Day Show* (1953–54)
The star of the first season of the show was Ezio Pinza, whose luxurious New York flat was the base for greetings and singing, usually with a

guest star invited for an evening of entertainment. In February 1952, Dennis Day, anchoring a more mainstream variety show, alternated weeks with the Pinza shows. Rich directed both stars' presentations during this late winter and spring of the alternating shows. From the fall of 1952 forward, Day was the show's sole star, and it bore his name the following and final season. Costarring were Verna Felton, Kathy Phillips, Cliff Arquette (as Charley Weaver), Hal March, Minerva Urecal, Lois Butler, Jeri Lou James, Ida Moore, Carol Richards, and Barbara Ruick. D: Stanley Shapiro, Joseph Stanley, John Rich. P: Paul Henning, Joseph Stanley. W: Parke Levy, Stanley Adams, et al. NBC, 30 min.

Our Miss Brooks (1952–56)

The popular radio sitcom about everybody's favorite high school teacher made a successful transition to the small screen. Eve Arden made the transition, too, as Connie Brooks, as did Madison High's often babbling principal, Osgood Conklin, played by Gale Gordon. Costarring were Richard Crenna, Gloria McMillan, Jane Morgan, Robert Rockwell, Gene Barry, Nana Bryant, Bob Sweeney, and Ricky Vera. Rich directed a full season of thirty-two episodes. D: Al Lewis, John Rich, et al. P: Larry Berns. W: Al Lewis, Joe Quillian. CBS, 30 min.

The 25th Annual Academy Awards (1953)

The Academy of Motion Picture Arts and Sciences' Oscars ceremony was telecast live, coast to coast, for the first time under Rich's direction with Bill Bennington on March 19, 1953, on NBC. It was hosted on the West Coast by Bob Hope from the RKO Pantages Theater in Hollywood and on the East Coast by Conrad Nagel at the NBC International Theater in New York City. Cecil B. De Mille's *The Greatest Show on Earth* was named Best Picture of 1952, while Gary Cooper won Best Actor for *High Noon,* Shirley Booth Best Actress for *Come Back, Little Sheba,* and John Ford Best Director for *The Quiet Man.*

Florence Chadwick Catalina Island Swim (1952)

The title swimmer, the first woman to successfully swim the English Channel to France, attempted to swim from Santa Catalina Island to Dana Point on the California coast, with millions watching the epic on television. Exhausted, she quit about a mile from the 15,000 people waiting on shore. Johnny Weismuller was in attendance. Rich and Bill Bennington directed the coverage of the event from one of the flotilla of seventy-five boats following Chadwick, who, in a later try, did successfully swim from Catalina to Palos Verdes. KNBH-TV, Los Angeles, 16 hours.

I Married Joan (1952–55)

Jim Backus and Joan Davis played Judge and Mrs. Stevens in this sitcom, which usually focused on the problems and adventures of their friends and neighbors. Costarring were Hal Smith, Geraldine Carr, Dan Tobin, Sheila Bromley, Sandra Gould, Wally Brown, and Sally Kelly. Rich directed a year of thirty-nine episodes. D: Hal Walker, John Rich, Marc Daniels, et al. P: Dick Mack, P. J. Wolfson. W: Phil Sharp, Sherwood Schwartz, Hugh Wedlock, et al. NBC, 30 min.

Where's Raymond? (1953)
Retitled *The Ray Bolger Show* (1954–55)

Capitalizing on the star's notoriety in the long-running Broadway comedy and movie of *Where's Charley?* this show presented the various adventures of Raymond Wallace, a Broadway star living in the suburbs. The show afforded Bolger plenty of singing and dancing opportunities. The cast included Richard Erdman, Sylvia Lewis, Allyn Joslyn, Betty Lynn, Charles Smith, Gloria Winters, Rise Stevens, and Charlie Cantor. Under both titles, the show ran for fifty-nine episodes. Rich directed the second season of thirty-six episodes. D: Marc Daniels, John Rich. P: Stanley Shapiro, Paul Henning, Jerry Bresler. W: Stanley Shapiro, Paul Henning, Maurice Richlin, Fred S. Fox, Don Johnson. ABC, 30 min.

Schlitz Playhouse of Stars (1951–59)

The Schlitz Brewing Company sponsored one of the more ambitious anthology dramas, which drew a wide variety of film and Broadway stars over the years. Rich's shows under the Schlitz umbrella title were several Westerns that aired after 1955, one with Steve Forrest, and "The Trouble With Ruth" in 1958 with Jeanne Crain. CBS, 60 min. in first season, 30 min. thereafter.

Colonel Humphrey J. Flack
aka *The Fabulous Fraud* (1953–54)

The stories about a Robin Hood-style swindler of swindlers, based on stories by Everett Rhodes Castle, became the basis for this sitcom. Alan Mowbray starred with Frank Jenks and Constance Bennett. Rich directed twenty shows, almost the entire season. P: Wilbur Stark and Jerry Layton. 30 min.

General Electric Theater (1953–62)

This long-running anthology series was a mixed assortment, with stories set in all eras and genres. Unlike many of its contemporary anthology dramas, this one specialized in uncomplicated and easily digestible entertainments, light dramas, and some comedies. Many film stars top-lined the show including Charlton Heston, Ronald Colman, Greer Garson, and Joan Crawford. Ronald Reagan hosted all but the first year of the show. Rich directed four installments, including "The Tallest Marine" with Red Buttons in 1958, and "They Like Me Fine" with George Gobel in 1960. Also in 1958 for the series, Rich wrote "Auf Wiedersehen!" with John Furia; it starred Sammy Davis, Jr., in his first dramatic television performance.

Dateline Disneyland (1955)

The Opening Day ceremonies at the far-from-complete Disneyland theme park in Anaheim, California, were covered live on ABC. The festivities included speeches and music and a parade and commentary. Walt Disney made his thereafter legendary comments about the park on this day: "To all who come to this happy place—welcome!" The commentators included Ronald Reagan, Bob Cummings, and Art Linkletter. Guests included Frank Sinatra, Danny Thomas, Irene Dunne, Jeanne Crain, Fess Parker, Buddy Ebsen, Johnny Green, Bonita Granville, Alan Young, and Gale Storm. Rich shared the directing with Stu Phelps. The Disneyland show overall won the Emmy Award for Best Action or Adventure Series of the Year. P: Sherman Marks, Walt Disney. ABC, 60 min.

Screen Directors' Playhouse (1955–56)

Prestigious filmmakers were asked to direct favorite short subjects for this television drama anthology. Leo McCarey, John Ford, John Brahm, and other screen directors participated. Rich directed "Apples on the Lilac Tree," with Joan Caulfield and Macdonald Carey, in 1956. NBC, 30 min.

Gunsmoke (1955–75)

The setting was Dodge City, Kansas, in the 1880s. The law was Marshal Matt Dillon. The storylines plumbed all of the Western themes and variants imaginable and offered extended looks at many side characters in town, including Longbranch Saloon owner Kitty Russell (Amanda Blake), Doc Adams (Milburn Stone), Deputies Chester (Dennis Weaver) and Festus (Ken Curtis), Quint (Burt Reynolds), Sam the

Bartender (Glenn Strange), and others played by Dabbs Greer, Claude Akins, Buck Taylor, Roger Ewing, Tom Brown, John Harper, Roy Roberts, et al. *Gunsmoke* ran for twenty years, longer than any other show with continuing characters in television history. Rich alternated every other episode during the 1957 season with Ted Post, directing thirteen in all. Through the years, Rich directed another six episodes of the one-hour series. D: Bernard J. McEveety, R. G. Springsteen, John Rich, William Conrad, Mark Rydell, et al. P: Norman MacDonnell, James Drackow, Leonard Katzman. CBS, 30 min. 1955–61, and 60 min. thereafter.

Hey, Jeannie (1956–57)

Jeannie Carson starred as Jeannie MacLennan, a Scot immigrant who's being sponsored in her new life by a New York cabdriver. Allen Jenkins and Jane Dulo costarred. Rich directed the pilot. D: James V. Kern, Leslie Goodwins. P: Charles Isaacs. W: Stanley Shapiro, et al. CBS, 30 min.

Conflict (1956–57)

This biweekly series alternated with the Western *Cheyenne* and mostly involved personal conflicts affecting everyday people. Some were repeats of the previous series *Warner Bros. Presents.* The show was coproduced by the National Association for Mental Health. Rich directed "Girl on a Subway" in 1957 with Natalie Wood, Charles Ruggles, James Garner, Murray Hamilton, and Joe Kearns. P: Jack Barry, Paul Stewart. ABC, 60 min.

Oh! Susanna (1956–58)
Retitled The Gale Storm Show (1958–60)

Storm starred as the social director aboard the cruise ship USS *Ocean Queen.* Costarring were ZaSu Pitts, Roy Roberts, Elvira (Nugey) Nugent, Ray Montgomery, James Fairfax, and Joe Cranston. D: John Rich, et al. P: Hal Roach, Jr. CBS, then ABC, 30 min.

Richard Diamond, Private Detective (1957–60)

The title investigator had a few advantages over other PIs in that he used his status as a former cop to lean on his old coworkers for information and shortcuts, and on his in-car telephone. The phone was often called by "Sam," the answering-service woman who was seen only from the waist down, to emphasize her beautiful legs. The part is trivia fodder today, as it gave Mary Tyler Moore her first recurring role, which was taken over by Rozanne Brooks. The half-hour drama costarred

Regis Toomey, Barbara Bain, and Russ Conway. Rich directed five episodes. D: John Rich, et al. P: Dick Powell. CBS, then NBC, 30 min.

The Eve Arden Show (1957–58)

After Arden's previous hit, *Our Miss Brooks*, was canceled the previous season, this sitcom attempted to continue to capitalize on the star's popularity. Arden played novelist Liza Hammond, loosely based on the life of actual writer Emily Kimbrough. Twelve-year-old twins and Liza's mother were usually featured. Costarring were Allyn Joslyn, Frances Bavier, Gail Stone, and Karen Greene. Rich directed most of the series. P: Robert Sparks, Edmund Hartmann. CBS, 30 min.

How to Marry a Millionaire (1958–59)

Based on the 1953 film starring Marilyn Monroe, Betty Grable, and Lauren Bacall, this sitcom upped the troika of eligible girls to a foursome of New York career girls. They were played by Barbara Eden, Lori Nelson, Merry Anders, and Lisa Gaye. Stacy Keach Sr. costarred. Rich directed the pilot. D: Danny Dare, et al. P: Nat Perrin. W: Dick Conway, Seaman Jacobs. Syndicated, 30 min.

The Rifleman (1958–61)

Chuck Connors starred as Lucas McCain, who's trying to raise his motherless son, Mark, on their homestead ranch near North Fork, New Mexico. Lucas carried a modified Winchester with a large ring that cocked the weapon as he drew, thus making him a split-second faster than anyone else. A seminal Western of the late 1950s, it made former professional baseball and basketball player Connors into a television star. Johnny Crawford played Mark, and the costars included Paul Fix, Joan Taylor, Patricia Blair, Hope Summers, Edgar Buchanan, Jack Kruschen, Thomas Gomez, Abby Dalton, John Anderson, Richard Anderson, and Bill Quinn. Rich directed four episodes. D: Tom Gries, Arthur Hiller, John Rich, Sam Peckinpah, Richard L. Bare, Lamont Johnson, Ida Lupino, et al. P: Jules Levy, Arthur Gardner, Arnold Laven. ABC, 30 min.

Bat Masterson (1958–61)

Gene Barry starred as the dapper ex-lawman William Bartley Masterson. The actual Masterson had been a deputy of Wyatt Earp's. In the series, Masterson roamed the West with a gold-topped cane. Rich directed a full season of twenty-two episodes. P: Andy White, Frank Pittman. NBC, 30 min.

Law of the Plainsman (1959)
aka *The Westerner*

> Michael Ansara originally played U.S. Marshal Sam Buckhart on two episodes of *The Rifleman* in 1959. Dayton Lummis and Gina Gillespie costarred. Rich directed four episodes. P: Arthur Gardner, Jules Levy, Arnold Laven.

Bold Venture (1959)

> Dane Clark starred as Slate Shannon, the skipper of the title adventure craft, which plied Caribbean waters from a base in Trinidad. Joan Marshall costarred as Sailor Duval, with Bernie Gozier as the narrator and Calypso singer King Moses. The series was based on the Humphrey Bogart–Lauren Bacall radio series of the same name. Rich directed six episodes. Syndicated, 30 min.

Peck's Bad Girl (1959)

> Torey Peck was a mischievous twelve-year-old who got into one jam after another. The sitcom was partly based on its star's reputation: Patty McCormack, who had starred in the successful bad-little-girl film *The Bad Seed* (1956), top-lined this series. Her parents were played by Wendell Corey and Marsha Hunt. Roy Ferrell and Reba Waters played Torey's friends. Rich directed six episodes. P: Stanley Rubin. CBS, 30 min.

Hotel de Paree (1959–60)

> After seventeen years in prison for killing a man in Georgetown, Colorado, Sundance ends up in 1870 in the same town at the title hotel, which is operated by two female relatives of the dead man. Earl Holliman played Sundance, whose gimmick was a glistening hatband that sometimes blinded his foes in strategic situations. Jeannette Nolan, Judi Meredith, and Strother Martin costarred. Rich directed thirteen of the one-season show's thirty-two episodes. P: William Self, Stanley Rubin. CBS, 30 min.

Markham (1959–60)

> Ray Milland played Roy Markham, an attorney who decided to solve cases instead of trying them. His adventures were global, his fees adjustable. Simon Scott played his employer, John Riggs. Rich directed two episodes. D: John Rich, et al. P: Joe Sistrom, Warren Duff. CBS, 30 min.

Tightrope (1959–60)

> Mike "Touch" Connors played an undercover police detective infiltrating organized crime. He often was so far undercover that the police he sometimes saved had no idea that he was on their side. D: John Rich,

Abner Biberman, et al. W: Stirling Silliphant, Bernie Giler, et al. CBS, 30 min.

Riverboat (1959–61)

The 100-foot-long title stern-wheel paddleboat was *The Enterprise,* which plied the waters of the Mississippi, Missouri, and Ohio Rivers during the 1840s. Darren McGavin played Gray Holden, the owner and captain who had won the boat in a card game. His crew included Burt Reynolds as Ben Frazer during the first season; other cast members included Dan Duryea, Jack Lambert, Jack Mitchum, William D. Gordon, Richard Wessell, and Noah Beery, Jr. Rich directed two episodes. P: Jules Brickem, Richard Lewis, et al. NBC, 60 min.

The Twilight Zone (1959–64)

Conceived, written, and introduced by Rod Serling, this anthology show mixed elements of science fiction, horror, and the spectrum of ironies. Rich directed two shows for this time-honored classic: "A Most Unusual Camera" in 1960 with Fred Clark and Jean Carson, and "A Kind of Stop Watch" in 1963 with Richard Erdman, Roy Roberts, and Doris Singleton. CBS, 30 min., except for eighteen 60-min. shows in 1963.

The Detectives, Starring Robert Taylor (1959–61)
Retitled *Robert Taylor's Detectives* (1961–62)

Screen star Taylor played Captain Matt Holbrook, a no-nonsense and efficient investigator leading a four-man, big-city police detective unit solving a variety of felonies. Tige Andrews, Russell Thorsen, and Lee Farr played the plainclothes partners; Ursula Thiess, Taylor's actual wife, played his girlfriend; and Adam West was added for the final two seasons. Rich directed six episodes. D. John Rich, Michael Ritchie, Ted Post, Tom Gries, Richard Donner, et al. P: Jules Levy, Arthur Gardner, Arnold Laven. ABC, 30 min., then NBC, 60 min.

Bonanza (1959–73)

One of the longest-running television series of all time was also the second-longest-running Western, at fourteen seasons ranking only behind *Gunsmoke. Bonanza* was based at the Ponderosa, a huge ranch near Virginia City, Nevada, soon after the discovery of the Comstock Silver Lode. The ranch was operated by the Cartwrights—patriarch Ben (Lorne Greene) and sons Adam (Pernell Roberts), Hoss (Dan Blocker), and Little Joe (Michael Landon). Victor Sen Yung played Hop Singh and Ray Teal played Sheriff Roy Coffee. Other ranch hands turning up in latter incarnations of the show included David Canary,

Mitch Vogel, Lou Frizzel, and Tim Matheson. Through the years, Rich directed eight episodes. D: John Rich, Lee H. Katzin, Tay Garnett, Paul Henreid, Jacques Tourneur, et al. P: David Dortort, Richard Collins, Robert Blees. W: David Dortort, Gene L. Coon, Michael Landon, N. B. Stone, Jr., Borden Chase, et al. NBC, 60 min.

Slezak and Son (1960)

Walter Slezak became Count von Slezak in this sitcom pilot. Slezak and his actual son, Leo Slezak, try to pawn off their supposedly high-born notoriety into getting a free posh New York hotel room. Costarring were Norman Lloyd and Neva Patterson. D/P: John Rich. CBS, 30 min.

The Brothers Brannigan (1960)

This crime adventure, set in Phoenix, Arizona, starred Steve Dunne and Mark Roberts as private investigators Mike and Bob Brannigan, with Rebecca Wells as their secretary. Rich directed the pilot. P: Wilbur Stark. 30 min.

The Aquanauts (1960–61)
Retitled Malibu Run (1961)

These adventures of a pair of salvage divers on the Southern California coast were the network's answer to the syndicated Sea Hunt series. The crew included Keith Larsen, Jeremy Slate, Ron Ely, and Charles Thompson. Rich directed seven episodes. P: Ivan Tors. CBS, 60 min.

The Outlaws (1960–62)

The lawless 1890s in Oklahoma was the setting for the first season of this show, which showed the lawmen from the outlaws' point of view. The second season shifted the point of view to the lawmen. Only Don Collier was maintained from the first season's trio, which included Barton MacLane and Jack Gaynor. The second season also costarred Slim Pickens, Bruce Yarnell, and Judy Lewis. Rich directed two episodes. P: Joseph Dackow. NBC, 60 min.

The Law and Mr. Jones (1960–62)

James Whitmore starred as Abraham Lincoln Jones, whose integrity to justice was signaled by his name and his offering his services gratis. The New York–set show, which costarred Conlan Carter and Janet De Gore, was one of the first brought back for a second season after fan mail railed against its cancellation. But its audience never grew exponentially. Rich directed thirteen episodes, half of its only full season. P: Sy Gomberg. ABC, 30 min.

The Americans (1961)

Two brothers in Harper's Ferry, Virginia, became divided after their father (John McIntire) was killed during the Civil War—one fought for the Union, the other for the Confederacy. Darryl Hickman and Dick Davalos costarred as the Canfield brothers. The episodes alternated the exploits of each brother. Rich directed two episodes. P: Frank Telford. NBC, 60 min.

King of Diamonds (1961–62)

Broderick Crawford starred as John King, a private investigator for the diamond industry who traveled the globe battling unsavory gem smugglers, fences, and the like, and getting involved with various women. Ray Hamilton costarred. Rich directed one episode. Syndicated, 30 min.

Pine Lake Lodge (1961)

A pilot for a potential series was wedged into *Mister Ed*, the sitcom about "a horse [who] is a horse, of course, of course." The pilot concerned Bill Parker, the owner-operator of a mountain vacation spa who is visited by Wilbur and Carol Post (Alan Young and Connie Hines, the stars of *Mister Ed*). William Bendix played Bill, with support from Nancy Kulp, Coleen Gray, John Qualen, Marjorie Bennett, Marlene DeLamater, and John Bryant. D: John Rich. P: Arthur Lubin. Syndicated, 30 min.

The Dick Van Dyke Show (1961–66)

One of television's great sitcoms concerned the two halves of Rob Petrie's existence: his family with wife Laura and son Ritchie in New Rochelle, New York, and his working life as a writer in Manhattan for the fictional comedy/variety television show *The Alan Brady Show*. Mary Tyler Moore costarred as Laura, with Larry Mathews as Ritchie. Jerry Paris and Ann Morgan Guilbert played neighbors who frequently dropped by. At the *Brady* show, the co-gag-writers were played by Morey Amsterdam and Rose Marie, and the bosses by Richard Deacon and Carl Reiner (as Brady). Reiner created *The Dick Van Dyke Show*. Rich directed forty episodes throughout the life of the show, including "Where Did I Come From?" "That's My Boy," "Sally and the Lab Technician," "Washington vs. the Bunny," "My Blonde-Haired Brunette" "Forty-Four Tickets," "To Tell or Not To Tell," "Sally Is a Girl," "Who Owes Who What?" "The Curious Thing About Women," "Never Name a Duck," "Bank Book 6565696," "The Attempted

Marriage," "Hustling the Hustler," and "What's in a Middle Name?"
D: John Rich. P: Carl Reiner. CBS, 30 min.

McKeever and the Colonel (1962–63)
A boys military school, Westfield Academy, was the setting of this
sitcom, which often included byplay between Cadet Gary McKeever
(Scott Lane) and the headmaster, Colonel Harvey T. Blackwell (Allyn
Joslyn). Costarring were Jackie Coogan, Elisabeth Fraser, Ellen Corby,
Charles Ruggles, Johnny Eiman, and Keith Taylor. Rich directed
four episodes. D: Don Weis, John Rich, et al. P: Tom McKnight, Bill
Harman. NBC, 30 min.

Gilligan's Island (1964–67)
Marooned together on a South Pacific island, well-to-do charter boat
renters and the crew, including the inept Gilligan, try to figure out
schemes to get back to civilization. This popular sitcom had enough sea
legs to exhaust every desert-isle possibility and character adventure.
Bob Denver starred as Gilligan, with Alan Hale, Jr., Jim Backus, Tina
Louise, Natalie Schafer, Russell Johnson, and Dawn Wells. Sherwood
Schwartz created the series. Rich directed the pilot and two episodes
and also functioned as a producer on shows he directed. D: Jack Arnold,
John Rich, Ida Lupino, et al. P: Jack Arnold, Robert L. Rosen.
W: Sherwood Schwartz, Al Schwartz, et al. CBS, 30 min.

Gomer Pyle, USMC (1964–69)
Jim Nabors's Gomer Pyle was the filling-station attendant in Mayberry,
North Carolina, on the old *Andy Griffith Show*. In this hit sequel, he
had joined the Marine Corps and was assigned to Camp Henderson in
California. The frustrated and barking drill instructor for the happy-go-
lucky and glad-to-please Gomer was Sergeant Vince Carter, played by
Frank Sutton. The cast included Forrest Compton, Ronnie Schell, Ted
Bessell, and Elizabeth McRea. Aaron Ruben created the show. Rich
directed at least thirty-two episodes. D: John Rich, Coby Ruskin, Gary
Nelson, et al. P: E. Duke Vincent, Bruce Johnson. CBS, 30 min.

Hank (1965–66)
Hank Dearborn was forced to quit school after his parents' deaths and
raise his younger sister. He was an ice cream truck driver near a college campus. Dick Kallman and Katie Sweet played the siblings, with
support from Howard St. John, Dabbs Greer, Lloyd Corrigan, Linda
Foster, and Dorothy Nuemann. Hugh Benson created and produced
the show. Rich directed the pilot and two other episodes. NBC, 30 min.

Hogan's Heroes (1965–71)

   A prisoner-of-war camp in Nazi Germany was the setting for this
   unlikely but popular sitcom, which elaborated on a rather comfortable if
   antagonistic relationship between the savvy prisoners and inept guards.
   Bob Crane starred as Hogan, and the cast included John Banner,
   Werner Klemperer, Robert Clary, Richard Dawson, Ivan Dixon, Larry
   Hovis, Kenneth Washington, and Sigrid Valdis. Produced by Bing
   Crosby Productions. Rich directed seven episodes. D: John Rich,
   Robert Butler, Ivan Dixon, Gene Reynolds, Howard Morris, et al. P: Ed
   Feldman. CBS, 30 min.

I Spy (1965–68)

   Robert Culp and Bill Cosby played espionage agents Kelly Robinson
   and Alexander Scott, whose adventures usually came infused with elements of humor and reality during their own idiosyncratically casual
   approach to derring-do. A landmark series executive-produced by
   Sheldon Reynolds, it featured Cosby as the first African American
   actor to star in a regular dramatic series. Rich directed the twenty-sixth
   episode, "There Was a Little Girl," in 1966, costarring Mary Jane
   Saunders, Harry Raybould, and Jose de Vega. D: Leo Penn, Mark
   Rydell, Robert Culp, John Rich, Earl Bellamy, Alf Kjellan, Richard C.
   Sarafian, et al. P: David Friedkin, Mort Fine. W: Gary Marshall, Jerry
   Belson, David Friedkin, Robert Culp, et al.

Run for Your Life (1965–68)

   Ben Gazzara played Paul Bryan, a lawyer given two years to live who
   decides to go on a globetrotting adventure to fill the remainder of his
   life (which, measured in television time, lasted longer than expected).
   The series was based on a 1965 installment of *Kraft Suspense Theater*.
   Rich directed four episodes. D: Robert Butler, William A. Graham,
   John Rich, Michael Ritchie, Ben Gazzara, Stuart Rosenberg, et al. P: Jo
   Swerling, Jr., Paul Freeman. NBC, 60 min.

McNab's Lab (1966)

   Broadcast under the umbrella title of *Summer Fun*, this pilot featured
   the misadventures of a small-town pharmacist, widower, and amateur
   inventor named Andrew McNab. Cliff Arquette, whose alter ego was
   folksy comedian "Charley Weaver," starred as McNab, with Sherry
   Alberoni, David Bailey, Paul Smith, Elisha Cook, Jr., and Gary Owens.
   D: John Rich. P: George Burns. W: Norman Paul, Elon Packard,
   William Burns. ABC, 30 min.

T.H.E. Cat (1966–67)

Thomas Hewitt Edward Cat, a former circus acrobat, hired out as a bodyguard in San Francisco for those expecting assault or assassination. He shunned weaponry, preferring to rely on his brains and quickness. Robert Loggia starred with R. G. Armstrong and Robert Carricart. Rich directed two episodes. D/P: Boris Sagal. NBC, 30 min.

That Girl (1966–71)

Ann Marie was a small-town girl trying to make it as an actress in New York. Her foibles with her boyfriend, Don, and her parents were recurring themes. Marlo Thomas, daughter of television star Danny Thomas, played Ann, with support from Ted Bessell, Lew Parker, Rosemary DeCamp, Bonnie Scott, George Carlin, Ronnie Schell, Billy DeWolfe, Morty Gunty, Frank Faylen, Mabel Albertson, et al. Bill Persky and Sam Denoff, who formerly wrote for *The Dick Van Dyke Show*, created this series. Rich directed twenty-two episodes throughout the life of the show. D: Jay Sandrich, John Rich, Ted Bessell, Saul Turtletaub, et al. P: Bernie Orenstein, Saul Turtletaub, Jerry Davis. ABC, 30 min.

Hey Landlord (1966–67)

Will Hutchins and Sandy Baron played bachelors who co-owned an apartment building. The support included Michael Constantine, Pamela Rogers, Ann Morgan Guilbert, Sally Field, Tom Tully, Jack Albertson, and Ann Doran. Richard Dreyfuss had a small role in a Rich episode. Rich directed six episodes of this one-season show. D: John Rich. P: Lee Rich, Garry Marshall, Jerry Belson.

Good Morning, World (1967–68)

The main characters also formed a Los Angeles radio disc-jockey team, "Lewis and Clarke," whose adventures on and off the air included romances and family life. Joby Baker and Ronnie Schell costarred with Billy DeWolfe, Julie Parrish, and Goldie Hawn in her pre-*Laugh-In* days as Lewis's gabby neighbor, Sandy Kramer. Rich directed seven episodes. D: Carl Reiner. P: Bill Persky, Sam Denoff. W: Bill Persky, Sam Denoff, E. Duke Vincent, et al. CBS, 30 min.

My World—and Welcome to It (1969–70)

The humor of James Thurber was the source of inspiration for this series about a New York cartoonist and writer whose Walter Mitty–like daydreams and fantasies were acted out for the audience. William Windom had one of his best-remembered roles as the scribe, James Monroe. Costarring were Joan Hotchkis, Henry Morgan (as a Robert

Benchley–like friend), Harold J. Stone, and Lise Gerritsen. Rich directed thirteen episodes of the single-season show. D: John Rich, Sheldon Leonard, Danny Arnold, et al. P: Danny Arnold. W: Melville Shavelson, Lawrence Marks, Bill Manhoff, et al.

The Brady Bunch (1969–74)

A widow with three daughters married a widower with three sons, and the household misadventures were myriad. Robert Reed, Florence Henderson, and Ann B. Davis starred with Maureen McCormick, Eve Plumb, Susan Olsen, Barry Williams, Christopher Knight, and Michael Lookinland. Sherwood Schwartz created the series. Rich directed the pilot and six episodes. D: John Rich, Peter Baldwin, et al. P: Lloyd J. Schwartz, John Thomas Lenox, et al. ABC, 30 min.

Headmaster (1970–71)

Retitled and reformatted as *The New Andy Griffith Show* (1971)

Andy Griffith played the title role at a coeducational prep school in California. Griffith became the mayor of a small North Carolina town after the mid-season shake-up, in a show that resembled the old *Andy Griffith Show*. The earlier incarnation costarred Claudette Nevins, Jerry Van Dyke, and Parker Fennelly. Rich directed two *Headmaster* episodes. P/D: Aaron Ruben.

Make Room for Granddaddy (1970–71)

This sequel to *Make Room for Daddy*, aka *The Danny Thomas Show* (1953–64), included some of the early series's cast: Danny Thomas, Marjorie Lord, Rusty Hamer, Angela Cartwright, Sid Melton, and Hans Conreid. The *Granddaddy* cast also included Sherry Jackson, Stanley Myron Handelman, and Rosy Grier. Rich directed one episode. P: Richard Crenna.

All in the Family (1971–79)

One of the most influential programs in television history, *All in the Family* broke new ground in its portrayal of bigotry and intolerance in the oafish character of Archie Bunker. Each week, Archie's bellicose attitudes toward people of color and/or people not exactly like his white, middle-age, macho-posing self usually resulted in some sort of comic comeuppance. Rich produced and directed almost one hundred episodes, the entire first four years of the show's great run. Carroll O'Connor created in Archie one of the most indelible characters in the medium's history. The show often challenged the censors with Archie's crass use of derogatory labels for racial or ethnic groups. Jean

Stapleton's portrayal of Archie's wife, Edith Bunker, was priceless as her shrill voice and "dingbat" antics (in Archie's estimation) often revealed to the audience more common sense than at first seemed possible. Recurring themes were Archie's opinions on the African American Jefferson family living next door, and his working life as a dock foreman at the Prendergast Tool & Die Co. Costarring were Sally Struthers as the Bunkers' daughter, Gloria, and Rob Reiner as her husband, Mike Stivic. Mike was, to Archie's distress, of Polish descent, and he often called his son-in-law "Meathead." Recurring characters were played by Mike Evans, Mel Stewart, Isabel Sanford, Sherman Hemsley, Betty Garrett, Vincent Gardenia, and Burt Mustin. CBS, 30 min.

Maude (1972–78)

This spinoff from *All in the Family* gave Edith Bunker's brassy cousin Maude Findlay her own show. Maude was the liberal flip-side of Archie Bunker—diametrically opposed politics, same intractably brash personality. She's living with her fourth husband in Tuckahoe. Beatrice Arthur starred with Bill Macy, Adrienne Barbeau, Rue McClanahan, Esther Rolle, Brian Morrison, Conrad Bain, et al. Norman Lear executive-produced. Rich directed the pilot only. CBS, 30 min.

Clarence Darrow (1974)

In one of the year's most distinguished and well-reviewed TV presentations, Henry Fonda repeated his one-man Broadway smash as the title lawyer. Darrow moves about a courtroom set, remembering his defense of clients in the Leopold/Loeb murder trial, Scopes "monkey trial," *Los Angeles Times* bombing trial, and other cases. The play was written by David W. Rintels and directed at the Minskoff Theatre by John Houseman. Fonda's performance in this TV version is roundly regarded as one of his best, enhanced by the intimacy of the medium under Rich's direction. The show has also been titled *Clarence Darrow Starring Henry Fonda* and, for a PBS reprise, *Henry Fonda as Clarence Darrow*. D: John Rich. W: David W. Rintels. P: Mike Merrick, Don Gregory. NBC, 90 min.

Good Times (1974–79)

A lower-class African American family's laughs and travails were the subjects of this spinoff of *All in the Family* and *Maude*. Esther Rolle was the maid on *Maude*, and in this show played the hard-working matriarch of a Chicago family whose father, played by John Amos, was often unemployed. Costarring were BernNadette Stanis, Jimmie "J. J." Walker, Ralph

Carter, Johnny Brown, and, later in the series, Moses Gunn. Norman Lear executive-produced. Rich directed the pilot only. CBS, 30 min.

Grandpa Max (1975)

The generation gap between grandfather Max Sherman and Paul, his protective son, was explored in this pilot. Larry Best played Max with Michael Lerner as Paul. Also in the show were Suzanne Astor, Dick Van Patten, and Brad Savage. D: John Rich. P: Aaron Ruben, John Rich. W: Aaron Ruben. CBS, 30 min.

The Jeffersons (1975–85)

This spinoff from *All in the Family* featured Archie Bunker's African American next-door neighbor George Jefferson, experiencing business success and moving to the East Side of Manhattan. As opinionated as Archie, George and his wife, Louise, settle into their new digs in white America. Sherman Hemsley and Isabel Sanford starred with Mike Evans, Damon Evans, Roxie Roker, Franklin Cover, Paul Benedict, Marla Gibbs, et al. Norman Lear executive-produced. Rich directed the pilot. CBS, 30 min.

Barney Miller (1975–82)

The life and times of the denizens of a big-city police precinct fed this hit sitcom, which Rich helped retool from its original try—an installment of a summer anthology called *Just for Laughs*. Rich urged that the title officer's family be practically deleted from the series and that the stories concern almost solely the officers. The second "pilot," directed by Rich, aired in January 1975 and afterward the show became a hit. Starring was Hal Linden with Abe Vigoda as Fish, Maxwell Gail, Jack Soo, Gregory Sierra, Ron Glass, James Gregory, Barbara Barrie, Linda Lavin, Ron Carey, Steve Landesberg, George Murdock, et al. Rich directed two other episodes. D: Alex March, David Swift, Maxwell Gail, John Rich, Theodore J. Flicker, et al. P: Noam Pitlik, Danny Arnold, et al. ABC, 30 min.

On the Rocks (1975–76)

This prison-set sitcom caused a stir when the National Association for Justice asked ABC to cancel it because it supposedly portrayed prison life as not so bad. Jose Perez starred with Bobby Sandler, Hal Williams, Rick Hurst, Jack Grimes, Mel Stewart, Logan Ramsey, and Tom Poston. Dick Clement and Ian LeFrenais based the series on their own British sitcom *Porridge*. Rich produced and directed the full season of twenty-three shows. ABC, 30 min.

I'll Never Forget What's Her Name (1976)

Rita Moreno starred as Rosa Dolores, a New York girl who has dreams of making it big in Hollywood. This pilot was aired as a segment of *On the Rocks* and featured Hamilton Camp, Yvonne Wilder, Jose Perez, and Rick Hurst. D/P: John Rich. W: Dick Clement, Ian LeFrenais. ABC, 30 min.

Charo and the Sergeant (1976)

The title comic actress, known as the "coochie-coochie girl" from her many variety- and talk-show appearances, marries a U.S. Marine sergeant and adjusts to American life in this sitcom pilot. Charo starred with Tom Lester, Noam Pitlik, and Dick Van Patten. D: John Rich. P: John Rich, Aaron Ruben. W: Aaron Ruben. ABC, 30 min.

Mother, Juggs and Speed (1978)

Based on the 1976 feature film of the same title directed by Peter Yates, this pilot concerned three paramedics who worked for the greedy Harry Fishbine, the owner of a private ambulance company. Ray Vitte, Joanne Nail, and Joe Penny starred with Harvey Lembeck as Fishbine. D/P: John Rich. W: Tom Mankiewicz. ABC, 30 min.

Dorothy (1979)

This four-episode sitcom set at the Hannah Huntley School for Girls starred Dorothy Loudon as the school's magnetic performing arts instructor. Costarring were Russell Nype, Linda Mantz, Priscilla Morrill, Elissa Leeds, et al. Rich directed all episodes. P: Jerry Madden. CBS, 30 min.

Billy (1979)

This replacement show concerned a nineteen-year-old whose fantasies were depicted onscreen in this sitcom version of the 1963 John Schlesinger film *Billy Liar.* John Rich Productions supplied the show and Rich directed all thirteen episodes. Steve Guttenberg played the title character with support from James Gallery, Peggy Pope, and Bruce Talkington. D/P: John Rich. W: Dick Clement, Ian LeFrenais. CBS, 30 min.

Benson (1979–86)

The one character who didn't seem half-cracked in the series *Soap* was the droll butler, Benson. In this spinoff, he was sent by the Tate household (from *Soap*) to help out with the household of Mrs. Tate's widowed cousin, Governor Gatling. It was as if he traded one brood of kooks for another. His competence is acknowledged and he is appointed to variously more important posts during the duration of the show until, by its end, he ran against Gatling for governor. Robert Guillaume starred with James Noble, Missy Gold, Inga Swenson, Jerry Seinfeld, Caroline McWilliams, Lewis J. Stadlin, Didi Conn, and Ethan Phillips. Rich directed two years of episodes, nearly fifty in all, and was executive producer on the series with Tony Thomas and Paul Junger Witt. D: John Rich, Jay Sandrich, Tony Mordente, et al. P: Susan Harris, Tom Reeder, et al. ABC, 30 min.

Amanda's (1983)
aka Amanda's-by-the-Sea

Bea Arthur starred in the title role as a woman who owns and operates Amanda's-by-the-Sea, a resort hotel overlooking the Pacific Ocean, in this attempt to recreate the British series *Fawlty Towers*. Costarring were Kevin McCarthy, Fred McCarren, Rick Hurst, Simone Griffen, Keene Curtis, and Michael Constantine. Rich directed the pilot. D: John Rich, Marc Daniels, Howard Storm. P: Elliot Schoenman. ABC, 30 min.

Condo (1983)

In this culture-clash sitcom, a white family on the skids led by an opinionated patriarch moves into a condominium next door to a Latino family on the rise led by the ambitious chief of a landscape crew. McLean Stevenson and Luis Avalos starred with Brooke Alderson, Yvonne Wilder, Julie Carmen, Marc Price, et al. Rich directed the entire season of episodes and was executive producer on the series with Tony Thomas and Paul Junger Witt. D: John Rich. P: Bernie Orenstein, Sy Turtletaub, Kathy Speer, et al. ABC, 30 min.

MacGyver (1985–92)

This action/adventure series starred Richard Dean Anderson as the title character, a former Special Forces officer who works for a think tank called the Phoenix Foundation to battle transgressors and enemies of peace throughout the world. He used his wits more than hardware to solve tough problems and avoided violence at almost all costs. Henry Winkler, Stephen Downing, and Rich executive-produced this popular series. Costarring were Dana Elcar, John Anderson, Teri Hatcher, Bruce McGill, Michael Des Barres, and Elyssa Davalos. ABC, 60 min.

Newhart (1983–86)

Bob Newhart returned to television as Dick Loudon, a writer specializing in how-to books who opens a colonial inn in small-town Vermont, deals with a neighborhood of eccentrics, and becomes a local media personality. The supporting cast included Mary Frann, Julia Duffy, Tom Poston, Steve Kampmann, Jennifer Holmes, William Sanderson, Rebecca York, Peter Scolari, Ralph Manza, et al. Rich directed the pilot episode. CBS, 30 min.

Mr. Sunshine (1986)

Professor Paul Stark had recently been blinded by an accident, then divorced. He dealt with dating and everyday challenges with a biting wit, hence the ironic title. Jeffrey Tambor starred with Nan Martin, Barbara Babcock, Leonard Frey, Cecilia Hart, and David Knell. Rich directed thirteen episodes and was executive producer of the series. W: David Lloyd, Bob Ellinson. ABC, 30 min.

Dear John (1988)

Judd Hirsch starred as a man who comes home to a "Dear John" letter—his wife has left him. He copes through therapy. Costarring were Isabella Hofmann, Jere Burns, Billie Bird, Tom Willett, Billy Cohen, Deborah Harmon, Harry Groener, Ben Savage, Jane Carr, and Olivia Brown. Rich directed seven episodes. NBC, 30 min.

Murphy Brown (1988–98)

Candice Bergen starred in this smart and funny time-honored series that ran for 247 episodes over eleven years. Murphy, a tough television news reporter, was also a single mother and hot-tempered recovering alcoholic. Rich directed one episode, which featured two other directors in supporting roles, Garry Marshall and Louis Malle, who was Bergen's husband. Costarring were Grant Shaud, Faith Ford, Robert Pastorelli, Charles Kimbrough, Lily Tomlin, Scott Bakula, Colleen Dewhurst, Alan Oppenheimer, Garry Marshall, Paul Reubens, Jay Thomas, Joe Regalbuto, and Pat Corley. CBS, 30 min.

Nearly Departed (1989)

Eric Idle and Caroline McWilliams played the deceased Pritchards, who haunt their old home, where only Grandpa can see them. Henderson Forsythe played Grandpa with support from Jay Lambert, Wendy Schaal, and Stuart Pankin. Rich directed six episodes. NBC, 30 min.

The Man in the Family (1991)
aka Honor Bound

Ray Sharkey starred as Sal Bovasso, a ne'er-do-well son who returns to Brooklyn reluctantly to live up to his promise to keep Carmine's Deli open. Rich produced the show and directed all thirteen episodes.

Costarring were Julie Bovasso, Anne De Salvo, Leah Remini, Billy L. Sullivan, Louis Guss, and Don Stark. ExP: Ed. Weinberger. ABC, 30 min.

Walter and Emily (1991–92)

The parents of a divorced sportswriter help him raise his son in this sitcom. Brian Keith and Cloris Leachman played the grandparents; Christopher McDonald played the scribe and Matthew Lawrence was the son. Support came from Sandy Baron, Shelley Berman, and Edan Gross. Rich directed thirteen episodes. NBC, 30 min.

Baby Talk (1991–92)

This sitcom, spun off from the *Look Who's Talking* movies, starred Julia Duffy, then Mary Page Keller, as the mother with Paul and Ryan Jessup alternating as the toddler, Mickey. Tony Danza supplied Mickey's amusingly rugged voice (in the same manner Bruce Willis had done for the films). Rich directed one episode. Costarring were Scott Baio, Polly Bergen, George Clooney, Julia Duffy, and William Hickey. ABC, 30 min.

Second Half (1993–94)

A slovenly, divorced Chicago sports columnist has weekend custody of his two preteen daughters in this sitcom created by its star, John Mendoza. Costarring were Ellen Blain, Brooke Stanley, Wayne Knight, Joe Guzaldo, Jessica Lundy, and Mindy Cohn. Rich directed six episodes. NBC, 30 min.

The Good Life (1994)
aka Bowman

The eclectic family of a Chicago loading-dock manager was this sitcom's subject. The series starred John Caponera with Eve Bowman, Jake Patellis, Drew Carey, Justin Berfield, Monty Hoffman, and Shay Astar. Rich directed the pilot episode only. NBC, 30 min.

Hudson Street (1995)

This sitcom about lives of policemen living in Hoboken, New Jersey, often referred to the actual city's favorite son, Frank Sinatra. Rich directed four episodes. Tony Danza starred with Lori Laughlin, Jerry Adler, Christine Dunford, and Reni Santoni. ABC, 30 min.

If Not for You (1995)

Hank Azaria and Elizabeth McGovern seem made for each other but are kept apart by their significant others and the denizens of his recording studio. Zeljko Ivanek, Peter Krause, Chris Hogan, Jane Sibbett, and Reno Wilson costarred. Rich directed six episodes. CBS, 30 min.

Mr. Rhodes (1996–97)

Tom Rhodes starred as Tom Rhodes, a hip novelist whose book was a commercial failure, but who's old enough to teach at his former prep school, where he's young enough to encounter old demons. Rich directed six episodes. Costarring were Lindsay Sloane, Alexandra Holden, Ron Glass, and Stephen Tobolowsky. NBC, 30 min.

Something So Right (1996–98)

A divorced single father and mother start over again. Mel Harris and Jere Burns starred with Emily Ann Lloyd, Billy L. Sullivan, Christine Dunford, and sometime costar Shirley Jones. Rich directed five episodes. ExP/W: Judd Pillott and John Peaslee. NBC, then ABC, 30 min.

Pistol Pete (1996)

This Western pilot starred Stephen Kearney as a town sheriff with Mark Derwin, David Carpenter, Brian Doyle-Murray, and Rick Hurst. W: John Swartzwelder, 30 min.

You're the One (1998)

Cynthia Geary starred as Lindsay Metcalf, a Southern belle who married a Jewish guy from Long Island. Costarring were Elon Gold, Jayce Bartok, Leo Burmeister, and Julie Dretzin. Rich directed all three episodes that aired. WB, 30 min.

Payne (1999)

This was Rich's second involvement with an American attempt to remake the British hotel comedy Fawlty Towers (see Amanda's above). John Larroquette executive-produced and starred as the appropriately named Royal Payne, with JoBeth Williams, Julie Benz, and Rick Batalla. Rich directed six episodes. ExP/W: Judd Pillott and John Peaslee. CBS, 30 min.

OTHER TELEVISION

The unsold pilots directed by John Rich in the 1950s included *The Reluctant Eye*, with Bobby Van as a private detective; *Two Boys*, which was shot on location in Texas for Paramount Pictures Television; and *The Paul Ford Show*, one of several attempts to establish Ford as a sitcom star. Other Rich-directed pilots that went unsold in the 1980s or later include *Chameleon,* which was written by David Lloyd and starred Madeline Kahn and Nina Foch; *The Dallasandros* for producer Aaron Ruben; *Moscow Bureau,* about a U.S. news operation, written by David Lloyd and starring Caroline McWilliams and William Windom; *Second Start* with Joanna Cassidy and Powers Boothe; and *Steubenville* starring Rick Hurst.

AWARDS

Emmy Awards
Academy of Television Arts and Sciences
Outstanding Directorial Achievement in Comedy, 1963, *The Dick Van Dyke Show*
Outstanding Directorial Achievement in Comedy, 1972, *All in the Family,* episode: "Sammy's Visit"
Outstanding Comedy Series, 1973, *All in the Family,* award shared with Executive Producer Norman Lear

Emmy Nominations
Outstanding Directorial Achievement in Comedy, 1962, *The Dick Van Dyke Show*
Outstanding Directorial Achievement in Comedy, 1971, *All in the Family,* episode: "Gloria's Pregnancy"
Outstanding Directorial Achievement in Comedy, 1973, *All in the Family,* episode: "The Bunkers and the Swingers," nomination shared with Bob LaHendro
Outstanding Comedy Series, 1974, *All in the Family,* nomination shared with Executive Producer Norman Lear

Directors Guild of America Awards
Most Outstanding Television Director, 1972, *All in the Family*
Robert B. Aldrich Award, 1993, for Outstanding Service to the DGA
Honorary Life Membership, 2003, occasionally awarded by the Guild since 1938; Rich was named as the thirty-sixth Life Member

Golden Globe Awards
Hollywood Foreign Press Association
Outstanding Production, Musical or Comedy Series, 1971, *All in the Family*
Outstanding Production, Musical or Comedy Series, 1972, *All in the Family*

Outstanding Production, Musical or Comedy Series, 1973, *All in the Family*

Golden Globe Nomination
Outstanding Production, Musical or Comedy Series, 1974, *All in the Family*

Producers Guild of America Hall of Fame
Inaugural Induction, 1992; *All in the Family* was included among twelve shows "that have set an enduring standard for American entertainment"

The Christophers
Christopher Award
Television Production Affirming the Highest Values of the Human Spirit, 1974, *Clarence Darrow*

NAACP Image Award
For the portrayal of race relations, 1973, *All in the Family*

American Cancer Society Award
For bringing attention to breast cancer, 1973, *All in the Family*

Environmental Media Award
Ongoing Commitment to Environmental Concerns, 1991, *MacGyver*

University of Michigan
Sesquicentennial Award, 1967
Honorary Degree Doctor of Humane Letters, 2002

DIRECTORS GUILD OF AMERICA

John Rich has been a member of Directors Guild of America (DGA) and its forerunners, the Radio and Television Directors Guild (RTDG) and the Screen Directors Guild (SDG), since the early 1950s. His efforts were significant in the merger of the SDG with the RTDG to form the DGA in 1960. For the Guild, Rich's many involvements include:

Alternate, National Board of Directors, 1954
Member, Western Directors Council, 1955 to the present
Member, National Board of Directors, 1955–69, 1971 to the present
Secretary/Treasurer & First Vice President, 1956–57

Member, Negotiating Committee, 1956, 1958, 1960, 2002, and 2004
Co-Chairman, Negotiating Committee, 1996
Founding member, DGA-Producers Pension Plan
Chairman, Board of Trustees, Pension Plan, 1966, 1968, 1970, 1992,
    1996, 2005, and 2006

Rich is also a member of the Writers Guild of America West, the Producers Guild of America, the Screen Actors Guild, the American Federation of of Television and Radio Artists, and the Caucus for Writers, Producers and Directors.

INDEX

Brittenham, Skip, 159
Broken Arrow, 93
Brooks, Jim, 1–2, 175, 184–85
Brooks, Mel, 29, 94
Brooks, Richard, 93
Brown, Hy, 49
Bull, Sheldon, 180
Burk, Arnold, 142
Burke, Cornelius J., 15, 128
Burns, Allan, 1–2, 184
Burns, George, 91–92
Burns, Jere, 175, 177–78
Buttram, Pat, 71, 100

Caesar, Florence, 30
Caesar, Sid, 28–30, 83, 181
Calvada Productions, 115
Cantor, Eddie, 35
Capra, Frank, 85, 87, 95–97, 203
Carol Burnett Show, The, 5
Carr, Jane, 175
Carsey, Marcy, 187
Carson, Johnny, 131
Carswell, Harrold G., 135
Carter, Jack, 28–29, 35
Casablanca, 65, 93
Cates, Gil, 203
Caulfield, Joan, 201
CBS Evening News, 134
Chadwick, Florence, 31–34
Chadwick, Sue, 91
Chaplin, Charlie, 79
Chasen's, 102, 140
Cheers, 185
Cimino, Michael, 171
City Lights, 79
Clarence Darrow, 144–47
Clary, Robert, 111
Clement, Dick, 150–52
Climax, 41
Clinton, Hillary, 167
Coach, 158
Coca, Imogene, 29
Coe, Fred, 25–26
Cohen, Ted, 199–200

Cohn, Bobby, 60, 68–69
Colgate Comedy Hour, The, 22, 26, 81
Coolidge, Martha, 203
Cooper, Hal, 107, 109
Corey, Wendell, 201
Correll, Charles, Jr., 160
Correll, Charles, Sr., 160
Cosby, Bill, 187–89
Cousy, Bob, 9
Crabbe, Buster, 33
Cranes Are Flying, The, 103
Cranston, Lamont, 52
Crisler, Fritz, 7–8
Cronkite, Walter, 135
Crosby, Bing, 11
Cukor, George, 66
Curtis, Tony, 69, 80–82
Curtiz, Michael, 93–94
Cyrano de Bergerac, 26

Dalton, Abby, 148–49
Daniels, Ann, 161
Darrow, Clarence, 144
Daves, Delmer, 93
Davis, Ann B., 113
Davis, Jefferson, 94
Davis, Joan, 35–37
Davis, Sammy, Jr., 123, 131–33
Day, Dennis, 34
Dear John, 175
December Bride, 114
Defenders, The, 113
DeMille, Cecile B., 88, 94
Denoff, Sam, 53, 55, 112
Denver, Bob, 106
DePew, Joe, 36
Diamond, Selma, 29
Diary of Anne Frank, 67
Dick Van Dyke Show, The, 2, 36,
    50–64, 106, 111–12, 114–15,
    184, 198, 200
Dillard, Mimi, 59
Diller, Barry, 148
Directors Guild of America (DGA),
    87, 90, 202, 203

Penn, Arthur, 20, 22–23, 41, 182
Perez, Jose, 152–54
Perkins, Rowland, 144
Persky, Bill, 53, 55, 112
Phelps, Stu, 87
Philco Playhouse, 23, 25, 41
Pillott, Judd, 177
Pinza, Ezio, 34
Place in the Sun, A, 67, 98–99
Playhouse 90, 41
Poindexter, H. R., 144
Poitras, Armand, 31, 33
Polanski, Roman, 159
Porgy and Bess, 121
Porridge, 151
Post, Ted, 43
Poston, Tom, 153
Powers, Stefanie, 69
Presley, Elvis, 71–77
Price, H. T., 127
Price Is Right, The, 177
Purlie Victorious, 122

Quinn, Stanley, 24

Radio and Television Directors Guild
    (RTDG), 86, 87, 89, 95
Rashomon, 123–24
Rather, Dan, 137
Ray Bolger Show, The, 114
Reagan, Ronald, 39–40
Reed, Robert, 113–14
Reiner, Carl, 29–30, 50, 52–55, 58,
    60–61, 67–68, 115, 175, 183
Reiner, Rob, 117, 123, 203
Release the pigeon, 196, 203
Reynolds, Gene, 158, 203
Rich, Pat, v, vii–viii, 30, 111, 182
Richardson, Tony, 43
Rintels, David, 144–46
Ritter, Thelma, 80
Riverboat, 40
Roberts, Jerry, viii
Roberts, Julia, 177
Roberts, Pernell, 42

Rolle, Esther, 141
Rose Marie, 51, 61, 62, 64, 198
Ross, Mickey, 121, 127, 184
Roustabout, 71–76
Ruben, Aaron, 92, 110–11, 200
Run for Your Life, 170

Sadowski, Edward, 16–17
"Saga of Cousin Oscar, The," 127
Sandler, Bobby, 153
Sanford, Isabel, 122
Sanford and Son, 200
Sarnoff, David, 97
Saval, Dany, 80, 83
Savalas, Telly, 69
Schaefer, George, 203
Schaeffer, Natalie, 106
Schaffner, Frank, 203
Schmittmer, Christiane, 80
Schwartz, Bernie, 69
Schwartz, Sherwood, 105–7, 113
Screen Actors Guild (SAG), 89
Screen Directors Guild (SDG), 85,
    86, 87, 89, 203
Screen Directors' Playhouse, 201
Seaton, George, 95
Segal, George, 69–70
Seinfeld, 185
Sennett, Mack, 44, 198–200, 202
Serling, Rod, 114
Shane, 75
Sharkey, Ray, 175
Sharp, Phil, 105
Shayne, Alan, 146–47
Shea, Jack, 20–21, 87, 203
Shepherd, Jean, 190–92
Sherin, Ed, 177
Shore, Dinah, 35
Sidney, George, 85–87, 95, 203
Silverman, Fred, 143, 152–54
Silvers, Phil, 107, 110
Simon, Danny, 29
Simon, Neil, 29
Singer, Abby, 194
Slaff, George, 98

Text design by Mary Sexton
Typesetting by Apex Publishing, LLC, Madison, Wisconsin
Text font: New Caledonia
Display font: Elroy

Caledonia was designed by William A. Dwiggins in 1939.
Linotype reworked the typeface in 1982 and released it as
New Caledonia, which you see in this volume. Its classic look
can be used in almost any application.
—courtesy linotype.com

Elroy is a Monotype Imaging font designed by Christian Schwartz.
—courtesy myfonts.com